LIES AND CONSEQUENCES

COVERING THE TRIALS OF KERRY MAX COOK

VANESSA E. CURRY

I0096659

SPARK Publications
Charlotte, North Carolina

LIES AND CONSEQUENCES:
Covering the Trials of Kerry Max Cook
Vanessa E. Curry

Designed, produced, and published by SPARK Publications
SPARKpublications.com
Charlotte, North Carolina

Stock Image Credit:
Cover: AnotherPerfectDay, ESB Professional, Miloje, Natasha Barsova, New Africa, pics five, STILLFX
Interior: AnotherPerfectDay, Flas100, iunewind, STILLFX

Printed in the United States of America

Paperback, August 2024, ISBN: 978-1-953555-80-9
E-book, August 2024, ISBN: 978-1-953555-61-8
Library of Congress Control Number: 2024906620

DEDICATION

To Dr. Kenneth R. Casstevens
1939–2006
My professor. My boss. My friend.
Thank you for your unwavering support.

CONTENTS

PART 1: Faulty Foundation

PART II: Under Review

PART III: New Trials

PART IV: A Possible Ending?

PART V: A New Approach

PART VI: The Waiting Game

FOREWORD

I met Vanessa Curry in the 1980s when she was a reporter/photographer for a competing newspaper in a small East Texas town and we were covering the same beat. She was competitive, aggressive, hardworking, and a good writer. It was our goal to "scoop" each other as often as we could, or if we were covering the same event, to write the better story. She made me work that much harder, and I respected her dedication and diligence as a reporter and writer.

When an opening became available at the *Tyler Morning Telegraph*, where I was working, I told Vanessa about it and encouraged her to apply. Not only could we use her skills to improve the quality of our newspaper, but I also figured if we became part of the same team, it would make my life easier. I was right—at least to a certain extent. The quality of our newspaper improved, but my challenger was now sitting at a desk next to me. Vanessa joined the Tyler paper in 1988, and for the next several years we challenged, encouraged, and cajoled each other to do the best we possibly could reporting and writing stories across East Texas, primarily from the state and federal courts. We were both dedicated to our craft and to excellence, but I have never known anyone who worked so hard at improving her writing as Vanessa. She would spend hours on a lede trying to make it "just right"—interesting, informative, and eye-catching using as few words as possible. She knew she had to hook the reader immediately or he or she was gone. Her example challenged me to work harder at improving the quality of my writing as well. During those years, Vanessa covered numerous court proceedings, including several sensational murder and capital murder trials. One of the most infamous cases in her career involved Kerry Max Cook and allegations that he had murdered Linda Jo Edwards, a young secretary at what is now The University of Texas at Tyler. Cook was convicted and sentenced to death for the 1977 crime. An appellate court granted him a new trial after ruling he had been denied counsel during an interview with a psychiatrist. Although Vanessa was not there to cover the first trial, she covered appeals and subsequent multiple retrials. She has spent hundreds—maybe even thousands—of hours listening to testimony, reviewing evidence, interviewing the major players, and poring over the details of this case. She knows this case well, but still has questions about what really happened between the young woman and the man accused of sexually assaulting her and mutilating her body. Cook served more than twenty years on death row in the Texas prison system, but after a series of missteps, prosecutors ultimately set aside the charge in June 2016. That decision was made after one of the key witnesses admitted he had lied under oath. Cook is currently a free man. Although Vanessa moved on from the Tyler paper years ago, this case is one that has traveled with her—the one that will not let her go. Is the voice of a young woman crying out from the grave for justice—justice that now may never be possible—what motivates her, or the cries of an innocent man who was unjustly convicted and spent a major portion of his life caged with society's worst criminals? Perhaps she is driven by her own desire—and society's need—to believe that the American judicial system really works and we can have confidence in it. Surely when the ultimate punishment of execution is a sentencing option, we can all agree that there is no room for error and injustice. Society needs a system free of ego and ambition at all costs, and deserves one focused on finding the truth, punishing the guilty, and protecting the innocent. Vanessa has invested several years in her own search for the truth in this case and shares that journey with us now. Join her as she traverses the multiple twists and turns of Cook's saga through the courts and lays bare the frailties and shortcomings of our judicial system, and try to decide for yourself what is true.

Marilyn Covey

AUTHOR'S NOTE

This is the book I swore I would never write. I first made that vow in 1994 after a Williamson County jury convicted Kerry Max Cook of capital murder and sentenced him to die for the 1977 mutilation slaying of Linda Jo Edwards.

As a reporter I had been covering the case for nearly two and a half years, including a 1992 retrial that ended when a different jury deadlocked 6–6 on a verdict. Both trials lasted more than a month.

I renewed that vow in 1996 when the Texas Court of Criminal Appeals again granted him a new trial—what would be his fourth. By that time, I had written more than one hundred articles (at two different newspapers) over a period of five years about this case, and frankly, my mind was simply fried from hearing and rehearing testimony and opinions.

People ask me all the time whether I believe Cook is guilty. My answer: My opinion doesn't matter.

I am neither a judge nor juror, only a public watchdog who had the difficult task of trying to fairly report the events involving this remarkable criminal case.

I changed my mind about writing this book for a variety of reasons. Foremost, I was one of the few people who could write about this precedent-setting Texas case because I had followed its developments for more than thirty years, covered two trials, and had access to the principal players. I not only want to share with the public what went on inside the courtroom but outside as well from a journalist's point of view.

The battle to prove guilt or innocence raged not only in the courtroom but in the court of public opinion.

I want to present a more complete account of events for those people attempting to educate themselves before forming an opinion. I also want to share how this case led me to reevaluate my beliefs about capital punishment because it forced me to consider the issue in reality, not as an abstract idea.

This nonfiction account is based upon court records, personal interviews, written and recorded news reports, personal observations, and a journalist's privilege of fair comment and criticism. This story is accurate to the best of my knowledge. It is not my intention to prove or disprove any of the allegations against Cook. I do hope, however, that readers will realize how lies, and the consequences of those lies, cheated Kerry Max Cook, Linda Jo Edwards, and society out of true justice.

PROLOGUE

Dateline: Fall 1991

Before I ever met Kerry Max Cook I had one strike against me.
To him, any journalist from Tyler, Texas, whether they worked in
print or broadcast, was unfair, blind to the truth, and hell-bent
on promoting his guilt. He lumped me in with a group he simply
referred to as "Tyler media"—words he pronounced with obvious
disdain. He made his reservations clear to me as I sat across from
him in the visitor's room at Ellis I Unit in Riverside, Texas. Tyler
media, he explained, always favored the "home team" prosecutors
and ignored revelations uncovered by *The Dallas Morning News* he
said proved his innocence. Although he agreed to give me a chance,
Cook's slow, carefully worded responses reflected a guarded mistrust.

With few exceptions, I've never been afraid to interview capital
murder defendants, although maintaining a meaningful dialogue is
always a challenge.

My ground rules are simple: Don't lie to me. Don't play games.
And don't forget that I don't take sides. It's a precarious relationship.
At any time, the defendant and/or attorneys can shut me out, leaving
my competition with exclusive access and my coverage appearing to
be one-sided.

In my experience, criminal defendants either don't trust reporters
at all or believe reporters— especially those from major news
organizations—are all investigators willing and eager to expose
corruption, which, of course, they always insist is the foundation of
the case against them.

Most of the time, I can overcome the first obstacle simply by
listening and earning their trust over time. The latter obstacle is

a lot more complicated. Most small to midsize newspapers don't have the staff and financial resources to launch an independent investigation. Given the *Morning Telegraph*'s conservative lean, the best I can promise a defendant is that I will cover their case fairly and accurately.

Cook was one of one hundred twenty-three other condemned men from throughout the state housed at what was known as "death row," located fifteen miles north of the execution chamber in Huntsville. It was the fall of 1991, nearly a month after the Texas Court of Criminal Appeals overturned his conviction and death sentence for the mutilation slaying of twenty-two-year-old Linda Jo Edwards. He granted me an interview despite my credentials as a reporter with the *Tyler Morning Telegraph*, grasping the opportunity to herald the ruling as proof of his innocence. After thirteen years on Texas's death row, Cook now had discovered something he thought he had lost forever. "I wake up at 7:30 a.m. every day and begin thinking about my case. It's been my job . . . for what, to me, has been my entire life. And all this time I've been screaming my innocence. I've never whispered it, I've screamed it, and now, finally, there's hope that justice is for everyone and not just a few," he told me.

Just a month before the interview, the name Kerry Max Cook barely registered on my radar as important news. That changed on the morning of September 18, 1991. Glowing yellowish-green letters spelled his name in a news alert on the screen of one of our outdated computers. Alerts are normal in my business, not necessarily as alarming as the word implies. But this one from the Associated Press bureau in Austin was different. It was a bombshell, the first of many to come in this case.

It didn't take long for Cook's name to catch the editor's eye as he scanned the bulletin. It was a Wednesday, the day of the week when the Texas Court of Criminal Appeals routinely releases its rulings. The court vacated Cook's capital murder conviction with a 3–2 decision granting him a new trial.[1] The unexpected news caught the

---

1 Texas created what is now known as the Texas Court of Criminal Appeals in 1876 to relieve the Supreme Court of its caseload in criminal and civil cases. In 1891, the state

newsroom off guard since the appeal had been languishing in the state's highest criminal court for a record-setting thirteen years. The case simply fell off the radar because there were only a handful of *Tyler Morning Telegraph* employees who had worked there long enough to remember Cook and the details of the 1977 slaying that had kept East Texas spellbound for months. I wasn't one of them. I was about to become a freshman in a central Illinois high school when the murder occurred. For me, capital punishment then was just one of a handful of abstract social issues ripe for a perfunctory research paper. Growing up in a small farm town during the 1970s (pre-internet) limited my exposure to such complex social issues via occasional news coverage. Although I began reading newspapers before I was in kindergarten, I don't recall any local capital murder trials or executions in the state. My knowledge of the criminal justice system during my childhood consisted of maybe one lecture in social science class and a field trip to the county courthouse.

Despite lacking a complete understanding of the capital punishment debate, I initially leaned toward the anti–death penalty stance because the thought of an innocent person being executed infuriated and frightened me. How could that scenario even be allowed to happen? In retrospect, I recognize my innate intolerance for injustice when I was in fourth grade. I recall watching a children's television program in which one of the characters was being mistreated by others. Frustrated by what I saw, I wrote my objections in a letter, addressed an envelope to the television station, and asked my mother for a postage stamp. The letter was never mailed, and I was reprimanded for not asking permission for the paper and envelope—another layer of injustice from my perspective.

---

removed that court's jurisdiction over civil matters. Initially, the court consisted of three judges, but in 1966 the number of judges was increased to five. In 1977, the bench again was enlarged to nine judges (a chief justice and eight judges).

* * *

I was still in the early stages of my journalism career when the assignment to write about Cook's appeal first landed on my desk the day of the 1991 reversal announcement. My induction into the realm of capital punishment reality came from my first capital murder trial just nine months before Cook won his appeal. I had covered the trial of Tony Chambers, who was convicted of raping and murdering an 11-year-old Tyler girl.[2] Chambers didn't have much of a defense since he confessed to strangling the girl with her own shoestrings and led investigators to where he had hidden the scalpel he used to carve on her skin. His death sentence came as no surprise, but finding the judge crying in a stairwell as she attempted to leave the courthouse unseen stunned me. It would be years before I would begin to understand her personal struggle between her faith and her civic duty.

Realizing the enormity of the court's decision in Cook's case stoked my journalistic impulses. Not a very dignifying description, I suppose, but it's difficult to explain the rush of excitement and slight panic I feel when I'm involved in a huge story. My pulse quickens. My palms sweat, and I tend to become a little panicky as I attempt to organize the jumble of thoughts bouncing around inside my brain. With the deadline for reporting Cook's overturned conviction just hours away, I had to research the case history, find and interview those people involved with the case for their reactions, and then write a coherent news story. A major story like this is controlled chaos that sends my mind on a roller-coaster ride from the depths of panic and uncertainty to the exhilaration of accomplishment. That ride never fails to thrill me.

My research started in the newspaper's clip morgue of previously published stories labeled and filed—physical files essential in the pre-internet world of journalism. The *Tyler Morning Telegraph*'s morgue—located in the sports department—

---

2 Chambers was executed by lethal injection on November 15, 2000.

consisted of two rows of green and gray metal filing cabinets three or four drawers high stuffed with manila file folders overflowing with yellowed pieces of aging newspaper. I yanked open the *C* file and ran my fingers through the alphabetical rank. No Cook. Frantic, I checked all possibilities. Nothing under *K* for Kerry, *E* for Edwards, or *L* for Linda Jo either. The file—if there had ever been one—was gone.

There are only a few things worse in the news business than interviewing someone without first doing your homework. News sources—especially public officials—involved in a major event don't have time to answer routine background questions. Ask those types of questions during a press conference and you will get labeled as a dumbass rookie. I couldn't just drive to Austin for a copy of the decision. Austin is at least four hours from Tyler, and I only had three hours until deadline. I read the Associated Press's summary and then headed to the Smith County courthouse three blocks away to interview Smith County District Attorney Jack Skeen, who at that point knew as much about the court's ruling as I did. Prosecutors and defense attorneys don't get early notice of the court's decision. They often learn about it from the first news reporter—usually from the Associated Press—to call asking for their reaction, and then their telephone rings throughout the morning with calls from numerous other reporters seeking interviews.

I patched a simple news story together that morning, answering the who, what, when, where, why, and how—the basic building blocks of every news story. The afternoon edition carried a three-deck headline on the front page that read "Kerry Max Cook Death Sentenced Overturned" in bold print with my byline and an old photograph of Cook that apparently had escaped notice of whoever pilfered the clip file.[3] It's not uncommon for a journalist to take files of their favorite cases with them when they move on to other jobs elsewhere, but their successor certainly is

---

3 All evidence strongly indicated a former reporter took the file when he left employment of the *Tyler Morning Telegraph*.

left at a disadvantage. With that deadline challenge met, I faced the reality of a much more daunting task—catching up on the details of a case *The Dallas Morning News* had been committed to investigating for at least a decade. The more I learned through my research, the more the story began to change—new questions as well as new evidence were uncovered, testimony changed, and legal issues became more entangled. I rebuilt the case file (creating a duplicate for myself as a backup), which became thicker with copies of old articles and other relevant materials. My competitive nature wanted me to be considered a major "player" in covering what a former prosecutor once called "the most important case in Smith County history." I did not doubt my ability to understand and write about the intricacies of this complicated case. I was, however, naïve about the magnitude of pressure from opposing camps, my media competitors, and the readers I would face and the impact that pressure would have on my attempts to be fair and impartial. I began my journey into the depths of understanding the elements of this case by meeting the people involved. That meant interviewing Cook face-to-face.

* * *

It was my first visit to Ellis I Unit[4] where Cook had been
incarcerated since his conviction in 1978. The route south from
Tyler skirted the piney woods of deep East Texas through a largely
rural area. The last leg of the journey was on State Highway 19,
a two-lane ribbon of concrete winding its way through forests,
fields, and small towns. The two-hour trip gave me plenty of time
to consider what questions to ask. "Did you do it?" was the first to
come to mind. "Stupid," I thought. "What did I expect his answer
to be?" I decided the best strategy in this initial visit was to just
listen. The road to death row headed west off of Highway 19, just
after the Trinity River bridge. A few miles down Farm-to-Market
Road 980, there was another right turn back north on a road
that led straight to the prison units. On the right, at the corner of
two intersecting double rows of razor-wire topped fencing, was
a plain brick tower with a glass-walled observation hut perched
on top. A sign hanging on the wall directed visitors to place their
identification cards in a metal bucket dangling from a long rope
running up one side of the tower. Once approved by the guards
above, the visitor was directed to a parking lot just outside a locked
gate leading into the prison.

David Nunnelee, who worked in public relations for the Texas
Department of Corrections, waited on the other side of the gate.
Media visitation rules required advance notice to allow Nunnelee
time to contact that inmate and then schedule a meeting time if
the inmate agreed. The process sometimes placed Nunnelee in
a difficult position, especially on one occasion when I received
confirmation of an interview and drove 110 miles to Riverside
for an early morning appointment, only to be told the prisoner
had changed his mind. In the half-dozen or more instances when

---

4 In 1999, Texas officials decided to move death row to Livingston, Texas, about sixty
miles west of Huntsville. The state prison unit that now houses death row inmates is
the Allan B. Polunsky Unit. Executions, however, are still carried out at the Walls Unit
in Huntsville.

I visited death row to interview various inmates, I also learned Nunnelee could be quite moody. There were times he and I shared meaningful conversations, while other times he appeared sullen and offered only brusque responses to any questions or comments. On the latter occasions, I could expect not even one second of extra time for an interview.

The prison entrance was nothing more than a narrow, fenced corridor that spanned the gap between the two rows of fencing. Security protocol required a gate at one end to be completely closed and locked before the gate at the other end could open. Once past the second gate, I followed the sidewalk into the brick building where I signed a logbook. Nunnelee then led me through another door into a larger room that reminded me of a grade school lunchroom. An elongated room contained two rows of small cells divided by a walkway extending from the end of the row to a secured door leading deeper into the prison. A guard used the pathway to escort Cook from inside the prison to a designated cell containing a single chair. The setup allowed us to sit face-to-face and have some privacy—at least visually—from other visitors. A full room would have made it difficult to maintain a private conversation, but Cook and I were alone that day.

On his side of the steel-framed plexiglass divider, Cook sat dressed in a white prison uniform. The thirty-five-year-old face peering back at me didn't quite match the image I had created in my mind based on the few newspaper photos I had seen of him. This person was not the skinny, wayward youth who I had seen in an old photograph sobbing as he was led away from the courtroom in handcuffs. This person was a round-faced man with a touch of gray in his short-cropped prison haircut. Our introduction was awkward but polite considering the surroundings and the purpose of our meeting. Cook appeared determined to tell as much of his story as he could—talking nearly nonstop for the entire two hours we had been allotted. I rarely needed to interject a question.

Cook was prepared to talk, and I was prepared to listen. A small round hole covered in wire mesh served as our conduit for communication. In a low, soft voice he told me about his childhood, his family, his trial, his life behind bars, and his hopes for a life on the outside. Cook insisted he did not know Linda and had never been inside her apartment. He denied killing her but admitted he left his fingerprint on her patio door while peeping into her apartment. I found myself wanting to believe him. But of course, I had my reservations too. As unfair as it may seem, a journalist has to suspect everything a source is telling her, especially when it involves someone accused of a crime. A journalist with even a little experience knows, however, that no one ever tells the entire story. Every story can contain elements of truth, subjective perception, and misinformation and lies—intentional or otherwise. Although not everyone who is convicted is guilty, the problem is finding the truth, and sometimes that task is impossible. Nothing, not even the justice system, is black and white.

By the time we finished the interview, I didn't know what to believe. Cook presented himself as friendly and sincere but the tone and pace of his voice reflected something else. He leaned toward the portal to speak as he recalled his time behind bars and his desire to be exonerated. The intensity of speech and his pleading eyes told me he wanted, and needed, me to believe he did not kill Linda. I thought about Cook's story while retracing my route back to Tyler. At the time, I had no idea how unfair his first trial had been or how prosecutorial misconduct would forever taint this case. I was convinced, however, that the judicial system had worked as I believed it should by overturning his 1978 conviction based upon an error. I learned much later that ruling was the key in opening Pandora's box in Cook's case.

Keeping pace with the process of the upcoming retrial required maintaining an open line of communication with all significant parties in Cook's case. That wasn't easy. The stakes in this game were extremely high. It's just human nature for individuals to reward those who offer support and to reject those who don't—a true conflict for a journalist who wants to be impartial. Cook, his attorneys, and his supporters certainly wanted me to believe he was innocent and to champion his cause through my newspaper articles. Prosecutors and the victim's family certainly wanted me to believe Cook was guilty and to write stories that supported that belief. And despite how they all might deny it, the fact is both sides played to the court of public opinion just as much as they attempted to play to the court of justice.

There is no doubt Linda's murder and the charge against Cook was an issue of public interest. The story had most of the elements of what makes something newsworthy—controversy, prominence, bizarre, currency, proximity, and impact—but every time I wrote a story I had to consider whether the information was truly something the public needed to know or was just part of opposing attorneys' agenda to sway the public. I was always caught in the middle.

Cook's expectations of me continue to be a point of contention in our relationship to this day.

* * *

I had a lot of catching up to do if I wanted to understand the complexities of Cook's case. Fishing out old newspaper clips, reading court records, and interviewing the principal people involved consumed every spare moment as I attempted to educate myself and rebuild the missing *Tyler Morning Telegraph* file about a case that opened my eyes to a reality I didn't want to admit existed—that the judicial system is fallible, the appellate process is dysfunctional, and the mess they can create is unfair to both victim and accused. The journey challenged and reshaped my core beliefs about journalism, public opinion, the judicial system, capital punishment, and—most of all—human nature.

PART 1

Faulty Foundation

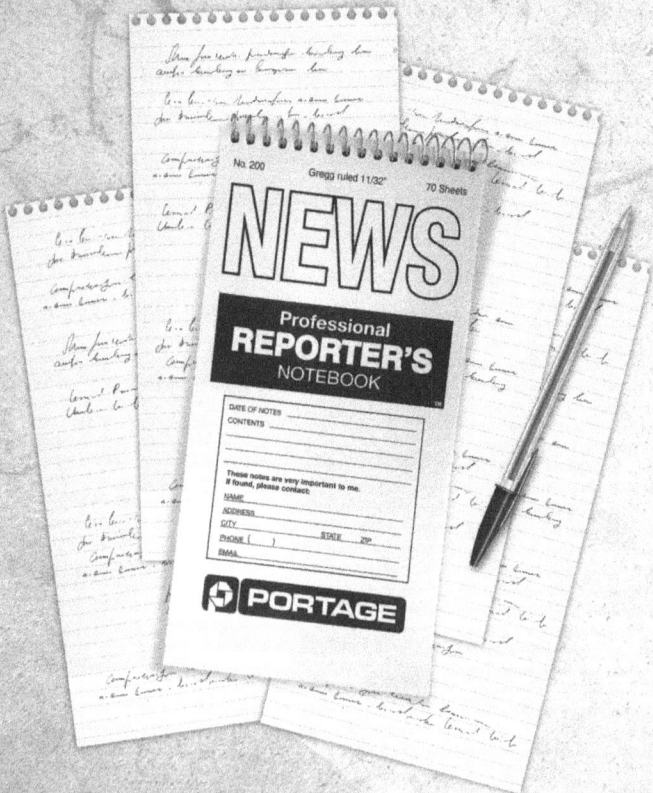

TIMELINE:

1977

Victim Knifed 25 Times

1978

June 22, 1978
Trial begins in the 241st District Court in Tyler, Texas.

June 28–29, 1978
Smith County jury convicts Cook and recommends a death sentence. Cook is sent to death row, located at the Ellis I Unit near Huntsville, Texas.

1979

1980

1981

Witness Says Cook Was Man In Apartment

1982

Cook Gets Death Penalty

1983

Tunnell Sets Death Date

1984

1985

1986

September 1987
Robert Hoehn, who testified at trial he was with Cook the night of the murder, dies of AIDS in Dallas.

1987

June 10, 1977
Linda Jo Edwards found dead in Apartment 169 of Embarcadero Apartments complex.

August 5, 1977
Kerry Max Cook arrested in Port Arthur, Texas, and charged with capital murder in connection with Edwards's death.

September 1977
Smith County grand jury indicts Cook on a capital murder charge that alleges he stole one of the victim's nylon stockings.

Officer Confirms Cook Fingerprints

January 1983
Jack M. Skeen Jr. takes office as Smith County District Attorney.

CHAPTER 1

Glimpse of a Murderer

Paula Rudolph pushed open the front door of her Embarcadero apartment and intuitively felt she had stepped into an awkward situation.

The fact that the door was unlocked at 12:30 a.m. annoyed her. She diligently secured the door whenever she left the apartment and was adamant her roommate do the same. That night, as she stepped into the entryway, she glimpsed a figure standing in the doorway of the spare bedroom to her left. The figure quickly stepped forward and closed the bedroom door. The encounter lasted just seconds, but Rudolph's face flushed with embarrassment for interrupting what appeared to her as an illicit visit between her boss, James "Jim" Mayfield, and her temporary roommate, twenty-two-year-old Linda Jo Edwards. The two had an intimate on-and-off affair despite Mayfield being married and nearly twenty years her senior.

"Oh, don't worry. It's only me," Rudolph called out as she hurried through the living room on her way to the opposite side of the apartment. She lit a cigarette and stood in the middle of her bedroom trying to calm a lingering feeling that something wasn't quite right.

Was it really Mayfield? "That's the only explanation that makes sense," she thought. She longed to go to bed, tired from a workday extended by a night out with a friend. She had work in the morning too, but that nagging feeling made her hesitate. "What should I do?" she thought.

Moments later she heard the patio door open and close. "Yes," she thought, "it must be Mayfield." It seemed a rational explanation, although she later recalled Mayfield always used the front door. She finished her bedtime routine and went to sleep, content she had resolved her conflicting feelings.

Rudolph awoke the morning of June 10, 1977, at about 6:30 a.m. and reluctantly got out of bed thirty minutes later. She shuffled into the kitchen, started the coffee pot, then turned to face the sliding glass door that separated the living room from the patio. She noticed the open outside gate, and her cat—normally put in for the night— was nowhere to be found.

"Odd," she thought. She also expected to see or hear Linda stirring since she had to start a new job at a local bank that Friday morning.

"Linda!" Rudolph called out.

No response.

"Linda?" she called again.

She walked hesitantly to the spare room, eased open the door, and saw Linda lying on the floor. A pool of blood surrounding her head and a blood-smeared arm were all she saw before she hurriedly retreated. Rudolph ran to her own room and made two telephone calls: first to Tyler police and then to a coworker at Texas Eastern University where she worked in the library.

"Linda has been severely beaten," she reported. Rudolph forced herself to return to Linda's room to determine if her friend was still breathing. She opened the door wider than before, and this time noticed blood all over the lifeless body.

Rudolph forced her hand inside her mouth to stifle a scream as the horror of what she saw registered as a reality. Linda was dead.

Still dressed in her pajamas, Rudolph locked the cat—that had suddenly reappeared—in her bedroom, poured a cup of coffee, and then went out front to wait for the police. She steadied herself against the stucco wall and drank the steaming liquid, attempting to steady her nerves.

It wasn't long before patrol cars, an ambulance, and a television news van converged at the scene. Steve Knight, a police reporter for the *Tyler Morning Telegraph,* arrived to find the complex quiet since most of the tenants already had left for work. But the area outside Apartment 169—Rudolph's—was active as officers came in and out of the small apartment, now cramped with investigators collecting and tagging evidence, taking photographs, and dusting for fingerprints.

The gruesome scene officials found inside stunned them. It was obvious the victim suffered a violent death. But the body sprawled out in front of them showed so many wounds, it was difficult to immediately determine the exact cause of death. Stab wounds riddled her torso. Blood clumped around her wounds, and a lock of hair cut from the top of her head appeared to be missing as well. Her right earlobe had been severed, as was one quarter of her lower right bottom lip. A stab wound in the right breast and multiple stab wounds in the vaginal area added even more macabre aspects to her death.

A pair of bloody scissors and a broken plaster statue lay near her body. A nylon stocking remained on one leg as if she had been surprised as she undressed. Her blue jeans lay crumpled on the floor nearby, and her panties had been cut from her body and discarded onto the floor. The television set and an iron remained on, apparently throughout the night. Nothing else in the room appeared disturbed.

Knight somehow managed to dodge investigators to get a quick look inside. The atrocity he saw left an indelible image for a reporter just a year out of college. "It kept me awake for a few days after that," he recalled.[5]

Hours later, a short news story and a photograph of the victim's covered body on a gurney appeared on the front page of the *Courier-Times*—the afternoon edition of the Tyler newspaper.

---

5 Telephone interview with Steve Knight, December 3, 2012.

It would be the first of two headline-grabbing articles published that weekend. Neither article provided much detail about the murder, except to say the search for an unknown suspect was ongoing. In an interview with an investigator, Rudolph described the man she saw as White, slender, wearing white or light-colored shorts, and having tan skin. His hair, she recalled, was silvery, medium length in a "touching-the-ear fashion."

"I know that Linda had been seeing my boss, Jim Mayfield. My first impression on seeing the figure was that it was he, even though I did not see the facial features nor hear him speak," she wrote in her statement to police.

A preliminary autopsy revealed Linda had been beaten repeatedly, stabbed, and mutilated with a pair of scissors and another unknown sharp object. Rudolph's father solved that mystery nearly a week later when he found a large, bloody vegetable knife crammed between the tightly packed clothes in Linda's wardrobe closet.

Rudolph couldn't stand the thought of spending another night in her apartment and left to stay with a friend while her father cleared out her belongings. Knowing now that she had slept soundly while her friend lay dead just down the hall made her shudder.

Rudolph wasn't the only one in Tyler afraid to fall asleep at night. Linda's murder set the town on edge, especially since her death was the second within a month connected to Texas Eastern University. Just weeks before, student James B. Becknell Jr. fatally shot assistant biology professor Dr. W. Carl Roddy[6] outside his campus office in an apparent dispute over a grade.

The murders shocked a community of residents who still considered Tyler a small, quiet town despite its population of nearly 70,000. In some respects, Tyler was, and still is, the center of East Texas because of its location between Dallas and Shreveport. It has a historic connection to the oil industry and serves as the hub for regional medical and educational institutions.

---

6 Becknell was convicted in December 1977 and sentenced to life in prison.

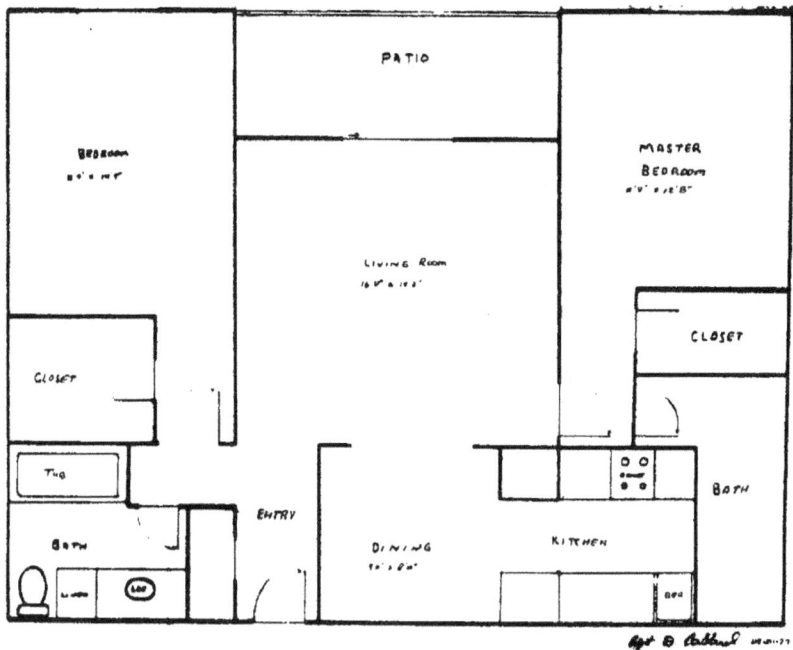

A diagram of Paula Rudolph's Apartment 169
at the Embarcadero complex in Tyler. The diagram was
admitted as evidence to help jurors visualize the layout.
Rudolph's bedroom was located to the right of the front door;
Linda Jo Edwards stayed in the bedroom located to the left.

As the Smith County seat, downtown Tyler also supports a hearty legal community as the home of the county courthouse, the US District Court Eastern District, and the 12th Court of Appeals of Texas. Broadway Avenue divides the city geographically, slicing through the downtown square and extending all the way to the city's southern boundary, where it becomes US Highway 69.

The 1970s brought the county's first-ever Republican sheriff and desegregation to the city's school district. New apartment complexes sprang up to accommodate a younger generation moving to larger communities with better amenities such as the newly built Broadway Square Mall. The Embarcadero Apartments—just off Broadway on Old Bullard Road—were located on what in 1977 was considered the outskirts of the city. The complex offered the advantage of being close to jobs, movie theaters, restaurants, and other activities, while maintaining relative distance. The Embarcadero was one of the newer apartment complexes in the area and, as its name implies, featured Spanish-style buildings with stucco exteriors. The complex appeared to cater to singles or young couples who enjoyed its swimming pool, tennis court, and clubhouse. Tyler's social scene also included a gay community—active, yet hidden from the judgmental eyes of a conservative mainstream.

News reporter David Barron grew up in Tyler and recognized how alternative lifestyles challenged the ideal small-town atmosphere its native residents thought still existed until the lurid details of Linda's murder became known. "People thought this [murder] is an example of what can happen when others begin moving into the community," he said. "It's like, 'What's our town coming to?'"[7]

---

7 Telephone interview with David Barron, December 10, 2012.

"I know that Linda had been seeing my boss, Jim Mayfield. My first impression on seeing the figure was that it was he, even though I did not see the facial features nor hear him speak."

–Paula Rudolph

CHAPTER 2

Just a Small-Town Girl

I came to know Linda Jo Edwards as a person, rather than just a murder victim, through my interviews with her brother, Jimmy, a tall, muscular blue-collar worker and family man. His blazing blue eyes filled with tears nearly every time we talked about Linda.

She grew up in Bullard, Texas, about fifteen miles south of Tyler. The town straddled the county line and was nothing more than a small cluster of homes and a few businesses in the 1970s. An old general store—the kind with a creaky screen door, wood-plank floors, and a low, open-top soda cooler—graced the center of town. Railroad tracks and a highway divided the population geographically north and south; Farm-to-Market Road 344 did the same east and west.

Linda lived on a farm with her parents Ray and Melba Sue, her sister Carolyn, and her brother Jimmy. Linda often got the better of her little brother by holding him down and tickling him until he cried for mercy. The two had inherited the same type of eyes—radiant color that drew attention and left a lasting impression. She had brown eyes and long, straight dark hair. She was taller and physically larger than most of her female classmates. She enjoyed horseback riding, playing basketball, and oil painting. Like a lot of farm girls, Linda dreamed of life in a city.

One of two photographs of murder victim
Linda Jo Edwards released to the media.

Her mother died in 1972, four months after being critically injured in a car crash. The incident happened as she rushed to a Tyler hospital to see Linda, who was being treated after a separate crash. Linda was only seventeen, but she took on the role of mother for her Jimmy until he was old enough to join the US Navy.[8]

8 Interviews with Jimmy Edwards and Carolyn Edwards Loftin, October 1991.

Just five months after her high school graduation, Linda married Bobby Lister, but the relationship ended badly in just a few years. She attended nursing school but lost interest and began working as a library clerk at Texas Eastern University.

Her coworkers were much older and wiser. They saw a personable, bubbly, but vulnerable and naïve young woman whose true beauty had yet to be realized. She craved attention, especially from men, and was too inexperienced in the world of relationships to recognize the dangers of falling in love with a married man.

The day of her death, Linda reportedly told Mayfield she intended to date other men—a declaration that angered him. She attempted to see him again later that night to talk but did not find him at his Lake Palestine home. Instead, she stopped by the home of a mutual friend, Dr. Andrew Szarka, a history professor at the university. After a brief visit Linda headed home where she met acquaintances at the Embarcadero tennis courts. She went to their nearby house for a drink, but appeared "nervous and apprehensive," her friends said, as if she were expecting someone. She left after about twenty-five minutes and returned to Apartment 169 about 10:30 p.m., where she met Rudolph as she was leaving the apartment.

Presumably it was the last time anyone—except for her killer—saw Linda alive.

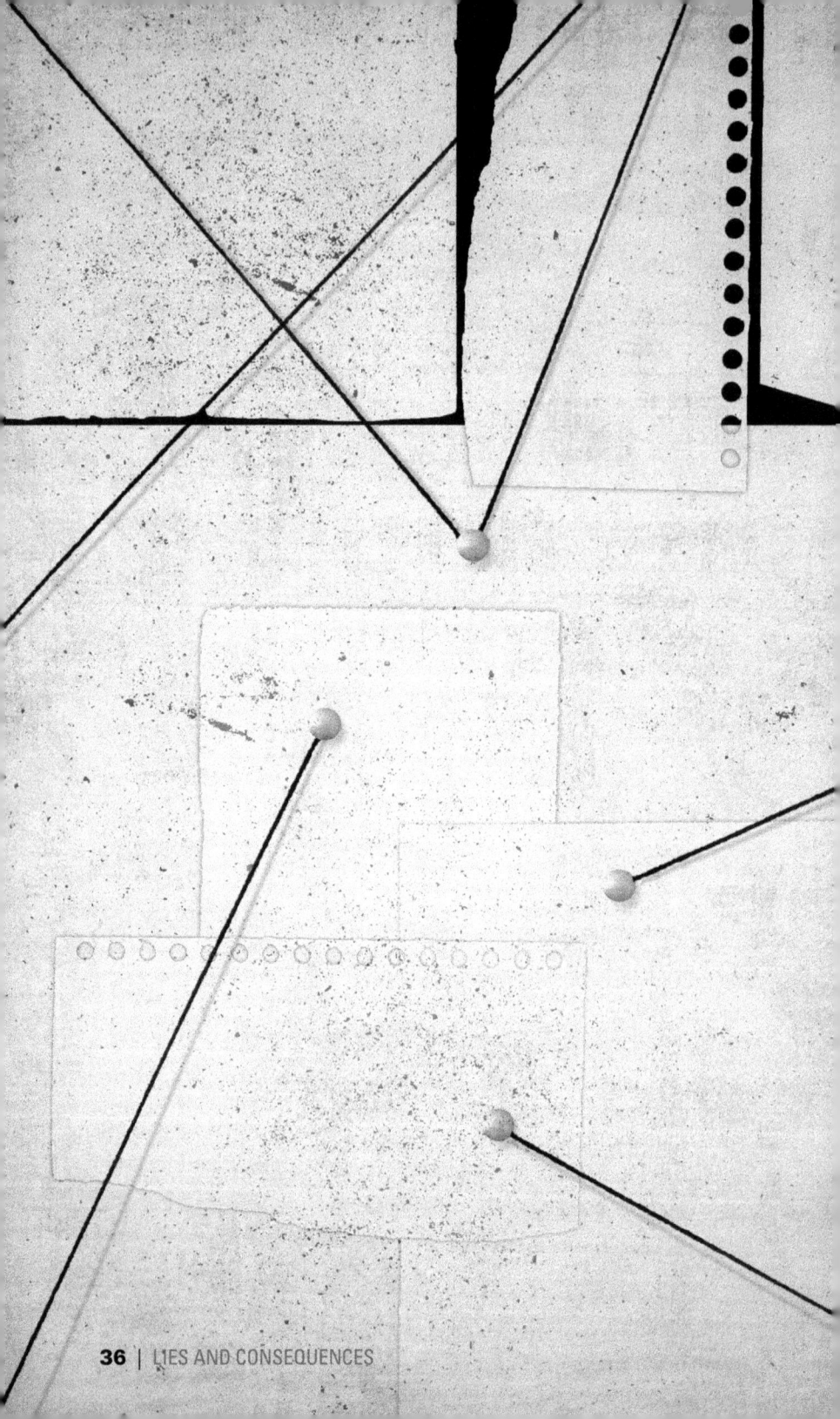

CHAPTER 3

The Affair

Linda's killer was on the loose, and people in the community remained guarded about their property and children. But some employees at the university's library were just plain scared. They had reason to fear Mayfield before the murder, but now they feared him even more because of the events in the prior weeks.

Mayfield's demeanor and physical appearance reflected someone who considered himself a distinguished man. He kept his gray hair well groomed, maintained a slim figure and a good tan from playing tennis, and he kept a sharp eye on the ladies. He had a master's degree in library science, and, as the university's director of library sciences, it was his job to create a library for the new Texas Eastern University. To do so, he oversaw the bulk purchases of books from discontinued libraries and other sources. He also worked with professors in the university's various departments to acquire books they deemed important to their respective disciplines, and he hired and supervised a team of clerks to sort, approve, catalogue, and shelve the books and periodicals.

In the university's early years, its campus consisted of the former Oran M. Roberts Junior High, an outdated brick building located just north of downtown Tyler. The library occupied the basement floor until administrators moved the entire school to its current location in east Tyler, where the main library consumed most of the floor above the student center.

Peggy McGill, Olene Harned, Ann White, Paula Rudolph, and Linda were among the library staff who processed the stacks of books and other materials. McGill, a widow, immediately recognized the type of man her boss was and, like many of her coworkers, feared retaliation for challenging his authority or interfering with his extracurricular social activities. "He had the most evil eyes," McGill said. "He would undress you with his eyes."[9]

Whether it was working in a darkened corner of the basement or being called to his office and invited to close the door, McGill knew to avoid being alone with Mayfield and to stand just out of reach of his roaming hands.

"He tried it on everyone and was very smooth about it," she said. "But he was the kind of guy that if you rejected him, he would fire you."

Office gossip recounted a previous affair with a former female employee, and it was only a matter of time before he set his eyes upon Linda.

At first there was a friendship. Because she was distraught about her divorce, she accepted Mayfield's invitation to live with his family until she could get back on her feet. Their affair began with a kiss at an office Christmas party. Mayfield had invited his employees to celebrate the holiday in his home. His repeated attempts to kiss McGill and others under the mistletoe were fruitless until Linda stepped up to the plate.

"They locked up in a long, passionate kiss," McGill recalled. "Thereafter you could tell she was totally infatuated with him."

At times, Linda spent more than an hour in his office with the door closed or met him behind the book-lined shelves. When her job processing newspapers backed up, Mayfield let her into the office after hours to catch up and to spend more time with her. During breaks with her coworkers, Linda could talk of nothing else but Mayfield.

---

9 Personal interview with Peggy McGill in Tyler, 2012.

The attention she received from her boss began to change her. She lost weight and took up tennis—Mayfield's favorite sport—creating a model figure. Mayfield thoroughly enjoyed his role as the man with a beautiful, young lover, but sternly warned his employees not to talk about the relationship. The affair was common knowledge among the library workers. The rest of the campus was none the wiser even when Linda accepted a position in the English department in an apparent attempt to distance herself from the inevitable gossip.

Within the month before her death, Linda moved into an apartment with Mayfield at the Embarcadero, and he filed for divorce. That arrangement only lasted a few days. The affair infuriated Mayfield's daughter, who stomped into the library one day to confront her father. The confrontation turned ugly, and sixteen-year-old Luella Mayfield publicly threatened to kill Linda during her tirade.

Mayfield soon realized he had made a mistake, risking his family life and career for someone who was no more than a child. His decision to return to his wife devastated Linda, who responded by taking an overdose of pills. In her suicide note, Linda addressed her lover by saying she "didn't want to go on living if we couldn't be together."[10] After she recovered, Linda attempted to start a new life. She applied for a job at a local bank and moved into Rudolph's apartment under the caveat that Mayfield was only welcome to visit as a friend, not as her lover.

But the suicide attempt drew the school administration's attention to the affair—a situation that would not be tolerated in conservative East Texas. Not only had Linda decided to leave, but Mayfield showed up to work one day to find a resignation letter prepared for him. His only choice was to sign it.

Mayfield had returned to the library Friday morning, June 10, 1977, to clean out his office when Rudolph's call reported the attack on Linda.

---

10 Mayfield later testified he destroyed the note.

He "went to pieces," and asked White to drive him to two area hospitals and then the police department in search of answers. His fruitless efforts led him to the victim's apartment, where he was greeted with the sights of emergency vehicles and reporters. The realization prompted conflicting feelings.

"He was upset and crying. And he looked back and watched kind of what was going on," White said. "And then he became angry, and he said that she had ruined him, that she had cost him his job."

Shocked by such a gruesome murder, library personnel braced for what they were certain would come next. They expected the police investigation into Linda's murder to focus on Mayfield because of the affair.

Mayfield voluntarily appeared at the Tyler Police Department on Friday afternoon, the day Linda's body was found, and talked to investigators for hours. Luella Mayfield also met with police. During a brief meeting in the school's auditorium days later, investigators also extended an offer to library employees to meet with them if they had any information to share. No one immediately came forward. Police appeared uninterested in Mayfield as a possible suspect and quickly ruled him out after confirming his alibi that he was home with his wife and daughter at the time of the murder.

Because of his history with the victim, Mayfield expected others to assume he had killed her. "You know what? Everybody's trying to blame me for Linda's death," Mayfield told McGill in a break room conversation. "You know I didn't do that, don't you?"

McGill shrugged her shoulders in response.

"He was upset and crying. And he looked back and watched kind of what was going on. And then he became angry, and he said that she had ruined him, that she had cost him his job."

—Ann White

CHAPTER 4

On the Trail of a Suspect

The task of finding Linda's murderer fell into the hands of Eddie Clark, a Tyler police investigator who, coincidentally, had grown up in Bullard and attended high school with the victim. Crime scene investigators discovered some fingerprints at the crime scene but who put them there, and when, remained a mystery.

Clark began his search to find the answer by casting a broad net, fingerprinting more than two hundred apartment complex residents. He also received assistance from psychologist Jerry Landrum, who also happened to live at the Embarcadero. Landrum reviewed basic information about the crime scene and developed a psychological profile of the killer.

Clark's search, however, appeared fruitless until one day he happened to walk past the open door to Apartment 147 where James Taylor lived. Although the detective had previously spoken to Taylor about the murder, Clark stopped to chat with him again, revealing characteristics mentioned in the profile. Something sounded familiar. Taylor suggested the detective check out a man who had lived with him briefly. The man, Taylor said, matched the psychological profile.

Clark followed the lead and found what he was looking for—a match to one of the fingerprints left on Rudolph's sliding glass door. A front-page headline in the *Tyler Morning Telegraph* on Saturday, August 6, greeted readers with the news that police were seeking a twenty-one-year-old Jacksonville man in connection with Linda's death. A three-column picture to the right of the story showed Police Captain Bob Bond holding up a poster-sized enlargement of Kerry Max Cook's mugshot obtained from a previous arrest record.

Cook's dark, full, shoulder-length hair was disheveled; his right eyelid appeared to droop, and his facial hair appeared patchy. He looked "wild." It's the type of picture that doesn't leave a good first impression.

Investigators refused to discuss how Cook became a suspect or a possible motive, but an arrest-warrant affidavit revealed his fingerprints had been found at the murder scene. The details of the psychological profile, however, were not public knowledge until Cook was arraigned on a capital murder charge.

In those days news reporters enjoyed relatively free access throughout the police station. Even Captain Bond formed close working relationships with some reporters, but when it came to discussing details of a crime, he remained tight-lipped. Bond did tell Tyler reporters that police had been looking for Cook for nearly two months and described their efforts as one of the city's most intensive manhunts.

The case made headlines again the next day in the Sunday edition of the *Tyler Courier-Times Telegraph*. The article announced Cook's arrest took place late Friday night, August 5, in the Texas Gulf Coast city of Port Arthur. Investigators found Cook at work at the Holiday Club after receiving a tip from Cherokee County Sheriff Danny Stallings, who was familiar with Cook's criminal history.

Cook was flown back to Tyler, denied bond, and booked into the city jail. Officers later moved him into a one-man cell at the Smith County Jail located on the sixth floor of the county courthouse just three blocks away.

ught
eath
lle Man

the head by an unknown object, detectives added.

Police searched the two-
bedroom apartment in
which Miss Edwards had lived
wo weeks for the murder
weapon without success until
ane 15, when the weapon, a
tchen knife, was found hid-
n behind some boxes in a
set near where the victim's
y was found.

he initial investigation
sed on detectives' attem-
o "get to know" Miss Ed-
s through interviewing
aintances and residents of
prawling South Tyler
nent complex.

ventually escalated into
fficers have referred to
if the city's most inten-
unhunts, involving as-
s three full- and part-

CT (Page 14, Sec. 1)

Staff Photo By Robert Langham

POLICE CAPT. BOB BOND SHOWS MUG OF COOK
Tyler Police Detectives Search For Edwards Murder Suspect

Reprinted by permission of *Tyler Morning Telegraph*

CHAPTER 5

A Wayward Youth

Kerry Max Cook was born in Stuttgart, Germany, in 1956, an Army brat who grew up moving from base to base with his parents Ernest and Evelyn Cook and older brother, Doyle Wayne. The military lifestyle left no time to establish roots or lasting friendships for the two young brothers.

The family returned to the United States in 1971, when Cook was fourteen. They found themselves back in Jacksonville, Texas, where his parents opened a restaurant.

Cook grew restless and bored with small town living and engaged in activities that caught the eye of local law enforcement officials. He called it joy riding, but the law defined it as theft. By his own account, Cook reported stealing more than forty cars, but he had other arrests for larceny, malicious mischief, and burglary. A local business owner also accused him of robbery, but the charges were later dropped. Cook retaliated by smashing the front window of the man's business.

He was tried as an adult in 1973 for taking a car and was sentenced to two years in state prison. Before being sent away, however, court officials ordered him to submit to a mental evaluation at the nearby Rusk State Hospital. In a hospital report, officials characterized Cook as a "typical rebellious juvenile," immature, and dependent. He was a self-described "momma's boy," who had the word "mom" tattooed on his left arm and admitted crying at night for his mother while at the hospital. A clinical psychologist noted his condition as "adjustment reaction of adolescence."

After being released from prison, Cook voluntarily committed himself to the hospital, saying he was depressed because he could not live up to the successes of his father and brother. "Situational anxiety reaction of adolescence" was noted on his record.

He again checked himself into Rusk State Hospital in May of 1976. His records noted his drinking, drug use, and claims that the Jacksonville Police Department harassed him. His diagnosis this time included the words "anti-social personality."

As an adult, Cook—a high school dropout—found himself wandering from city to city, staying with people he met along the way. He spent time in the Dallas, Houston, and Tyler areas looking for a job and a place to belong. Although he always denied being homosexual, Cook frequented gay bars and socialized within the gay community. He worked as an auto-transport driver, a construction laborer, a dancer, and a bartender. On one of his trips to Dallas, Cook met Taylor at a bar known as the Old Plantation. Taylor was an older man who worked as a truck driver and discretely lived a homosexual lifestyle in Tyler.

In the summer of 1977, Cook moved in with Taylor at the Embarcadero. A walking path to Taylor's apartment led past the back of Rudolph's apartment. It was along this path that Cook said he noticed a figure in a window of that same apartment. The figure was of a woman undressing—a scene Cook recounted to a handful of other guys, even pointing out the exact window.

Taylor contended he had a casual sexual relationship with Cook, but eventually asked him to move out. He later told a Smith County grand jury that he finally realized Cook was a freeloader who drank a lot of his booze and failed to contribute to the household.

He was a self-described "momma's boy," who had the word "momma" tattooed on his left arm and admitted crying for his mom at night while at the hospital.

-Report from Rusk State Hospital
on Kerry Max Cook

CHAPTER 6

Pretrial Battles

As he sat behind bars following his August 5, 1977 arrest, Cook's parents frantically searched for legal help and used all the money they had—$500—to retain Cherokee County attorneys John Ament and LeRue Dixon to defend him. The latter attorney's employment perplexed Cook since Dixon, a former state's attorney, had prosecuted him four years earlier for car theft. Cook had his doubts, but Dixon and Ament immediately requested an examining trial, a move that put a damper on any suggestion they weren't going to try their best for their client.

An examining trial is a hearing before a judge to determine if there is probable cause to present the felony charge to a grand jury. In most cases, the defense lets the case go directly to a grand jury.

The August 19 hearing before Smith County Court at Law #2 Judge Bill Coats was brief and to the point. District Attorney A. D. Clark III (no relation to investigator Eddie Clark) presented the state's evidence.

Clark called Rudolph to the witness stand to testify about the man she saw closing the door to Linda's bedroom that night. She testified she went to bed after hearing the patio door open and close, believing it was Mayfield.

"I thought I recognized the person who was there," Rudolph told the judge. "I didn't really find it that unusual or any cause for worry or alarm."

Tyler Police Sgt. Doug Collard took the stand next and testified he collected fingerprints from the frame of the sliding glass door about 9:00 a.m. the morning the victim was found. He said the fingerprints belonged to Cook and, in his opinion, had been placed there in the previous six to twelve hours.

Clark argued that Cook's fingerprints found at the scene within the approximate time of death was enough probable cause to hold the defendant and present the case to a grand jury. Dixon, however, insisted the state failed to provide the necessary proof, noting Rudolph did not identify Cook as the man she saw in the apartment that night; in fact, Cook did not match her description as having silver hair.

Judge Coats's ruling came quickly—bond denied, remanded to jail, proceed to grand jury.

In September 1977, a grand jury returned an indictment on a capital murder charge after a daylong session in which they heard testimony from four witnesses. The witnesses included Robert Hoehn (pronounced Hane), a Tyler hairdresser who was the only person who said he could account for Cook's actions (other than Cook himself) during the hours before the murder.

Hoehn told a grand jury he met Cook through mutual acquaintances, and although he had not known Cook for very long he characterized him as someone who acted as if "he owned the world" and "like someone owed him a living." He said Cook did not get along with his own family, and, as for his sexual orientation, Hoehn said Cook was a gay man who took on "the feminine roll [sic]."

"I am gay, and I know he was gay," Hoehn said. The night of the murder Hoehn said Cook pointed out the window where he had watched a woman undress and encouraged Hoehn to do the same. Hoehn said he refused.

That bedroom window belonged to Linda—the murder

victim Cook insisted he never met. He adamantly defended that claim publicly for the next fifteen years.

One of the most bizarre accusations claimed in the indictment was the allegation Cook stole one of the victim's nylon stockings. Prosecutors later argued the stocking was used to carry away parts of her sexually mutilated body that were never found.

Prosecutors convinced a grand jury that there was enough evidence against Cook to proceed to trial. What they didn't share, Cook's defense later claimed, was testimony favorable to the defense—known as exculpatory evidence. Their claim helped form the foundation of Cook's later attempts to prevent his retrial.

The defense filed a writ of habeas corpus with the 241st District Court. The writ is a way for a defendant to claim unlawful imprisonment, again forcing the state to present evidence in support of the arrest. Within the week of the indictment, Cook was brought back into court. Clark again took the lead in establishing a case for Cook's detention as a suspect.

Rudolph returned to the stand, repeating her testimony from the previous hearing, although she faced stronger cross-examination from the defense.

"I thought the person was Mr. James Mayfield," she said. "The figure didn't quite fit, not quite."

She said she thought there was something unusual about what she saw, but believing the man was Mayfield was a "logical explanation of what I perceived."

Pushed to be more precise, Rudolph replied, "I will not swear under oath who it was." She suggested that "in my own time" she may be able to make an identification, but now she was confident Mayfield was not the person she saw.

Collard again identified that a fingerprint found on the frame of the sliding glass patio door belonged to Cook and said the print was about six to twelve hours old when found.

The hearing also featured testimony from Landrum, the psychologist who had developed the profile for investigators. He testified he believed the person who killed Linda was a "homosexual, bisexual" person who had undergone recent psychiatric treatment, likely had used drugs, held a "pathological hostility toward his mother or all women," and had a problem with sexual performance.

For its part, the defense presented testimony from Cook, his mother, and Dixon. Their testimony addressed only the defendant's work history, financial status, and willingness to appear in court if he was released on bond.

District Judge Glenn S. Phillips denied bond at the end of the four-hour hearing and Cook returned to the Smith County Jail to await trial.

For Rudolph, the hearings and interviews with prosecutors required frequent trips to the downtown Tyler courthouse. During one of these visits—sometime between the writ hearing and Cook's trial—Rudolph found herself in the courthouse basement near the elevators. Her sister-in-law accompanied her that day, with both looking forward to shopping after Rudolph finished with business. As they stood there with a few other people, Rudolph suddenly gripped her sister-in-law's arm and squeezed it rather hard.

"What's the matter?" a startled sister-in-law asked Rudolph, who stood frozen in fear as she stared at one of the men in the crowd.

"That's the man I saw that night in my apartment," she responded, pointing to Cook.

"I thought the person was Mr. James Mayfield. The figure didn't quite fit, not quite."

–Paula Rudolph

CHAPTER 7

A Visit with Dr. Death

As summer slipped into fall, Cook's defense team filed several motions, including a motion for a speedy trial, but it wasn't until November that the prosecution took a big step in its attempt to secure a death sentence.

Without advance notice, investigators handcuffed and shackled Cook and drove him to Dallas for an interview with Dr. James Grigson, a noted forensic psychiatrist who earned the nickname "Dr. Death"[11] for his record as a state's witness in capital cases.

District Attorney Clark conducted a press conference in his office a few months later to announce Dr. Grigson's involvement in the case, much to the chagrin of Cook's defense attorneys, who knew nothing of the interview in advance and were not able to counsel Cook prior to or during the interview. Their letter to Cook advising him not to communicate with or talk to any doctor who wanted to interview him came in February 1978 in hopes of preventing another surprise.

As the new year rolled in, the defense filed a litany of pretrial motions, including requests for a gag order, a change of venue, and

---

11 In the 167 capital murder cases in which Grigson testified during his career, nearly all ended with a death sentence. In those cases, he testified the defendant was certain to kill again.

a court-ordered deposition of Mayfield to learn more about his relationship with the victim and his whereabouts the night she was murdered. Ament and Dixon knew this was a big case, one that attracted a lot of media attention and public interest. A gag order prevented anyone involved in the case—including prosecutors, investigators, jailers, etc.—from publicly discussing the case. The change of venue meant moving the trial out of Smith County where it would be unlikely the public (i.e., potential jurors) could be influenced by media coverage. The defense knew their battle was not only against the evidence presented in court, but also against public opinion, and they wanted a jury of citizens totally unfamiliar with the case.

As for Mayfield, the defense couldn't understand why investigators never seriously considered him a suspect or investigated his alibi more thoroughly. The defense got their chance to question him nearly seven months after Cook's arrest. In his statements, Mayfield admitted his affair with Linda, but insisted he was at home with his family the night she was killed.

Judge Phillips approved the gag order but declined to move the trial out of Tyler. And in one other significant matter, the judge ordered the state to disclose plea agreements with any witness in exchange for testimony. Prosecutors claimed there were none.

Reprinted by permission the of Texas State Historical Association.

Dr. James Grigson

CHAPTER 8

On Second Thought

Attorneys began questioning potential jurors on June 5, 1978, nearly a full year after Linda's murder. After thirteen days of questioning, attorneys selected eight men and four women to hear evidence in the case of *The State of Texas v. Kerry Max Cook* (No. 1-77-179).

Attorneys expected the presentation of testimony to take three to four weeks, but in the end, it took longer to seat a jury than to try, convict, and sentence Cook to death. Judge Phillips took the added precaution of sequestering the jurors for the duration of the trial that began June 22, 1978.

Cook's trial would be the first capital case to be tried in Smith County's 241st District Courtroom. Legislators created the new court—the fourth district court for Smith County—that April, and county officials decided to renovate the second-floor law library and central jury room to accommodate the new courtroom and judge.

The courtroom—still in use today—is located across from two public elevators that service the courthouse. A third elevator located just around the corner is used to securely transport inmates from the top two floors where they are housed to the courtrooms or the sally port in the basement where they can be transported by a secured vehicle to a state prison.

The courtroom itself is significantly smaller than the 7th and 114th District Courtrooms located on the same floor. The jury box, off to the left in the northwest corner of the room, allows jurors to see the witness stand, judge's bench, and opposing counsel, but not necessarily the rows of wooden benches used for public seating.

Spectators packed the courtroom to hear the opening statements in the case. Cook's parents sat on a wooden pew just a few feet behind the defense table, but no one from the victim's immediate family attended.

Assistant District Attorney Mike Thompson immediately set the tone for the entire state's case, telling jurors that Cook's "lust for blood and perversion" led him to kill the subject of his voyeuristic wanderings at the Embarcadero Apartments.

Thompson, thirty-five, was a local, graduating from Chapel Hill High School, a small community just east of Tyler, and Tyler Junior College before earning a bachelor's degree at Stephen F. Austin State University and a law degree from The University of Texas Law School. He was District Attorney Clark's go-to guy. Thompson was a very serious man, likable, tall, and gaunt, with a low monotone voice that cracked. The prosecutor reminded news reporter Barron of the fictional character Ichabod Crane. Outside the courtroom, Thompson had a profound stutter, but inside the courtroom he spoke clearly and had "a way with words."[12]

Thompson outlined the state's evidence, telling jurors that witnesses would testify that Cook became sexually aroused that night while engaging in homosexual acts and watching the movie *The Sailor Who Fell from Grace with the Sea.* And Cook's fingerprints found on the victim's patio door put the defendant at the scene at the time of the murder, he said. Thompson also said another witness would testify Cook revealed details about the crime during a jailhouse conversation. The prosecutor called his first witness after the defense deferred its opening statement.

---

12 Interview with Tyler attorney Randy Gilbert, 2012.

Collard, now a lieutenant with the Tyler Police Department, repeated his earlier testimony about Cook's fingerprint but elaborated about where it was found and identified. He said Cook's fingerprint had to have been left when the defendant pulled the door shut while standing inside the apartment. Collard said that in his opinion, the fingerprints had been left there about six to twelve hours before being discovered.

A comparison between the print lifted from the patio door and a known print taken from the defendant contained twenty points of exact matches. Only ten points are required to make a positive identification, he said.

Throughout Collard's testimony, the prosecution also presented as evidence dozens of photographic slides taken at the crime scene. He also identified the victim's clothing, some of which had been cut off her body by her attacker. A strong, foul odor filled the courtroom as officials unsealed the plastic bag containing the victim's clothing.[13] The odor lingered as jurors watched intently as each slide projected on the courtroom wall took them on a virtual tour of the crime scene, including pictures of the victim's bloody corpse lying in the middle of the floor.

The second day of proceedings included the testimony of two teenage brothers—Randy and Rodney Dykes (Taylor's nephews)—who testified Cook showed them the victim's bedroom window through which he had watched a woman undress. Jurors also heard from Rudolph, who identified a plaster statue,[14] a pair of scissors, and a fourteen-inch-long knife police identified as murder weapons found inside the apartment.

She also repeated her earlier testimony, detailing the events leading up to the moment of her gruesome discovery, except this time she pointed to Cook and identified him as the man she saw that night inside her apartment. Cook instantly reacted. "That's—" he began to blurt out before Dixon silenced him. Rudolph, whose

13 Interview with David Barron, 2012. Barron was a *Tyler Morning Telegraph* reporter who covered Cook's first trial in 1978.
14 The statue was called *The Bookworm.*

voice and hands sometimes shook during her testimony a reporter noted, continued her testimony, saying the defendant fit the "silhouette" and "the figure that is burned into my mind."

Under intense cross-examination, however, Rudolph admitted she did not see the figure's facial features and that she initially thought the man was Mayfield. The news account of her testimony did not report whether the prosecution or the defense pursued a line of questioning to explain how Rudolph was now able to identify Cook—an identification she first made when she saw Cook weeks earlier standing at the basement elevators.

The next morning's newspaper headline about the trial missed the significance of the witness's identification. The headline simply read, "Victim's Friend Gives Testimony."

"lust for blood and perversion"

–Smith County prosecutor
Mike Thompson suggests
a motive during trial

CHAPTER 9

Mounting Evidence

Until this point in the trial, the prosecution's case had focused on who killed Linda, but it hadn't explained why. That question would be addressed during the third day of testimony—a rare Saturday session—when Hoehn testified he visited Cook in Taylor's apartment at the Embarcadero.

Hoehn, who testified he was a homosexual, said he went to the apartment that night to deliver beer and ended up staying to watch the movie *The Sailor Who Fell from Grace with the Sea* on cable television. The movie involves the suggested mutilation of a cat by a group of boys and the impending murder of the main male character.

At one point during the movie, the witness said, the two men went for a walk, and Cook attempted to get him to look into Linda's window. Hoehn said he refused.

When they returned to the apartment, Hoehn said Cook became a "little excited" and the two engaged in sexual activity. Afterward, Hoehn said, he went to the bathroom and, when he returned, found Cook exiting the kitchen with a knife. He quoted Cook as saying, "Let's cut it up" or "Let's cut it out."

After the movie, Hoehn said, he drove Cook to the store to buy cigarettes and let him out of the car at the apartment complex about 12:30 a.m. The jury and a curious courtroom audience spent most of the day watching the movie, except for the portion Hoehn said he and Cook did not see when they went for a walk.

When the trial resumed on Monday, the prosecution presented Smith County inmate Edward Scott Jackson—known as "Shyster"—as a witness. Jackson testified that, while viewing pictures in *Playboy* and *Hustler* magazines sometime between September 2 and 15 at the county jail, Cook confessed to killing Linda. The witness claimed Cook detailed how he cut, stabbed, and mutilated the victim.

The "revelation" prompted another angry denial from Cook, who blurted out, "He's lying," as he attempted to stand. Dixon restrained him and ordered him to be quiet.

Jackson said Cook described how he stabbed Linda and cut off a portion of her hair. Under cross-examination, Jackson denied defense allegations that he was lying in exchange for leniency on his own murder charge.

The prosecution wrapped up its evidence with the testimony of Tyler pathologist Dr. V. V. Gonzalez, who performed Linda's autopsy. He said he believed Linda was alive as her killer took up to ten minutes to mutilate her body with a pair of scissors. The witness said he found numerous wounds to the victim's sexual organs, which were so mutilated he could not determine if she had been raped. He also told jurors the victim had been stabbed between twenty and thirty times in her chest, neck, and back with the pair of scissors and a kitchen knife.

Jackson's incriminating testimony was buried deep within the next day's newspaper article. The headline that day simply stated: "Defense Due to Begin in Cook Trial." Burying the lede reflected more lackluster coverage of the trial testimony. The reporter's failure to recognize the importance of particular testimony and to explain intricate legal issues for readers created information holes I would have to fill years later. A journalist's role in accurately and completely recording historic events is greatly appreciated by a researcher attempting to piece together crucial elements of a story.

"He's lying."

—Kerry Max Cook interrupts the testimony of Shyster Jackson

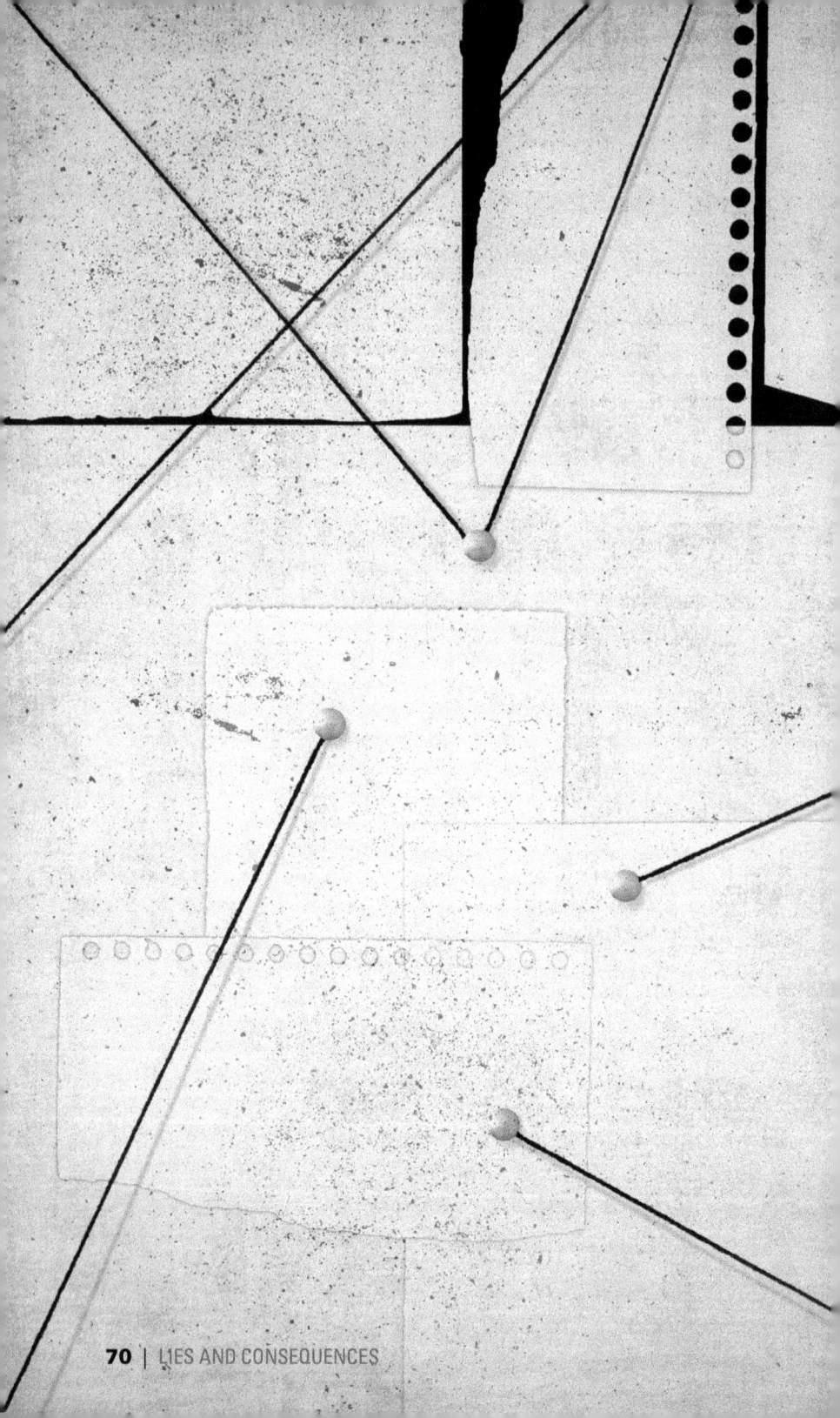

CHAPTER 10

Final Arguments

Cook's defense consisted of three witnesses, all Smith County Jail inmates, who testified Jackson told them he fabricated the confession story in a deal with prosecutors. Witness William Fomby told jurors Jackson considered his testimony to be an "ace in the hole" to get his charge reduced to manslaughter.

Jackson's court-appointed attorney, Woody Roark, testified as a rebuttal witness for the state. Roark said there was no plea agreement in exchange for Jackson's testimony.

The presentation of testimony consumed five days. On the sixth day, jurors heard final arguments—the attorneys' last chance to summarize and evaluate the evidence to convince the jurors of Cook's innocence or guilt.

Thompson cut to the chase, arguing the evidence proved beyond a reasonable doubt that Cook killed Linda. He repeatedly referred to the defendant as a "pervert" and a "sexual psychopath" whose actions—mutilation—mirrored suggestive scenes from the movie.

The prosecutor claimed the evidence wove a sickening scenario in which Cook stuffed the body parts he cut from Linda's body into a nylon stocking and took them with him. "I wouldn't be surprised if he didn't eat those body parts," Thompson told the jury.

The remark drew a quick objection from defense attorney Ament, an objection the judge sustained and instructed jurors to disregard. Readers likely questioned the missing body parts comment since news reports of the trial did not report any such testimony.

"This man," Thompson concluded in referring to Cook, "is a ghoul as he walks among you."

Defense attorneys argued the state had failed to prove all the elements of the indictment, but specifically targeted the fingerprints and Rudolph's identification. Dixon argued experts could not tell at what time Cook's fingerprint was left on the patio door and, he reminded jurors, a fingerprint on the pair of scissors had yet to be identified. The defense attorney also called the jurors' attention to the time element, saying it would have been impossible for Rudolph to have seen Cook in her apartment because Hoehn testified he dropped the defendant off at the complex at the same time. He also reminded the jury that her description of the man did not match Cook.

The charge against Cook consisted of five counts: murder in the course of aggravated rape, burglary with the intent to commit aggravated rape, burglary with intent to commit aggravated sexual abuse, burglary with the intent to commit aggravated assault, and burglary with the intent to commit theft. To convict, jurors had to find the murder occurred during the commission of at least one of the other alleged offenses.

It took the jurors four hours to return a guilty verdict—an announcement made after 10:00 p.m. on Wednesday, June 28, 1978. Cook left the courtroom sobbing. He and the jurors returned to the courtroom the next morning to begin hearing testimony in the punishment phase of the trial. That phase took only a day to complete.

"This man is a ghoul as
he walks among you."

–Mike Thompson, prosecutor

CHAPTER 11

The Penalty Phase

Sometime between that late hour and when the trial resumed the next morning, prosecutors and defense attorneys met behind closed doors to discuss a possible deal that could have saved Cook from a death sentence and presumably brought another possible suspect to justice. Negotiations between the prosecution and the defense are not uncommon but are conducted privately to prevent tainting the jury if a plea is not reached. The details of the meeting during Cook's 1978 trial remained secret for decades.

The proposed deal was a bust, and back in court the prosecution called sixteen witnesses addressing the defendant's "bad" reputation in the Jacksonville area. The witness list included psychiatrist Grigson, who testified Cook was "the most severe" type of sociopath who would continue to be a threat to society.

Psychologist Landrum added the icing on the cake, saying he believed Cook not only was a continuing threat but had "no chance" of being rehabilitated. The defense challenged Landrum's remarks, attempting to get the witness to concede that treatments for sociopaths had been improving over the years. Landrum disagreed.

During closing arguments, Thompson portrayed Cook as a sexual deviant who deserved to die: "But I proved to you beyond a reasonable doubt that that man is one of the worst perverted killers that this county has ever seen, and I hope to God you take his life. I hope you take his warped, twisted, and perverted mind out of existence so he can never perpetrate what he perpetrated on that young woman that night."[15]

The guilty verdict put the defense attorneys in an awkward position during their closing arguments. Despite promoting Cook's innocence, Ament's job now was to convince jurors his client should not be executed. He reminded the jury that executing Cook would not bring Linda back and there was a chance Cook could be rehabilitated.

Dixon appealed to the jury's emotions. "I wish I knew some nice Biblical phrases and words of eloquence . . . and beg you for mercy," he said. "The best thing I can say is please don't kill him."[16]

Jurors deliberated about an hour before finding that Cook acted deliberately, that he constituted a continuing threat to society, and that his actions were unreasonable in response to provocations, if any. Those findings constituted an automatic death sentence.

In an exclusive interview with news reporter Barron immediately after the trial, Cook denied knowing the victim, claimed he had never been inside her apartment, and denied knowing who killed her. He said he regretted the problems his conviction caused his family and vowed to one day prove his innocence.

"I'll prove I didn't do it. If it takes me ten years, twenty years, I'll prove I didn't do it," he said.[17]

He couldn't have realized then just how close his statement came to being prophetic. It would be at least thirteen years before he would even be given a chance.

---

15 David Barron, "Cook Found Guilty of Capital Murder," *Tyler Morning Telegraph*, June 29, 1978, 1.

16 David Barron, "Cook Found Guilty of Capital Murder," *Tyler Morning Telegraph*, June 29, 1978, 1.

17 David Barron, "Convicted Killer Has Found 'Peace,'" *Tyler Morning Telegraph*, June 30, 1978, 1.

"I wish I knew some nice Biblical phrases and words of eloquence...and beg you for mercy. The best thing I can say is please don't kill him."

—Defense attorney LaRue Dixon

CHAPTER 12

Climate of Deceit

Cook unknowingly made his mark as the first defendant in Smith County to be sentenced to die after the US Supreme Court effectively reinstated the death sentence in 1976. Before then, Edward Eldon Corley, convicted in the 1974 rape-slaying of a twenty-year-old Chapel Hill woman, was the county's only representative on death row.[18]

Despite Cook's conviction and death sentence, there remained a core group of citizens—specifically a handful of Mayfield's former employees—who believed Cook's trial represented the quintessential "kangaroo court," a slang term that originated during America's frontier days to mean a defendant's rights were grossly ignored.[19]

Cook's defenders didn't hide their opinions, but there was nothing they could do to help him. Their opinions, however,

---

18 Corley was convicted in 1975 in McClennan County, to which his trial was moved on a change of venue. Although the murder was committed in Smith County, Texas records reflect the county of conviction.

19 In the early eighteenth century judges roved (hopped) from venue to venue exacting justice, their pay based upon the number of trials over which they presided and the amount of fines they levied. The practice tended to promote quantity, rather than quality, of justice. Thus, the term "kangaroo court" came to mean a trial in which proper procedure, precedents, and due process were denied.

were based on Mayfield's reputation and their strong belief he had something to do with Linda's murder. Cook's trial left many in the group with no confidence in the judicial system. "I feel like that boy's life was ruined," library staff member McGill recalled. "There was just too much politics . . . and he [Cook] was a nobody."

Cook's hopes of getting a new trial, however, had to be based on legal issues, not public opinion. There were professionals (in addition to his defense attorneys) in another camp who believed he was the victim of a "kangaroo court" for specific legal reasons.

To fully understand the basis of the challenges levied over the next two decades questioning the fairness of Cook's trial, one must first understand the legal culture within Tyler County and Smith County from 1977 to 1981.

Cook's trial came on the cusp of the most tumultuous four years in Smith County's legal history, although his case was just a blip on the lifeline of city and county government at the time. Corruption—both real and perceived—within the city's and county's justice system created a dark, indelible stain that would come back to haunt officeholders for decades.

Self-described journalist David Ellsworth chronicled the depth and breadth of that corruption in his book *Smith County Justice*, a 662-page exposé about the biggest drug bust in the county's history and its aftermath. The nonfiction account centers on the police chief's ruthless pursuit of a club owner and a hit list of other residents believed to be part of a growing underworld of sex, drugs, and crime. Two undercover narcotics officers resorted to falsifying or planting evidence, intimidation, and perjury to make cases against more than one hundred people.[20] An attempted cover-up involved even more layers of lies and deception within the city and county legal system that included various means of retaliation and retribution against anyone—citizens and authorities alike—who stood in the way. It was Smith County's version of Watergate.

The Smith County judicial system meted out "justice" to those

20 One of those undercover officers, Kim Ramsey Wozencraft, wrote the book *Rush*, a supposed work of fiction about the two.

citizens caught up in the web of deceit. The undercover officers were so believable that at one point in this sordid tale Texas billionaire and future US presidential candidate H. Ross Perot provided them shelter.

Tyler and Smith County authorities repeatedly defended their actions and launched their own battle to deflect mounting criticism from defense attorneys, *The Dallas Morning News*, and other media sources, as well as those people within the ranks of the city, county, or state systems willing to speak out and risk their careers. Mounting pressure from a federal investigation eventually forced the officers to admit the truth. They served prison sentences for their roles in the ordeal, but the police chief was acquitted on federal charges.

Ellsworth himself was revealed as a fraud. His real name was Joe Werner, and when he wrote *Smith County Justice,* he was a fugitive from California wanted on a 1965 theft charge. Despite his own stained reputation, Ellsworth's book became a collector's item for competing reasons—those who want to bury the past and those who don't. The latter group still believes the "powers that be" in Tyler are on a search and destroy mission to wipe out every copy of *Smith County Justice.*[21]

The scandal surrounding the undercover drug operation in Tyler left a plethora of "human flotsam" in its wake, Ellsworth noted, but his story also included peripheral characters already associated with Cook's case or who became familiar years later in his retrials—Doug Collard, Joe Tunnell, and Sheriff J. B. Smith to name a few.

Smith took office in 1976 but became an apparent victim of retribution by the district attorney's office when certain officials believed he wasn't supporting the Tyler Police Department's efforts in the drug busts. Smith was suspended from office during his first term while facing a litany of charges alleging misconduct. Smith successfully beat the charges with the help of his attorney, Joe

---

21 Whether true or not, the previous scarcity of the book had reportedly driven the price from $300 to $500 a copy. A quick Google search also reveals a copy offered by someone claiming to be Kenneth Bora himself, who for $2,000 also will sign the copy. The book was reprinted in 2014 and is available in soft cover for about $34.

Tunnell. He went on to serve an unprecedented six consecutive terms of office as Smith County sheriff.

And then there is Hunter Brush, the Tyler attorney who succeeded District Attorney Clark after defeating him in the 1978 primary. Brush's assistants prosecuted the tainted drug cases developed by rogue undercover officers. It was Brush's second turn at the post, having served from 1967 to 1970. In his first term of office, Brush surrounded himself with what one local legal historian recalled was the best group of assistant prosecutors of their time.[22] But his second term wasn't reminiscent of the first and forever would be linked to government corruption in Ellsworth's book.

With Cook locked away and the appeal process just beginning its long journey, interest in the case—with a few exceptions—began to fade in Smith County, especially when the focus turned to the drug scandal.

Just three months after the end of Cook's trial, prosecutor Thompson went to his sister's Tyler home, put a gun to his head, and pulled the trigger. He left behind a wife and four children. His sudden death led some people to speculate for decades if he had become despondent over Cook's prosecution, but his reason behind such drastic action remains a public mystery to this day.

District Attorney Brush inherited Cook's case and faced defending the state's prosecution of Cook within months of taking office. The Texas Court of Criminal Appeals in Austin agreed to hear oral arguments in Cook's appeal in February 1980, but when the date came, Smith County prosecutors failed to show.[23]

---

22 Interview with attorney Randy Gilbert, 2012.
23 Brush told the Tyler media his office had not been notified of the upcoming hearing in Cook's case, although a defense attorney's assistant said a copy of the confirmation letter sent to the Austin court also was sent to prosecutors. The district attorney also said he did not see a front-page news story about the upcoming hearing published the Friday before the hearing. Judge Phillips, who presided over Cook's first trial, expressed being "shocked and appalled" about the lack of Smith County representation in a terse letter to Brush. "I'm not trying to run your office . . . However, I do believe that the people of this County are entitled to better representation from your office than was provided in this instance and I also believe that the weeks and weeks of effort put forth in my court in the trial of this case deserves better representation," Phillips wrote.

During these arguments, opposing attorneys are allowed to argue why or why not an appeal should be granted. Justices also have the opportunity to ask attorneys questions or to clarify an issue. The court uses this information in their continued deliberations. At the time, Brush's office was preparing for the upcoming trial of a key defendant in the undercover drug bust. A state's attorney in Austin with no knowledge of the case was asked to fill in thirty minutes before the hearing began.

Within his first year in office, Brush also faced prosecuting his first capital murder cases. Andrew Lee Mitchell of Tyler was convicted and sentenced to die for fatally shooting Troup fireworks stand employee Keith Wills during a robbery that netted less than $150. His appeal would take twelve years to play out and reveal another questionable law enforcement investigation. In time, Brush publicly expressed "great doubts" about Mitchell's guilt. James Sessions of Jacksonville received a death sentence in 1980 for killing Clifford McDougal of Troup during a robbery at the victim's home.[24] McDougal's wife, Belle, also died in the attack. A defense attorney later alleged prosecutorial misconduct in appealing that case too.

Mitchell, Sessions, Cook, and Corley remained the only Smith County representatives on death row when Jack M. Skeen Jr. took over the district attorney's office in 1983.

---

24 Sessions died in prison of natural causes in 1999.

CHAPTER 13

Skeen's Tenure Begins

The aftermath of the tainted Tyler drug bust began to dissipate as a new decade dawned, but the cloud of suspicion cast over the legal system in Smith County still hovered like a fine mist as the 1982 election season began to take shape.

Federal Judge William Wayne Justice ordered Sheriff Smith reinstated to the office he had been suspended from the year before, and cases against ninety-seven defendants from the 1979 undercover drug operations were dismissed because of the lack of credibility of two narcotics officers. District Attorney Brush decided enough was enough and announced he would not seek reelection.

The open position attracted contenders Skeen for the Democrats[25] and J. R. "Dick" Brumbelow on the Republican side. Both were uncontested in the primaries, but Skeen cruised to victory in the general election after Brumbelow dropped out. So, in 1982, Smith County voters put their trust in Skeen to uphold the laws and seek justice for crime victims. Skeen was relatively new to the political scene, having served as an assistant district attorney, the City of Tyler's attorney, and later as a Tyler Municipal Court Judge.

---

25 Later in his career, Skeen switched to the Republican party.

Since his father and grandfather were East Texas natives who raised their families in Tyler, Skeen was educated in the Tyler school district and at Tyler Junior College before earning his undergraduate degree at The University of Texas in Austin. He earned his law degree from Baylor University School of Law before returning to Tyler.

Skeen faced the difficult job of attempting to rebuild public trust in the district attorney's office. It didn't help matters much that Skeen and former District Attorney Clark are first cousins—Skeen's father and Clark's mother are brother and sister—a fact that didn't become an issue until Cook's conviction was overturned more than a decade later.

When he took office in 1983, Skeen couldn't have known he would eventually oversee the prosecution of some of the most high-profile criminal cases in Smith County history. But along the way, he established a reputation as a tough prosecutor who pursued justice even in controversial cases involving law enforcement officers as defendants.

During Skeen's first decade in office, Smith County reportedly led the state in obtaining the longest prison sentences for major crimes and the second longest for lesser violent crimes, according to a Sam Houston State University study.[26] Concerning capital punishment, Skeen set the bar high when it came to securing a death sentence in Smith County. Seventeen defendants received a death sentence during Skeen's nearly two decades at the helm, with the first coming in 1985 and the last in 2001. He also inherited four capital murder cases in which a death sentenced was imposed. As of 2023, fourteen of the defendants (seventy seven percent) his office tried had been executed. Of the remaining cases in that category, two won appeals, and one remains on death row. Of the four inherited cases, one won a new trial but agreed to plead guilty for a life sentence, one was freed after pleading guilty to lesser

---

26 Evan Moore, "Justice Under Fire: 'Win at All Costs' Is Smith County's Rule, Critics Claim," *Houston Chronicle*, June 11, 2000. Efforts to obtain a copy of this study from Sam Houston State University were unsuccessful.

charges and was freed for time served, one died in prison of natural causes, and then there is Cook. In comparison, Skeen's successor, Matt Bingham, added only five defendants to Texas death row during his fourteen-year tenure.

Skeen's first capital murder trials in 1985 ended with convictions and death sentences, but the Texas Court of Criminal Appeals overturned both on appeal. Thomas L. Dunn received a death sentence in the stomping death of Francis Willington but won his appeal a year later with a ruling that the trial court had erred by admitting a confession he allegedly gave a Smith County investigator. The appellate court ruled the investigator illegally coerced T. L. Dunn into confessing by suggesting that by doing so he would not receive the death sentence. T. L. Dunn was removed from death row but served time for rape. Decades later, he confessed to killing Willington and another woman and received a life sentence.

Bonnie Erwin received a death sentence for the 1982 kidnapping and murder of Patrick Brooks. That sentence was overturned when the appellate court ruled the trial court failed to compel a witness to appear to give testimony that reportedly favored the defense. Skeen decided not to retry the case because Erwin already was serving life without parole plus 105 years in a federal prison after being convicted of engaging in a continual criminal enterprise.

The T. L. Dunn and Erwin cases, in themselves, appear to reflect a continuation of questionable law enforcement practices in Smith County. Although the high court's written opinion clearly notes the trial judge's error in admitting the alleged confession (and, of course, the investigator's method of obtaining it), Skeen would learn in Cook's case that the errors of others within the legal system can mean guilt by association for prosecutors.

CHAPTER 14

A New Generation

In retrospect, the late 1970s and early 1980s offered many changes to the legal system within Smith County. As the drug scandal reached its peak and then faded, county officials continued to work on updating outdated jail facilities. The county was outgrowing the limited space provided by the 1950s-era courthouse, which had housed the sheriff's department in the basement and reserved the top two floors for jail space. Although it was convenient and secure to simply transport inmates to court without ever leaving the building, the cramped accommodations were attracting unwanted attention from state jail inspectors, who warned county administrators the facility was falling out of compliance.

County commissioners secured and renovated the sixteen-story former Carlton Hotel at the corner of Broadway Avenue and Elm Street, just a block south of the courthouse. It housed not only the sheriff's department but the adult probation office as well. The building served the county for the next thirty-plus years before the sheriff's department moved part of its operations to more modern facilities at the downtown square.

As for the jail, the county built a new facility on Elm Street—about one block east of the old Carlton Hotel—that opened in 1986 with a 276-bed capacity, an exercise yard on its roof, and a tunnel under the brick streets of Tyler to allow secure transport of inmates to and from the courthouse. The county also constructed its first of two low-risk jail facilities in North Tyler by the end of the decade but continued to use the fifth floor of the courthouse to house trusties—nonviolent offenders who are trusted to work outside their cells under supervision. Court administrators began using the sixth-floor cells to lock up trial evidence and other court records.[27]

A modern jail added a new physical dimension to the downtown skyline, but there were more changes to come in the 1980s, when the old guard of justice in Smith County gave way to a different generation of judges and prosecutors. Judge Phillips, the first judge of the 241st District Court, resigned for health reasons in 1985 and was replaced by the appointment of Tunnell to the bench. Tunnell—who had successfully represented Sheriff Smith—went on to serve two terms, presiding over Cook's first retrial before he retired. In 1986, voters elected Court at Law Judge Bill Coats as judge of the 7th District. By the end of the decade, the 114th District Court also would get a new judge: Cynthia S. Kent, the first female district judge to be elected in Smith County.

During their tenures, Tunnell, Coats, and Kent would preside over the most infamous capital murder cases in Smith County history.

---

27 On a late afternoon in 1996, court reporter Steve Awbrey took the jail elevator to the sixth floor and was on the opposite side of the room when a deputy making his 4.30 p.m. rounds accidentally locked the main door, barring Awbrey from the exit and leaving him behind bars. Awbrey found a pile of surplus table legs and used one to extend through the steel bars and push the elevator button. He wrote a note seeking help, attached it to a table leg, and attempted to toss it into the elevator. It took five tries to succeed and then send the elevator back down, where his note was found by a jail trustee. Awbrey was rescued after spending about thirty minutes locked up.

Photo of the Smith County courthouse.

PART II

Under Review

TIMELINE:

1987

December 9, 1987
Texas Court of Criminal Appeals upholds Cook's conviction in an 8–1 vote.

December 28, 1987
Doyle Wayne Cook, brother of Kerry Max Cook, is fatally shot during an altercation.

1988

July 8, 1988
Scheduled execution date for Cook, but order is stayed in June by US Supreme Court. Texas Court of Criminal Appeals ordered to review again.

Smith County Grand Jurors Hear Cook Testimony

1989

Cook Says Second Trial Will Prove Him Innocent

Expert Identifies Second Fingerprint

1990

January 17, 1990
In a 7–2 vote, Texas Court of Criminal Appeals upholds Cook's conviction for a second time.

Blames Publicity for Move

June 13, 1990
Texas Court of Criminal Appeals grants defense motion for rehearing.

1991

April 27, 1991
Cook's father, Ernest Cook, dies.

September 18, 1991
Texas Court of Criminal Appeals overturns Cook's conviction and death sentence.

Kerry Max Cook Death Sentence Overturned

CHAPTER 15

Inside Out

The aftermath of Cook's sensational 1978 trial followed the typical cycle surrounding most major news events. All the buildup, the hype, the emotions and then it's over and life goes on, or as my mother always says, "the herd moves on." The attorneys move on to their next case, big or small. The media returns to its daily routine. The public finds another issue to discuss in the local coffee shops. The defendant's parents are left to deal with the stigma of having a convicted murderer for a son. The victim's family continues mourning their loss but believes justice has been served.

Linda's murder entwined the lives of strangers as if they were a braided rope, but the conviction and sentence unraveled that connection, freeing those life strands to continue separate, but parallel, paths. Those involved went on with their daily lives but shared the consternation of awaiting a decision on Cook's appeal for the next thirteen years. Cook's arduous journey through the appellate system eventually re-entangled those strands into a legal fabric of justice—or injustice—depending upon one's point of view.

Cook left Smith County in handcuffs and shackles in 1978— transported from civilization to a prison cell on death row at the Ellis I Unit in Riverside, Texas. His stay in the Smith County Jail— as lonely and frightening as it was—paled in comparison to what

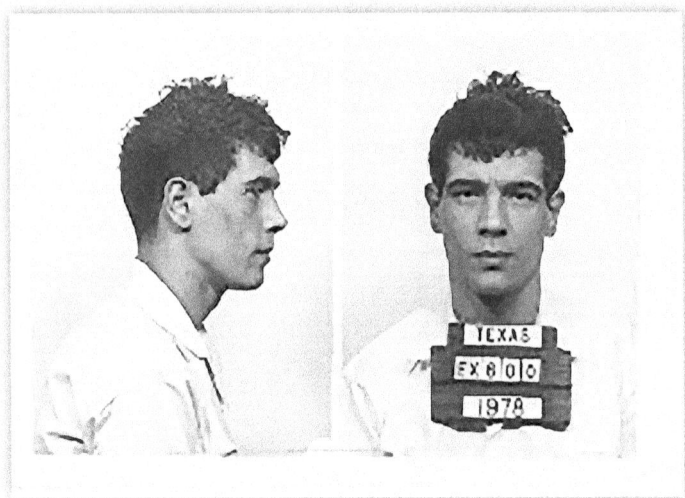

An intake photograph taken of Kerry
Max Cook after he arrived at the Texas
Department of Corrections to begin
serving his sentence on death row.

he was about to face in a state prison. That ball of emotions—fear,
disbelief, anger, and hurt—sat in the pit of his stomach like a rock.
He had few possessions and no money, cut off from the outside
world by concrete and steel and guarded day and night in the most
active death row in the country. He went in as Kerry Max Cook,
but as far as state officials were concerned, he was a number—600.

At Ellis I Unit, Cook faced a life for which he was not totally
prepared—a life not necessarily in his control. He was told when
he could shower, exercise, eat, and sleep. Guards watched his every
move, inspected his mail, and regulated his visitors. And he fended
for himself against the predators who lived inside the same walls.

More than anything, he had time. Time to think about every
detail of his trial repeatedly. He thought about it night and day,
trying to make sense of any of it. He dreaded the isolation from his
family and his attorneys. And then there was the stark reality—the
thought that someday guards would appear at his door, shackle

him, and drive him to Huntsville, where he would be strapped to a gurney and injected with a lethal dose of chemicals.

He tried not to think about what it would feel like to struggle to breathe and then slowly slip into unconsciousness, to never wake again. The thought of that final moment fueled his reoccurring nightmares, especially when Texas resumed executions in 1982.[28] Carrying out a death sentence was no longer an abstract idea for those awaiting their fate on death row.

Twice during my journalism career, I voluntarily spent the night locked in a jail cell just so I could at least experience something I often wrote about. I also was arrested in 2011 on a trespassing charge by a police officer working as a security guard for a public event. My unwise decision to argue with the officer cost me a few hours in jail and a few hundred dollars in bail. I remember feeling like I didn't exist as I sat on a cold bench outside the office where I would be photographed, fingerprinted, and required to answer a litany of personal questions. I had to remind myself that I wasn't a reporter just visiting. I was an inmate who wasn't allowed to speak unless spoken to by an officer. When I was granted permission to go to the restroom, I was locked in a bare holding cell by myself and promptly forgotten. I pounded on the door to no avail, waiting for what seemed like eternity before I finally noticed a small white intercom button on the wall. The guard seemed in no hurry to come and return me to the intake area of the jail. Finally, I was taken for arraignment before a justice of the peace, who denied my request to be released on my own recognizance. It was a little unsettling to realize the next step was being strip-searched and dressed in an orange jumpsuit, especially since another female inmate warned me about being locked in a certain cell with a certain group of women. Fortunately, I was able to make bail through a bondsman before that happened. I considered spending the weekend in jail just so I could renew my request for a public recognizance bond (no money required, just a promise to return

---

28 Charles Brooks Jr. from Tarrant County became the first Texas inmate to be put to death after the US Supreme Court reinstated the death penalty.

to court when called) before a different judge on Monday, but I quickly changed my mind when I saw what was being served for dinner. Prosecutors never pursued the trespassing charge, but I learned the consequences of being stubborn and how much an officer can embellish a report. My two voluntary one-night incarcerations and later arrest, however, pale in comparison to Cook's experience.

Cook's innermost thoughts about his trial and his new life behind bars aren't mine to tell. They are his and his alone. Only Cook and those who have stood in his shoes can adequately describe that experience. It is, however, important to review some key events of Cook's life behind bars to understand the reality of capital punishment in our society and not simply engage in an abstract exercise about the American criminal justice system. No doubt, Cook's every action and reaction will forever be scrutinized by opposing sides to condemn or justify the sentence imposed upon him in 1978. In either case, his time on death row is part of an unforgettable murder case.

Cook's introduction to J-23—the area of prison at Ellis I Unit known as death row—proved to be a harsh reality. His age, his slight build, and prevailing rumors of him being a homosexual made him an easy target for more experienced inmates. Although Cook repeatedly denied being gay, there were acquaintances who swore otherwise. By his own account, Cook was "punked out"—a prison term describing someone who must subject himself to the sexual pleasure of another in exchange for protection. Killing the person who attempts to take that control is the only way to prevent being a prison punk. Cook told me he became a target within the first three months of his incarceration, and one day during recreation another inmate twice his size gave him a choice: take off all his clothes and submit or fight the man holding a handmade knife.

Cook submitted, and his attacker finished the task by carving "good pussy" on his buttocks. The attack was more than he could handle emotionally, and within a few days he managed to pilfer a small razor blade and cut himself in what he described as his first suicide attempt behind the walls of death row.

Prison records noted only "small puncture wounds" on his arm, and a clinical psychologist who evaluated the incident noted the injuries were only superficial and "almost ludicrously small."

"I suspect he was seeking attention," wrote psychologist W. J. White, who also expressed doubts Cook represented a serious suicidal threat.

It wouldn't be the only time Cook harmed himself. Other documented incidents reveal a disturbing obsession with self-mutilation, often directed at his penis or testicles. Prison documents show eight incidents involving Cook cutting himself between 1979 and just months before his conviction was overturned in 1991. One of the most serious cases occurred in May of 1986 when he gave authorities a bizarre account of attempting to tattoo his penis and an ensuing infection. The swelling prevented him from urinating, so he inserted a hollowed ballpoint pen in an attempt to get relief. The pen barrel broke off and he attempted to remove it using a razor blade.

Before his dad's death in 1991, Cook was hospitalized after another suicide attempt in which he nearly severed his penis and cut his testicles and throat with a razor blade. He left a note: "I really was an innocent man. Amy Joanne, Mama, Daddy, Doyle Wayne. I can't do it anymore. I love you." Prison officials videotaped a bloodied Cook being taken from his cell to the prison infirmary before he was transferred to a hospital.

His despondency prompted episodes of self-mutilation or suicide attempts and often followed being sexually assaulted by other inmates and/or his intense emotional reaction to others seeing the crude tattoos on his buttocks, he told me.

Cook found it difficult to "fit in" socially on death row. He periodically wrote letters to the warden or other jail officials requesting to be removed from J Wing. "This places me in an extremely depressing state of mind. I am not strong enough right now to adequately cope . . . with the . . . pressure I have in my life currently," he wrote in a 1988 request.

For the most part Cook kept to himself, although there are two recorded incidents of physical altercations with other inmates. Twice, guards also found him in possession of a homemade knife, and once he was restricted to his cell for fifteen days for possessing marijuana.

He spent most of his time working on his case and writing letters to anyone he thought could help him prove his innocence. He researched legal issues in the law library and typed his own legal briefs or requests for copies of court opinions. When he thought his appeals attorney, Harry Heard, wasn't doing enough, he wrote the judge, the warden, or a court official to voice complaints or seek more information. He worked briefly in the Death Row Work Program and earned a General Equivalency Diploma in 1989. In 1991 he married by proxy a twenty-year-old Tyler woman named Amy Joanne Ticer.[29] The two had been introduced through another inmate who was involved with Ticer's mother.

Ticer told a news reporter she strongly believed Cook was innocent. "I'm going to stand by him through it and that's why I don't have to wait for the outcome of the court to marry him," she said. "I know he is a good person."[30] But their marriage fell apart within months, despite constant letters and visits. Cook contends the relationship succumbed to pressure from Ticer's mother, but others contend Ticer's interest in another man was the clincher.

Cook's relationship with immediate family members waxed and waned throughout the years. There were times he felt abandoned as their lives continued separate paths whereas his remained relatively stagnate day after day, year after year. He learned of his brother's murder in December 1987 through a telephone call from his father and had to mourn alone in his cell. Years later, as his father's health deteriorated, Cook desperately attempted to talk to him by telephone.

---

29 The ceremony was performed in Jacksonville at the home of Cook's parents. His father stood in for him as the groom.

30 "Death Row Inmate Awaiting Review of Case Gets Married," *Dallas Morning News,* July 6, 1990.

"My father lies near death in a Jacksonville hospital," Cook wrote in a note to a guard captain, seeking telephone privileges. "Speaking to him by phone may be my last opportunity to spend time with him alive." The request was granted, but Cook was never given the opportunity to make the call. Ernest Cook died on April 27, 1991. A prison chaplain told him of his father's death the next morning.

His determination to find someone to push his appeal consumed most of his time. Longview attorney Harry Heard had presented Cook's initial appeal, but those pleadings languished in the Texas Court of Criminal Appeals. As luck would have it, Cook also captured the attention of attorney Robert McGlasson during a visit to death row. McGlasson sent colleague Scott Howe to talk with Cook, and Howe vowed to take over the appeal.

Cook also called upon Jim McCloskey of Centurion Ministries, a New Jersey–based ministry assisting prisoners it believes have been wrongly convicted. McCloskey and Houston attorney Paul Nugent helped free Clarence Lee Brandley in 1990 after he spent nine years on death row for the murder of a sixteen-year-old girl in Conroe, Texas.

McCloskey agreed to take the case after reading Cook's own written account.

The tide was about to turn, and Cook felt confident he now had the attention his case needed, although it was difficult for him to keep up with any new developments. Most of the time he learned of court decisions via the radio or television news or other inmates who had somehow gotten word from the outside.

CHAPTER 16

The Appellate Battles

In Texas, a capital murder conviction that results in a death sentence is automatically appealed to the Texas Court of Criminal Appeals in Austin, the state court of last resort for criminal cases. The Texas Supreme Court hears appeals in civil matters. In America, only two states—Texas and Oklahoma—have separate high courts for criminal and civil cases. After a conviction a defense attorney submits a written document outlining arguments addressing why they believe the defendant did not receive a fair trial. The appeal, however, must address issues involving the trial proceedings. Prosecutors are given an opportunity to rebut the allegations and then the justices determine whether all the applicable laws were properly applied. In a death penalty case, all nine Texas judges are required to participate in the appeal.[31] The appellant's (defendant's) guilt or innocence is not an issue. In essence, the court is "grading the papers" of the lower court.

---

31 Texas established the Court of Appeals (three judges) in 1876 to ease the caseload at the Texas Supreme Court. Initially, the Court of Appeals had jurisdiction in both civil and criminal cases. In 1891, the state removed the court's civil jurisdiction and renamed the court the Texas Court of Criminal Appeals. In 1966, the number of judges on the Court of Criminal Appeals was increased from three to five. In 1977, the court again expanded to consist of eight justices and one chief justice. The court may sit in panels of three judges to consider noncapital cases. All justices must sit in capital murder cases.

Ament and Dixon had done what they could to defend Cook during trial, but they weren't up for taking on the appeal. That job fell into the hands of Harry Heard, a Longview attorney. Heard took somewhat of a shotgun approach to the appeal, casting a relatively wide net in hopes of hitting some target worthy of consideration. He attacked the technical aspects of the state's case, alleging the state failed to prove any of the elements in the indictment that elevated the charge to capital murder. For example, the state couldn't prove sexual assault because the prosecution's own witness testified the body was so mutilated it was impossible to test for the presence of semen. Heard also presented a smattering of other points, including a shot at Assistant District Attorney Mike Thompson for repeatedly referring to Cook as a "pervert" and suggesting he had eaten the missing body parts—actions the defense contended were prejudicial and inflamed the jury. His meatier arguments concerned the testimonies of inmate Edward Scott Jackson, psychiatrist Grigson, and psychologist Landrum. The trial judge erred, he said, by misapplying laws addressing the admissibility of information obtained from a jailhouse snitch (Jackson) and information gleaned from a psychiatric interview without first advising the defendant of his right to remain silent and to have his counsel present.

Heard raised twenty points of error in his written appeal and defended them in oral arguments in 1980 before the Texas Court of Criminal Appeals—a hearing at which Smith County prosecutors failed to appear. All he and Cook had to do was wait. And wait. And wait.

Although opposing sides face deadlines for their submissions, the court itself is not under legal obligation to issue a decision within a certain time limit. The process may take months or even years depending upon the issues involved, allowing the case to slip from the public eye until a decision is issued.

In Cook's case, a decision on his initial conviction took nine years—one of the longest periods of any death penalty case in the country at the time. Why did it take so long? No one really knows, although a *Dallas Morning News* article on the subject suggested Cook's files had been misplaced and forgotten—slipped through the proverbial crack—for an undisclosed period.[32] By comparison, Smith County capital murder defendants T. L. Dunn and Bonnie Erwin, who were both convicted in 1985, spent less than two years on death row before the court overturned those convictions and ordered new trials. From 1978 to 1987, the State of Texas executed twenty-six death row inmates who had lost their appeals.

Decision day in Cook's case finally came on December 9, 1987, when the court released a thirty-eight-page opinion upholding his conviction and death sentence in an 8–1 decision. Presiding Justice John Edward "Jack" Onion Jr. wrote the opinion for the majority. Justice Sam Houston Clinton was the lone dissenter (twenty-two-page opinion). The court concluded trial evidence, both circumstantial and direct, could support the essential elements of the crime beyond a reasonable doubt. As for the prosecutor's choice of words ("I wouldn't be surprised if he didn't eat those body parts"), the appellate court noted the lower court immediately sustained the defense's objection and instructed the jury to disregard the statement. The defense, however, did not request a mistrial and therefore did not preserve an error for review. In other words, if the defense had requested and been denied a mistrial, then the appellant would have an issue to review.

The admissibility of Jackson's testimony depended upon whether the conversation between Jackson and Cook occurred before or after August 29, 1977. A change in the law allowed such testimony only after that date. Although Jackson had testified he believed the conversation occurred between September 2 and 15 of that year, he confused several dates during the trial. The Texas Court of Criminal Appeals ruled it was the trial court judge's responsibility to judge the credibility of the witness and that there

---

32 "Cook Thinks He's Step Closer to Justice, but Patience Wanes after 10 Years on Death Row," *Dallas Morning News*, March 6, 1988; "Cook Murder Appeal Undecided: Court Recesses without Ruling on Case That Earlier Was Delayed 8 Years," *Dallas Morning News*, January 29, 1989.

was evidence to support the presentation of his testimony before the jury. Heard also had attached evidence of Jackson's retraction and an alleged "deal" with the state; however, the majority ruled that material was not properly presented to the court and therefore could not be considered.

The final issue in the opinion addressed Dr. Grigson's testimony concerning future dangerousness. This point of alleged error concerns the defendant's Fifth and Sixth Amendment constitutional rights—the right against self-incrimination and the right to counsel. In the US Supreme Court case *Estelle v. Smith*, the court ruled a defendant must be warned that he has the right to remain silent and that anything he says can be used against him in court. The defendant also has a right to consult with an attorney before being interviewed by a law enforcement representative or someone acting on their behalf, for example, a psychiatrist. Although evidence clearly showed Cook had not been warned of his rights before Dr. Grigson interviewed him, the court had to decide whether that error prevented the defendant from receiving a fair trial. To do this, the court applied standards established in the 1986 *Satterwhite v. State* decision also involving what is known as the "harmless error" test. The issue then is determining the weight of the constitutional error as part of the verdict. The appellate court determined that even if Dr. Grigson's testimony had not been admitted, there was still sufficient evidence to answer the question of future dangerousness. This evidence included Landrum's testimony (which was not subject to *Estelle v. State* because he did not interview Cook personally to reach a decision on the future dangerousness issue), the testimony of thirteen other witnesses who testified the defendant was not known as a peaceful and law-abiding citizen, and the brutal nature of the crime itself. In Justice Onion's words: "The admission of Dr. Grigson's testimony was harmless beyond a reasonable doubt."

In his dissent, Clinton challenged the sufficiency of the evidence against Cook. "The evidence may be sufficient when one picks and chooses certain items, but a rational reviewer of all facts is left with serious questions whether a rational trier of fact could find guilt beyond a reasonable doubt," he wrote.

Clinton characterized Hoehn's testimony as being "the most prejudicial" and Jackson's as "the most incriminating." He discussed Paula Rudolph's identification at length, questioning her ability to identify Cook only by the shape of his body. He also noted investigators found other unidentifiable fingerprints inside the apartment, that Jackson's testimony included information suggesting Cook may have met Linda before her death, and that Jackson's subsequent sentencing on a manslaughter charge supported a "deal" for his testimony. Finally, Clinton challenged the timing of events on the night of the murder, noting there was not enough time for Cook to have committed the murder and then be seen by Rudolph about the time Hoehn testified he dropped off the defendant in the parking lot.

The appellate court's ruling set in motion two competing paths of action in a race against time. Near the end of May 1988, Cook returned to Tyler to appear before 241st District Judge Joe Tunnell, who set July 8 as his date of execution. Cook, now thirty-one, had less than two months to live. His life now depended upon Robert L. McGlasson, Scott W. Howe, and Eden E. Harrington, three attorneys associated with the Texas Resource Center, a federally funded community defender organization representing death row inmates in post-conviction appeals. Cook grabbed McGlasson's attention during a visit to death row.

McGlasson promised to investigate his case and sent attorney Howe to interview him. The three attorneys who took over Cook's appeal in 1988 scrambled to either petition the Texas Court of Criminal Appeals to reconsider its December decision or to appeal the decision to the US Supreme Court. In the meantime, they also had to request the execution be stayed as they continued pursuing the appeal. The stress of his impending execution, the rush to file more appeals, and the onslaught of new publicity were more than Cook could bear. His case was back in the public eye. That same year, Cook granted an interview request from television reporter

Nita Wilson from KETK–Region 56 in Tyler. In that recorded interview, Cook admitted looking through the window of the victim's apartment but insisted that was all he did.

"I never entered her apartment," he said.

"Did you know the victim?" Wilson asked.

"No, ma'am I didn't," Cook responded.

As for his fingerprint found on the sliding glass door: "It's mine," he said. "But I never entered that woman's apartment. I looked in the window. I never entered the apartment."

What happened in the next three and a half years constituted somewhat of a battle of egos between the Texas Court of Criminal Appeals and the US Supreme Court. Cook's defense team petitioned the nation's highest court to stay the execution and asked the court to review the Texas court's upholding the conviction. It was the US Supreme Court's turn to "grade the papers" of the Texas court.

The US Supreme Court agreed to review the lower court's decision and, in the meantime, agreed to stay the execution—just twelve days before Cook was scheduled to die. Within seven months the US Supreme Court remanded the case to the Texas Court of Criminal Appeals, instructing that court to reconsider its earlier decision in light of *Satterwhite v. Texas*. In other words, the US Supreme Court disagreed with how it applied the standard of harmless error.

The panel of Texas justices took another year to ponder the issue and again affirmed Cook's conviction and death sentence in a 7–2 decision returned on January 17, 1990. Justice M. P. "Rusty" Duncan III wrote the majority opinion in which the court expressed controlled disdain for what appeared to them as an indefinite task. The US justices, Duncan argued, were asking the Texas court to make a determination they themselves could not clearly define. "It is virtually impossible to make any empirical rules or guidelines that would produce unassailable results," Duncan noted. From reading the decision, the US Supreme Court, it seemed, did not want the lower court to determine whether the state's case against the defendant was sufficient on the issue of future dangerousness without Dr. Grigson's testimony, but rather on whether the state proved beyond a reasonable doubt that the psychiatrist's testimony did not contribute to the verdict obtained. Justice Duncan likened the task to US Justice Potter Stewart's attempt to define pornography.[33] The Texas court then concluded, "After reviewing the evidence at both the guilt/innocence and punishment stages of the trial and taking appropriate account of the vile, offensive, and sordid facts, and in light of what the Supreme Court state in *Satterwhite v. Texas, supra,* we find beyond a reasonable doubt that the improper admission of Dr. Grigson's testimony did not contribute to the appellant's punishment."

Clinton dissented again, but this time he was joined by Justice Marvin O. Teague. The opposing opinion took aim at the majority's supporting comment claiming the prosecutors only had made a "passing reference" to Dr. Grigson's testimony during closing arguments to the jury. Clinton, however, noted numerous references to Dr. Grigson's testimony in the state's opening and closing statements, and therefore it very likely contributed to the final verdict.

It appeared the Texas Court of Criminal Appeals had made up its mind, but five months later, in June 1990, it took an about-face and decided to reconsider the issue again. It would be more than a year before the court reversed its previous two decisions and determined: "It is impossible to conclude that the jury was convinced of Cook's future dangerousness . . . without the aid of Dr. Grigson's testimony. Our ultimate concern here is whether the Grigson testimony contributed to Cook's punishment. We cannot say, 'beyond a reasonable doubt' that it did not."

But as it was, the ruling opened a Pandora's box for a complicated case that was about to get even more complicated.

---

33 Stewart was an associate justice of the US Supreme Court from 1958 to 1981. He is remembered for how he identified pornography. "I know it when I see it," he said. Artemus Ward, "Potter Stewart," Free Speech Center, August 10, 2023, https://firstamendment.mtsu.edu/article/potter-stewart/.

CHAPTER 17

External Investigation

On the day the Texas Court of Criminal Appeals finally overturned his conviction, Cook learned the news from a reporter who was interviewing someone else in the visitation room. "I've been waiting for this moment, it seems, for all my life," Cook told another reporter. "There's no words in the annals of the English language to describe how I feel right now."[34]

The thin thread of hope that had kept him going now began to thicken with support not only from the court's decision but from his new legal team and the results of *The Dallas Morning News* investigation.

The Dallas Morning News began its investigation on September 12, 1978—within three months of Cook's death sentence. On this date, Dallas newsman Donnis Baggett, Texas Ranger Stuart Dowell, and businessman Don Trull met in a Smith County area motel room to hear a story by none other than Edward Scott "Shyster" Jackson.

Jackson was now a free man after pleading guilty to a manslaughter charge and serving twenty-one months of a two-year sentence for killing a man during a barroom fight. Jackson had been

---

34 Vanessa Curry and Associated Press, "Kerry Cook Due New Trial, Court Decides," *Tyler Morning Telegraph*, April 19, 1991, 1.

jailed on a murder charge when he testified in Cook's trial and swore under oath there was no deal with prosecutors in exchange for his testimony. That is not what he told the men in the motel room that day, and what he had to say would start *The Dallas Morning News* reporters on a twelve-year investigative path that would raise serious doubts about the fairness of Cook's initial prosecution.

Jackson claimed prosecutors did not overtly offer him a deal but made it clear to him that he would benefit for testifying against Cook. Jackson recanted his trial testimony, saying prosecutors coached him on what to say and left him alone in a room with photographs of the crime scene for him to study. He said he even took a lie detector test to bolster his credibility on the witness stand, but Jackson said jailers gave him sedatives to calm him and ensure he would pass. "I would have told them I was Superman and the needle [of the polygraph machine] wouldn't have wiggled, I was so sedated," Jackson said.

He told the men Cook never discussed the case with him nor ever admitted to killing Linda Jo Edwards. Jackson, however, refused to sign an affidavit or take a polygraph test about his new testimony unless he was granted immunity for perjury, according to *The Dallas Morning News* report. His recantation appeared in a June 15, 1979, article written by Baggett and Howard Swindle. It was the first public hint that evidence against Kerry Max Cook was beginning to unravel.

Baggett and Swindle were big guns at *The Dallas Morning News*. After graduating from Stephen F. Austin State University in 1973, Baggett worked briefly for the *Longview News-Journal*—just thirty-five miles east of Tyler—before he landed a Dallas reporting job in 1976. He eventually worked his way up to state editor and assistant managing editor. Swindle, who came to *The Dallas Morning News* in 1979, was an investigative reporter who loved to expose corruption, solve real mysteries, and write about true crime.

Baggett and Swindle collaborated on several articles about the Cook case, but Baggett also took aim at the Smith County District Attorney's office. The string of articles alleged ineptness at the highest levels of the Smith County criminal justice system and outlined its effect on Cook's trial. The headlines set the tone for what would become a bitter battle with Smith County prosecutors.

- March 19, 1978—"Critics cite lack of management by Smith County DA," Baggett.
- March 26, 1978—"Smith County DA blames court system for backlog," Baggett.
- June 15, 1979—"Lie helped sentence man to death, inmate says," Baggett and Swindle.
- June 18, 1979—"Death-row dreams haunt condemned 'mama's boy,'" Baggett and Swindle.
- June 27, 1979—"DA belittles recanted testimony," Baggett.
- September 5, 1979—"Tyler sex murder conviction appealed," Baggett.
- February 14, 1980—"Death scenario called 'impossible,'" Austin bureau of *The Dallas Morning News*.

The Dallas Morning News's independent investigation remained somewhat stagnant as Cook's appeal sat in the Texas Court of Criminal Appeals—a long delay in the normal appeal process that made the news in 1986 when *The Dallas Morning News* reported that Cook's case was the oldest undecided death-penalty case in the state. In the meantime, David Hanners inherited the case in *The Dallas Morning News* echelons of investigative reporters. For Hanners, a future Pulitzer Prize and George Polk Award winner, the Cook case became his white whale.

Hanners, who began his investigation in earnest in 1988, poked holes in the state's case in published articles throughout the next four years.

In a 1988 article,[35] Hanners revealed the details of that plea offer discussed between opposing attorneys before the punishment phase of Cook's first trial. The offer involved a life sentence if Cook implicated a second man. Cook reportedly offered investigators some information indicating Robert Hoehn was the main attacker and that

---

35 David Hanners, "Convicted Man Called Innocent Disclosure Sheds Light on 1977 Tyler Slaying," *Dallas Morning News*, March 3, 1988.

Cook could lead them to where the body parts had been buried. The offer was withdrawn when Cook's statements couldn't be corroborated, according to accounts. Prosecutors would again visit the possibility of Hoehn and Cook committing the crime together during a grand jury investigation in 1992 and again with affidavits obtained in 2013.

In a seventy-one-column-inch article published on February 28, 1988, Hanners's investigation concluded Cook was "railroaded" because of "questionable police tactics, over-zealous prosecutors and a weak defense." Subsequent articles detailed conflicting statements made by Landrum, opinions from legal experts who said police failed to pursue other clues in the investigation, and Collard's testimony about the age of Cook's fingerprints—deeming it "false and misleading."

Concerning Landrum, Hanners reported the Tyler psychologist who told jurors the defendant was a sociopath and sexual deviant who couldn't be rehabilitated had concluded in a separate evaluation report that Cook was nothing more than a trouble making adolescent in need of counseling. The report was made two years prior to Linda's murder when Landrum evaluated Cook at Rusk State Mental Hospital.

Within months of the Texas Court of Criminal Appeals granting Cook a new trial, Hanners wrote articles claiming discrepancies in the original autopsy report and that "vital" evidence was withheld from Cook's defense attorneys. Hanners also wrote a story based on the statements of a man named Richard Engle. Engle claimed Hoehn—who died of AIDS in September 1987—made a deathbed statement indicating the wrong man was serving time for Linda's death.

In all, Hanners authored more than thirty major newspaper articles from 1988 to 1991. The sensational headlines heralded problem after problem with Cook's prosecution. Hanners sought out legal experts to draw conclusions and provide opinions about the questionable evidence he found. Subsequent articles repeated earlier findings to provide a supportive link to his investigation.

Hanners's articles clearly shredded the illusion of fairness by Smith County law enforcement officials in Cook's case. In retrospect, however, I believe the articles also laid the foundation for a more controversial role, blurring the line between investigative reporting and advocacy journalism without readers realizing it. The headlines continued the punch attack on the Smith County justice system.

- February 28,1988—"Inmate Was Railroaded, Inquiry Suggests: Attorneys, Police Criticized in Slaying Case"
- March 1, 1988—"Execution Hearing for Cook Halted"
- March 3, 1988—"Convicted Man Called Innocent: Disclosure Sheds Light on '77 Tyler Slaying"
- March 4, 1988—"Ex-DA Says Cook Confessed but Texas Death-Row Inmate Denies Claim"
- March 6, 1988—"Cook Thinks He's Step Closer to Justice, but Patience Wanes after 10 Years on Death Row"
- April 10, 1988—"Psychologist Reviews on Inmate Disputed: Sentencing Testimony, Prior Opinion Conflict"
- April 12, 1988—"No Probe Planned by Agency: Testimony in Murder Trial Raises Questions"
- May 7, 1988—"Cook Execution Date to Be Set at May 19 Hearing, Judge Says"
- May 20, 1988—"Cook to Die For '77 Murder, Judge Rules"
- May 26, 1988—"Cook Case Psychologist Faces Ethics Inquiry"
- June 4, 1988—"Ruling Stirs Renewed Hopes for Cook Stay"
- June 24, 1988—"High Court Petitioned in Cook Case: Death Row Inmate's Attorney Expects Ruling Soon on Psychiatric Testimony"
- June 29, 1988—"Cook's Execution Stayed: Supreme Court Agrees to Review Accused Killer's Case"
- June 30, 1988—"Cook Apparently Tried Suicide before Winning Execution Stay, Officials Say"
- July 3, 1988—"Clues Not Pursued in Slaying: Tyler Police Work Was 'Sloppily Done'"
- July 26, 1988—"State Requests Review of Death Penalty Case"

- October 9, 1988—"Key Testimony in Cook Case Said to Be False: Fingerprint Evidence Disputed"
- January 15, 1989—"Criminal Behavior Forecast Questioned: Appeal by Cook Challenges Prediction"
- January 19, 1989—"Court Asked to Overturn Cook Sentence"
- January 29, 1989—"Cook Murder Appeal Undecided: Court Recesses without Ruling on Case That Earlier Was Delayed 8 Years"
- December 23, 1989—"'90 Mirrors '80 for Death Row Inmate Cook"
- January 18, 1990—"State Court Affirms Cook Death Penalty: Appeals Judges Restate 'Harmless Error' Ruling"
- January 21, 1990—"Ruling Raises Issues, Cook's Attorney Says Condemned Man's Bid for Retrial Dealt Setback"
- June 14, 1990—"Court Grants Cook New Hearing: Criminal Appeals Panel Reverses Itself in 1977 Murder Case"
- July 6, 1990—"Death Row Inmate Awaiting Review of Case Gets Married"
- August 21, 1990—"Inmate Cook Makes 4th Suicide Attempt"
- November 23, 1990—"Report in Cook's Case Examined: Experts Say Conclusion Wrong, Theory Unlikely"
- September 19, 1991—"Cook's Sentence Rejected: New Trial Ordered in '77 Tyler Killing"

Hanners's investigation also created a ripple of collateral complaints. Respective professional peers filed formal complaints against Landrum with the Texas State Board of Examiners of Psychologists and against Collard with the International Association for Identification's Latent Printer Certification Board. Part of the complaint against Landrum stated the Tyler psychologist had given improper testimony in Cook's original trial because he allegedly did not have sufficient evidence to express an opinion about the defendant's propensity for violence. Landrum later sued Hanners and *The Dallas Morning News* for libel but lost his case when Judge Joe Clayton granted a pretrial motion for summary judgment. The judge ruled the article constituted fair comment.[36]

The complaint against Collard pertained to his testimony about the age of Cook's fingerprints found on the sliding glass door. Experts contend there is no scientific way to determine the age of a fingerprint.

Hanners's news articles buried the Tyler competition, frankly because the Tyler newspaper couldn't or wouldn't compete. Newspaper editors chose to follow the developments in the case by using Associated Press stories based upon copyrighted reports from *The Dallas Morning News*. Most of the stories published by the Tyler newspaper appeared with no bylines and were buried somewhere on an inside page.

Hanners's investigation kept Cook's case in the public eye and helped attract the interest of Centurion Ministries.

---

36 Fair comment and criticism are protected by the US Constitution. Fair comment is a legal term for a common law defense in a defamation case. In this case, Hanners drew a fair conclusion by stating the facts—Landrum's separate contradicting statements.

CHAPTER 18

Positioning

The Texas Court of Criminal Appeals final reversal constituted a lucky break for Cook since his case happened to be caught in the net of a bigger issue that affected several death sentences in Texas. The US Supreme Court decided in 1981 a psychiatrist could not examine a defendant without permission and that any information obtained during the examination could not be used unless the defendant first was warned that information could be used during trial. The new rules applied retroactively; it just took time for that landmark decision to trickle through the Texas court system.

Cook wasn't the only Smith County defendant to benefit. By the end of 1992, the Texas court overturned the convictions and death sentences assessed against James Joseph Wilkens Jr. and Edward Eldon Corley on grounds of inadmissible psychiatric testimony.[37]

After nine years of dormancy in the Texas Court of Criminal Appeals and another four years of the appeal bouncing back and forth from state and federal court, District Attorney Jack Skeen found the proverbial ball back in his court in 1991 when the

---

37 Wilkens was convicted in 1988 for the shooting deaths of Richard Wood and four-year-old Larry Wayne McMillan Jr. Corley was convicted of abducting and fatally shooting Vicki Lynn Morris in 1974.

reversal finally came down. He would decide the future of Cook's case—one of the most challenging cases in the county's history. Skeen expressed confusion over the court's September 18 decision to reverse itself and announced he would request the state's highest court to again reconsider its decision. "It's the same law, the same issue, just a different outcome. It's hard to understand," Skeen told reporters.

Skeen's decision to continue the appeal is puzzling considering the Texas Court of Criminal Appeals and the US Supreme Court already battled over that issue and the Texas court relented. Under the circumstances, the prosecution's course of action appeared a waste of time or a tactic to gain more time to review the evidence. The task of writing the request and supporting brief was assigned to Amy Blalock, an assistant district attorney just a year out of law school. In a fifteen-page motion, Blalock requested the Austin-based Texas Court of Criminal Appeals reinstate Cook's conviction because it misapplied the standards in evaluating the weight of testimony about the defendant's future dangerousness. The state agreed Cook's attorney was not given proper advance notice of the interview with Dr. Grigson, but contended the error was harmless. The court rejected the motion within weeks—a decision that shouldn't have surprised prosecutors since the same court had just voted against that very issue.

The next step for prosecutors meant asking the US Supreme Court to reconsider the issue—another highly unlikely event. But first, prosecutors had to be licensed to stand before the country's highest court because the Texas Attorney General's office declined to present the case on Smith County's behalf. Blalock filed a one-hundred-thirty-six-page-page petition[38] in January 1992 addressing the same issue concerning Dr. Grigson's testimony. The prosecution noted that at the time Dr. Grigson interviewed Cook, the law did not require the defendant be warned of his right to remain silent or to confer with his attorney prior to the interview. Although that

---

38 The petition sent to the US Supreme Court is known as a writ of certiorari.

law changed in 1981 and was applied retroactively, Blalock argued it should not have applied. She also argued the Texas Court of Criminal Appeals misapplied standards evaluating the weight of Dr. Grigson's testimony and ignored other evidence.

The US Supreme Court rejected Smith County's arguments without comment in mid-April 1992, leaving prosecutors with the options of retrying Cook or dismissing the charges. Chief Felony Prosecutor David Dobbs told reporters that prosecutors would review all the evidence in the case and convene a grand jury to hear additional testimony as the state attempted to reconstruct its case against Cook.

As prosecutors contemplated their options, the defense team changed faces. Attorney Scott Howe, who had represented Cook through the ping-pong battle between the appellate courts, stepped aside to allow Houston attorney Paul Nugent to take the helm.[39]

Cook returned to Smith County Jail in March 1992. The reversal didn't mean correction officers would just open the prison gates and let him walk free. Cook still stood charged with capital murder and remained jailed under bond. The ride back to Tyler gave him the rare opportunity to see the world beyond the Ellis I Unit again, even if it was only through a pane of glass as he sped down the highway in a patrol car. As he gazed at the fields of grass and livestock, trees, houses, and cars, he allowed himself the pleasure of embracing hope and yet, he dreaded returning to what he considered the den of injustice, he told me later. Four years prior, he had come to Tyler and stood before Judge Tunnell and heard the time and date of his execution. He had come so close to being strapped to a gurney with a needle stuck into his arm, slowly descending into an endless sleep. Those thoughts still made him shudder.

Now, however, there was a chance. As he recounted to me later: Maybe—just maybe—the powers that be in Smith County could right the wrongs of the past and set him free, he thought

---

39 Howe had moved to Massachusetts and said he found it too difficult to adequately represent his client from two thousand miles away.

as deputies led him handcuffed and shackled into the bowels of the six-story county jail.

Dobbs met him in a jailhouse hallway, ostensibly to determine whether Cook preferred to stay at the Ellis I Unit or the Smith County Jail while awaiting the outcome of the state's appeal to the US Supreme Court. Prosecutors wanted Cook to remain on death row and weren't happy when Judge Tunnell ordered him returned to the Smith County. Tunnell dismissed their complaints, leaving prosecutors frustrated and without recourse.

The brief encounter sparked outrage from the defense team, who later added the incident to their list of misconduct complaints against the prosecution. The defense alleged Dobbs intended to interrogate Cook without his attorney present.

Up until that point the defense team had been publicly playing nice with prosecutors, suggesting the two sides were working together to reach an amicable resolution. But the defense soon changed the tone, making loaded comments aimed at increasing public pressure: "I hope he [Skeen] does the right thing and [does] not try an innocent man a second time for something he did not do," McCloskey, of Centurion Ministries, said. Cook chimed in after the US Supreme Court rejection: "I hope that all the legal hoopla is over. If District Attorney Jack Skeen is interested in justice, he will put aside ego and politics to prove to Texas there is justice in Smith County," he said.

McCloskey wasn't what I expected of a businessman who left a successful career to pursue a spiritual calling—an atypical midlife crisis. He was still a suit and tie kind of guy, a middle-aged man of average height, with a band of graying hair ringing his balding head and just a hint of a northeastern accent. He could blend right in whether the venue was a boardroom or a courtroom.

He went about his selfless work with passion and dedication that reflected a deep desire to right a wrong not for vindictive glory but as a servant to those in desperate need. His calling was a ministry of action, not words.

Centurion Ministries wasn't affiliated with a religion or church, but it was aptly named after the Roman soldier who questioned Jesus's crucifixion by proclaiming, "Surely, this one is innocent." Based in New Jersey, the organization's sole purpose was, and still is, to seek justice for those McCloskey believed had been wrongly convicted of a crime, especially those serving a life term or under a death sentence.

Most of what I knew about McCloskey and his nonprofit ministry initially came from a green trifold brochure he sent me as an introduction. He was a very open person, willing to talk any time he could spare a minute from his work. There were periods of time we would talk on the telephone nearly every week, and sometimes a month would lapse between conversations.

McCloskey and his team of investigators had reviewed every detail of Cook's case and concluded the man who had been locked away for more than thirteen years had "absolutely nothing to do with the death of Linda Jo Edwards."

I met McCloskey in person for the first time just before the spring of 1992. He had flown into Tyler and was staying at a La Quinta Inn on the city's southwest loop. I interviewed him in the hotel lobby.

Just the week before, McCloskey had concluded a case in Los Angeles where his two clients had been freed after serving more than seventeen years in prison.[40]

For the next two hours, McCloskey laid out his case—six points of testimony or evidence he believed raised serious questions about conviction. He insisted Paula Rudolph's testimony had changed over a period and that a photograph taken of Cook the day after the murder for his driver's license clearly showed he did not match the description she gave. He had a signed affidavit from an expert who stated it is impossible to determine the age of a fingerprint, and he characterized testimony that Cook "fled" Tyler after the murder as a lie. He also noted that Shyster Jackson recanted his

---

40 Clarence Chance and Bentley Powell had been convicted for the 1973 death of a sheriff's deputy. McCloskey and his investigator spent four years reviewing the evidence and tracking down witnesses who admitted police coerced their testimony. The investigation led to the discovery that a key jailhouse informant had failed two polygraph tests and received special treatment in return for his testimony.

trial testimony, and that the pathologist shifted the time of death to fit the timeframe in which Cook was at the apartment complex, although witness testimony put him in the parking lot at about the time Rudolph claimed she saw him in her apartment.

McCloskey also challenged the characterization of Cook as a "homosexual crazed killer" by stating a woman Cook once dated said he is "very normal and had no sexual inadequacies."

During our conversation, McCloskey expressed optimism about Smith County prosecutors' willingness to review his evidence. "I have great faith the district attorney here will review the case objectively and do the right thing," he said.

That hope soon faded.

McCloskey was so convinced of Cook's innocence that when Skeen decided to retry Cook and seek a death sentence, McCloskey refused to consider that prosecutors honestly believed enough credible evidence existed to bring before a jury. In his mind, the decision was based upon an inexcusable mixture of ego, vengeance, and ignorance. The die was cast, and McCloskey and the defense hunkered down for a fight they knew would be long, difficult, and bitter.

"I have great faith the district attorney here will review the case objectively and do the right thing."

–Jim McCloskey, Centurion Ministries

CHAPTER 19

Rebuilding the State's Case

Skeen was an old-school politician who worked hard to maintain good relationships with law enforcement agencies and voters while supporting the rights of crime victims and prosecuting offenders to the fullest. He wasn't about to simply give in, even though he faced sorting out the mess he inherited. His approach to Cook's case took two paths now: asking the Texas Court of Criminal Appeals to reverse itself once again and reviewing all the evidence in the case as well as new information brought to light by an independent investigation.

Skeen convened a grand jury in May 1992 to begin reviewing evidence beyond the reach of the public eye. He addressed the proposed plea agreement by calling former prosecutors to testify. Transcripts of the grand jury testimony revealed that former District Attorney Clark testified Cook's defense attorneys approached him with a plea proposal in 1978 after a jury found Cook guilty of capital murder but before the punishment phase of his trial began. Defense attorneys John Ament and LeRue Dixon approached prosecutors with an offer to save their client from a death sentence in exchange for testimony against another attacker, he said. "Cook was prepared to testify against Robert Hoehn . . . that Hoehn was the real actor who had done most of the mutilation," Clark said. "I told them I wasn't interested." Clark said Hoehn had passed a polygraph test and state prosecutors were convinced only one person—Cook—was involved in killing Ms. Edwards. "We told him, 'No deal. No dice. We weren't interested in any kind of deal.'"

Former Assistant District Attorney Thomas Dunn's testimony before the same grand jury supported Clark's. Dunn said a defense attorney proposed the deal and told prosecutors Cook's involvement in the murder was limited to hitting the victim in the head three times. Cook's attorneys said their client could show investigators where Hoehn had buried the missing body parts, the prosecutors testified. The proposed plea deal fell through when Dunn and police investigator Eddie Clark checked the backyard of Hoehn's former residence based on information from Cook and found nothing. A *Dallas Morning News* article published in 1988 revealed details of the meeting between prosecutors and defense attorneys. Prosecutors contended then that Cook had confessed—a statement Cook denied. Prosecutors could not compel Ament or Dixon to testify before the grand jury about the same exchange because to do so would violate attorney–client privilege. The law gives a client the right to refuse to divulge confidential communications as well as prevents defense attorneys from disclosing it. Similar legal privileges are afforded in communication between spouses, doctor/patient, and clergy/parishioner. Testimony about the plea deal couldn't be used in the state's attempt to prove the charge, but it could be used to show grand jurors the strength of the state's case. Grand jury proceedings are not public, allowing jurors to hear testimony and ask questions. A grand jury doesn't decide guilt or innocence, only whether members believe there is enough evidence to hold the case over for a trial.

About the only thing a reporter can do while the grand jury is meeting is to stand outside in the courthouse hallway and watch who goes into the grand jury room and how long they stay. This may or may not be good material for a news article. I recall seeing

Cook under guard in the basement hallway near the grand jury room. I'm not sure why he was there since he could not be compelled to testify, but I do recall he was surrounded by a group of women (at least three) whom I did not recognize but obviously were acquainted with Cook. When I approached Cook to talk, the women quickly surrounded me and questioned me about my intentions. They told me I couldn't talk with Cook and blocked my approach by crossing their arms and forming a horizontal line between me and Cook. Cook stood against the wall smiling and didn't say a word.

Cook's defense team wasn't the only point of pressure facing Skeen. Judge Tunnell set a May 8, 1992, deadline for Skeen to announce whether Cook would be retried. The deadline came after the US Supreme Court declined to reinstate Cook's conviction and death sentence and a defense attorney requested the judge set a bond. "Cook has a right to reasonable bail and now that the last legal hurdle is overcome, I hope prosecutors open their minds and look closely at other legitimate suspects," Nugent told reporters. "There is very strong evidence pointing to two others and very little pointing to Kerry Max Cook." He declined to elaborate on the identity of the "two others."

Those who knew Skeen and how he worked knew one thing: His tendency to think and rethink an issue could drag on for extended periods without someone holding his feet to the fire. Tunnell had the power and authority to do just that. Through my years as the Smith County reporter covering the courthouse, I learned to endure and appreciate many of Skeen's quirks. My tenure as court reporter fell within the final era of true "open" government—a time before courthouse shootings and terrorism forced local authorities to install metal detectors, bulletproof glass, and security doors. I routinely roamed the halls with the freedom to pop into nearly anyone's office or courtroom anytime within reason. At my office three blocks away, I could simply pick up the phone and call an official directly, and often he or she answered the phone.

Skeen recognized the importance of maintaining an open-door policy—both literally and figuratively—with the media, especially if the reporter earned his trust. Skeen always was professional, but he was a tough person to quote. Whether being interviewed in person or giving final arguments before a jury, he believed repetition got his point across. He never grasped the concept of a giving a "sound bite."

Skeen's approach could drive some judges crazy. One of my favorite stories involved Skeen and Tunnell, who had given the district attorney a time limit for his closing arguments during a trial. When time ran out and Skeen kept talking, Tunnell simply excused the jury. Skeen kept talking even as the last juror exited the courtroom and the bailiff closed the door. Some claimed they could still hear Skeen's voice from the hallway.

During closing arguments, Skeen worked himself into a frenzy—his face and neck turned a mottled red and his voice cracked with emotion. I never could determine if it was real emotion or contrived, but it didn't matter—he was effective. During one-on-one interviews outside the courtroom, I tried to keep up with Skeen, writing frantically to get his every word. I grew tired of basically writing the same thing, just three or four different ways, so I learned to turn on a tape recorder and sit back and nod my head in understanding until he was through. That strategy didn't work well for a telephone interview, and inevitably, just after we would finish and hang up, my telephone would ring shortly afterward. It was always Skeen with "one more thing" he needed to tell me or to make sure he had gotten his point across.

Tunnell was quite a character too.

As a Democrat, Tunnell was only one of two sitting judges of that political party in Smith County in the 1990s. His political philosophy came out more in making policy decision with other judges than it did on the bench. And he certainly wasn't afraid to butt heads with his Republican colleagues even though he often came out on the losing side of a vote.

When he was appointed to the 241st District Court in 1985, Tunnell was sixty-seven years old and entering the last chapter of his legal career. The World War II veteran had been a teacher before he turned to a career in law. He was a native of neighboring Van Zandt County, where he had served as district attorney, and then moved to Tyler, where he served as an assistant US attorney for the Eastern District. In private practice he successfully defended Sheriff J. B. Smith against allegations of misconduct.

On first impression, Tunnell could be intimidating. He appeared stern, rarely smiled, and his gruff speech gave him the persona of being a curmudgeon, or, in Texas terms, one tough old bird. The judge also exhibited a great skill in the art of sarcasm. He wore a Panama hat, smoked a pipe, and refused to wear the traditional robe on the bench. A suit was just fine with him. During the long days of hearing testimony, Tunnell often closed his eyes, leaned back, and rocked slowly in his high-back chair while chewing on the earpiece of his dark-rimmed eyeglasses. Those who didn't know better would swear he was sleeping, but he was quick to coherently rule on an attorney's objection without lifting an eyelid.

Tunnell could play the game of politics with the best of them, but when it came to his courtroom, he took his legal duty seriously, even if it meant making a ruling he knew would be unpopular. He wasn't shy about raking police officers or prosecutors over the coals when he believed they had crossed a line.

He once threw out the confession of a young robbery suspect— the son of a longtime news reporter—because he believed evidence showed investigators had improperly coerced him during interrogation. The confession proved to be the only solid evidence prosecutors had, and without it they had no case.

In early 1992, as Skeen and Dobbs continued their attempt to piece together records and testimony in Cook's case, they were in Tunnell's court preparing to pursue a capital murder charge against Rickey Lynn Lewis, a Black Tyler man accused of killing a forty-five-year-old man and raping his fiancé—both White—while burglarizing their home.

After weeks of questioning potential jurors, Tunnell declared a mistrial, ruling prosecutors had failed to provide racially neutral reasons for excluding some Blacks from the jury panel. Skeen was furious, arguing and rearguing the state's reason for excluding certain jurors, but to no avail. Although Tunnell's ruling didn't necessarily mean he believed the prosecutors were racists, Skeen feared the perception it left in the public's mind.

In the meantime, Tunnell pressured Skeen to decide whether Cook would be retried. In April 1992, just one week after the US Supreme Court refused to reinstate Cook's conviction and death sentence, Tunnell gave Skeen the deadline. Skeen's answer to the retrial question would determine whether a bond hearing would be necessary.

Although grand jurors continued to review evidence and hear testimony in the case, Skeen told news reporters he had yet to find any evidence to prevent him from pursuing a retrial.

News of the US Supreme Court's refusal in late April didn't surprise prosecutors, who continued presenting evidence to a grand jury as Tunnell's deadline crept closer and closer. The decision, however, set Nugent in motion. He insisted his client deserved bond since the conviction had been reversed and it was as if Cook had just been arrested. He publicly expressed hope prosecutors would continue investigating evidence uncovered by Centurion Ministries.

May 8, 1992, marked the day of Cook's return to the 241st District Courtroom. The room appeared much the same as it had more than a decade ago—a décor by now outdated. The jail had changed, of course. Instead of simply riding down the elevator from the jail cells floors above, deputies escorted Cook through the connecting underground tunnel and up the reserved elevator to the second-floor courtroom.

Cook recalled a surreal feeling of sitting behind the defense table facing the jury box as he huddled over notebooks and folders spread out before him. He was not allowed to speak to reporters. The courtroom quickly filled as a television videographer and a still photographer stood crammed against the wall. Evelyn Cook, Jimmy Edwards, and Ray Edwards were among the nearly fifty people who came to watch the afternoon proceedings.

Skeen's announcement stirred an otherwise quiet courtroom. The state intended to retry Cook on the capital murder charge and to seek the death penalty, he said. Tunnell immediately set an October 5 trial date and warned Skeen that if the state was not prepared to begin jury selection at the end of September, he would consider arguments on the bail issue.

The news disappointed Evelyn Cook, who told news reporters later she had high hopes of taking her son home with her that day. "It's just been so long," she said. "Enough is enough." The Edwardses sat solemnly during the brief Friday hearing and took the news in stride. It was difficult for them to sit in the courtroom so close to the man they wholeheartedly believed ended Linda's life.

"I believe the state has what it takes to convict him again," Jimmy Edwards told me later.

CHAPTER 20

Pretrial

Skeen's decision turned up the heat on an already simmering pot. The dispute over the facts in the case set the stage for an epic series of courtroom battles, a challenge acutely more intense between Dobbs and Nugent—two pit bull legal adversaries. Eventually the animosity they shared toward each other reached a rolling boil that went beyond Cook's case.

Dobbs was the fair-haired boy of the Smith County District Attorney's office. A native Tylerite, he graduated from Robert E. Lee High School[41] two years after a jury's verdict sent Cook to death row in 1978. Dobbs followed in his father's footsteps in the legal field after earning a bachelor's degree at Southern Methodist University (SMU) and then his law degree at SMU's School of Law. It didn't take long for Dobbs to rise to the rank of chief felony prosecutor for Smith County—taking a leading role in prosecuting more than fifteen capital murder cases during his dozen years heading Skeen's team of prosecutors.

Dobbs usually made an immediate impression on everyone he met. What he lacked in height, he made up for with good looks and charm. He reminded me of one of those all-around good guys who

---

41 In 2020, school trustees voted to change the name to Tyler Legacy High School.

was everyone's friend in high school. His wavy blond hair and energy helped maintain his youthful appearance, but in the courtroom his legal acumen reflected the mind of a seasoned attorney. He worked hard, but he usually found a few minutes to talk with most reporters, even *Dallas Morning News's* Hanners, who Dobbs tolerated out of necessity—a case of keeping his friends close and his enemies closer.

As for our relationship, maintaining balance with Dobbs always was a challenge considering his persistent and persuasive nature. In writing about the "home" team (anyone and anything in Smith County) it is always important to remain neutral—a difficult task to self-regulate since I worked daily with the people on my beat. Reporters sometimes work so closely covering news events involving the same people it's difficult to remember we are supposed to be impartial observers. You really get to know someone—prosecutors and defense attorneys alike—especially when you spend hours and hours with nothing else to do but "shoot the breeze" while waiting for a jury to return a verdict.

Readers who complain about a news story "favoring" the prosecution forget how the legal system works. Of course, the prosecution tends to get more coverage during a trial—they are the ones who have the burden of proving the allegations against the defendant. The defense is not required to prove anything. But I never was so naïve to believe either side when they insisted they had no intentions of trying their case in the media—no matter how adamantly they denied it. The battle outside the courtroom in this case at times became just as intense as the one before the jury.

The funny thing about working with Nugent was his name. I couldn't get the name of rock singer Ted Nugent out of my mind— like a song that keeps replaying over and over until it drives you crazy. I had to work hard to stop myself from saying what I was thinking every time I called Nugent at his Houston office. I called so much his secretary eventually recognized my voice, and we would sometimes chat before she would put the call through.

Nugent didn't talk about himself or his work much, but I learned a lot about his approach to helping those he believed had been wrongly convicted by reading the book *White Lies: Rape, Murder, and Justice Texas Style.* Nugent gave me a copy of the book (autographed by Clarence Lee Brandley), a gift I initially considered returning since I didn't want to feel I owed Nugent anything.[42] The book recounted the fight to free Brandley, a Black janitor, sentenced to die for killing a White high school girl. Reading about the injustice Brandley suffered made me angry, but the book proved to be a great resource. Years later I returned the favor when I loaned Nugent a negative of a picture I took of him and Cook together. The negative was never returned.

Nugent, a Suffolk University Law School graduate, was a partner in the law firm of Foreman, DeGeurin & Nugent, as in Percy Foreman, one of the best-known trial lawyers in America, whose clients included James Earl Ray and Charles Harrelson.[43] Mike DeGeurin is another highly prized defense attorney who helped Brandley win his freedom. For me, Brandley's wrongful conviction served as a striking example of how a person's skin color can affect how law enforcement investigators pursue evidence. It's almost as if it becomes the suspect's burden to prove innocence when skin color is involved.

Nugent and I established a good working relationship over the telephone because it would be months before we could finally meet in person. I found him to be just as personable as Dobbs, although a lot more serious and somewhat reserved about his personal life. He struck me as someone who led a simple, back-to-basics kind of lifestyle while working in an upscale Houston law firm. It wasn't until much later that I learned he had six children.

Skeen's decision and Tunnell's deadline forced both sides to ramp up preparations for the next step in the case. The next step, however, wasn't a trial. Cook's defense team went on the offensive, believing the state should be barred from retrying the case on grounds of prosecutorial misconduct—a potential double jeopardy issue that required a hearing and judicial review.

A defendant, by law, cannot be tried twice for the same offense. So,

---

42 Written by British journalist Nick Davies and published in 1991 by Pantheon Books.
43 James Earl Ray was convicted of assassinating Martin Luther King Jr. Harrelson, a convicted murderer, is the father of actor Woody Harrelson.

for example, if a defendant is found not guilty of murder, the state cannot come back and try the same defendant for the same crime even if they have new evidence. As the saying goes, the state gets only "one bite at the apple" to prosecute a defendant on a specific charge. But if the initial conviction is overturned, it's as if the first trial never occurred. In Cook's case the Texas Court of Criminal Appeals majority agreed he could be retried.

Nugent, however, began working on a claim that since the state's first conviction was gained illegally, the state should be barred from trying it again—thus putting his client's life in jeopardy twice. The allegations about to be unleashed weren't just Nugent's efforts of going through the motions to cover all the bases. Evidence collected by McCloskey and his team compounded by *The Dallas Morning News* investigation raised a lot of questions—questions with answers that eroded the charges against Cook, or at least created reasonable doubt if the case went to another jury.

Their challenge to retrying the case came in the form of filing a writ of habeas corpus. Whereas a direct appeal addresses possible errors during the trial, a writ is allowed to address claims based on facts outside the trial record.

Unbeknownst to prosecuting and defense attorneys, Tunnell was giving the case some deep thought and began seriously considering moving the trial out of Smith County. He expressed his concerns about Cook receiving a fair trial with an administrative judge and began inquiring about the availability of a courtroom in northeastern Texas. He also requested a budget increase, telling the county officials a trial might be moved out of the county. Tunnell didn't specify what trial in that request. He didn't reveal his concerns until July, when he proposed a change of venue, citing extensive publicity surrounding the case.

"It is appearing to the satisfaction of the court that a trial, alike fair and impartial, cannot be had in Smith County," Tunnell said in his order.

The decision marked a legal, but rarely used, judicial move; considering a change of venue is usually requested by the defense.

In this case, Tunnell exercised his judicial prerogative to act on his own—a motion made *sua sponte*,[44] a Latin term meaning "of one's own will" or an act of authority without prompting from another party. The judge gave attorneys until August 7 to prove him wrong. The defense didn't oppose moving the trial, although they did have some concerns as to where it would be held. Not Skeen. He wanted the trial in Smith County, telling Tunnell in a hearing that moving it was not only unnecessary but too costly. To support part of his objection, Skeen presented the judge with thirty-five signed affidavits from county residents who expressed the opinion that Cook could receive a fair and impartial trial in Smith County.[45] For added emphasis, Skeen included an affidavit from one of Tunnell's neighbors.

The state's arguments didn't sway Tunnell, who ordered the trial moved to the 26th District Court in Georgetown, a city of about 14,800 located just north of the state capital of Austin. Taking time to address the double jeopardy issue and change of venue forced Tunnell to reschedule the trial date, ordering jury selection to begin November 2.

Tunnell said he had followed Cook's case closely during the original trial but contended the greatest publicity came in the previous few years. He said the detailed media coverage—especially from a newspaper with a large coverage area—cast doubt on the initial police investigation and other issues. He did not name *The Dallas Morning News*, but the source of his reference was clear. "In my view, those articles are read with keener interest in Smith County and adjoining counties than other counties," he said in his order.

Tunnell also scheduled an August 21 hearing to consider nine pretrial motions Nugent filed as part of his renewed offensive attack. If successful, the defense could prevent the state from presenting certain key testimony and possibly gut the prosecution's entire case.

---

44 A rookie reporter once asked me how to contact Sua Sponte, believing it to be the name of a female Hispanic attorney.
45 Parties usually present about three supporting affidavits.

CHAPTER 21

A Second Look at Mayfield

Nugent wanted access to Mayfield and his two alibi witnesses. The only way he could get it was if the judge agreed. In a motion to compel the victim's lover, his wife, and his daughter to participate in a deposition, Nugent claimed if Mayfield testified truthfully, his testimony likely would provide evidence vindicating Cook.

Dobbs disagreed, arguing that allowing the defense to question witnesses before the trial was akin to a trial before a trial. The chief prosecutor also contended the defense failed to give a good reason as required by law.

Judge Tunnell granted the motion, ordering Mayfield, Elfriede Mayfield, and Luella Mayfield, aka Luella Finley or Frances Raitano,[46] to appear before attorneys on September 21 in Houston. He reminded prosecutors that what was said during the deposition would not necessarily be admissible at trial. The arraignment seemed to accommodate the witnesses, who all lived in Houston.

In the meantime, Nugent attacked the state's case from another angle, first asking Tunnell to dismiss the indictment against Cook and then upping the ante to request the state be barred from retrying the case based

---

46 She had married and used the names Frances Raitano and Luella Finley, although it is unclear if the last names reflected multiple marriages. She also used two different first names.

on "systematic" prosecutorial misconduct. The crux of their complaint centered on Collard's testimony about the age of the fingerprints. The defense argued that prosecutors presented that evidence in two hearings and before a grand jury knowing it was false—that there is no scientific method of determining the age of a print. The defense later expanded its claims of prosecutorial misconduct to include claims that then District Attorney Clark failed to disclose and intentionally suppressed information about Luella Mayfield's death threat against the victim, that Shyster Jackson was given a "secret" deal in exchange for his testimony, and that a prosecutor lied to jurors, telling them in closing statements that the defendant fled Tyler and never returned. To this point, the alleged misconduct concerned former prosecutors, but Nugent took his claim a step further—characterizing that little jailhouse welcome home meeting Dobbs had with Cook in March 1992 as an illegal interrogation.

Nugent also wanted the court to suppress Rudolph's testimony, contending she only identified Cook after prosecutors used an "impermissibly suggestive" identification procedure. This claim was based on Centurion Ministries investigation, which concluded Rudolph gradually changed her testimony over time.

The Houston depositions never occurred after an undisclosed disagreement concerning the questioning process. Tunnell rescheduled the depositions for October 8 in Tyler and agreed to allow the media to cover the questioning as long as reporters did not record the testimony.

On the scheduled date, the defense team came loaded for bear, relishing the thought of finally being able to question the victim's married lover and his alleged alibi witnesses, including the daughter who made a death threat just days before the murder.

The Mayfields and their daughter appeared at the courthouse flanked by attorney F. R. "Buck" Files Jr.—the same attorney Mayfield retained in 1977. Mayfield took the stand first and for three hours answered a litany of questions about his extramarital affair. Mayfield stopped the questioning three times to confer with Files, and at one point Dobbs complained Nugent was badgering the witness.

"What was your daughter's reaction to you moving in with your lover?" Nugent asked.

"She wasn't pleased," Mayfield replied.

"Wasn't she furious?" Nugent shot back.

"Yes," Mayfield answered.

Mayfield said he saw Linda at least four times on the day of the murder, even going with her to look for a new apartment. But, he said, he was home asleep hours before she was murdered. Mayfield also testified he took "at least four" polygraph tests after Linda's death, passing most but failing others.

Nugent turned his attention to Luella—who now went by the last name Raitano—grilling her about her relationship with the victim and her reaction to the affair. Raitano said she and Linda had a "sister-like relationship," until she learned her father and Linda were lovers. She admitted threatening Linda.

"I told her to stay away from my father or I'd kill her. I said it to her face . . . but I was just upset," Raitano testified.

"What was Linda saying when you threatened to kill her?" Nugent asked.

"I don't remember. It was so long ago," Raitano replied.

Raitano said she never acted upon her threat and on that night went straight home after work and went to bed.

Elfriede Mayfield's testimony was brief. She didn't remember a lot about the discussions she had with her husband in 1977, but she confirmed that both her husband and daughter were home in bed that night. Mrs. Mayfield and Raitano also testified they passed polygraph tests. In interviews after the meeting, Files portrayed the Mayfield family as cooperative witnesses who had nothing to hide.

"I don't know how anyone could be more cooperative. We did this fourteen years ago and we're doing it again today," he told reporters.

Nugent appeared somewhat subdued after the hearing, apparently frustrated with the lack of detailed answers he received. But at least he had their testimony on record and could now begin to work on finding other evidence to enhance the reasonable doubt angle of the case. It was a good start, anyway, for Nugent knew he would soon get another chance to chip away at their stories, and the next time it would be in front of a jury.

CHAPTER 22

Boundaries

Judge Tunnell allowed defense attorneys to argue their handful of pretrial motions in separate court hearings, noting Collard's improper testimony and allegations that prosecutors influenced Rudolph's eventual identification of Cook as the killer.

"It's a sham of the founding fathers' intent if you can have the district attorney take false evidence that he knows is false and present it to a grand jury," Nugent said in challenging Collard's testimony.

Rudolph returned to the stand and insisted under oath that no one had persuaded her to identify Cook. She went on to explain her initial assumption that Mayfield was the man she saw standing in the doorway that night.

"What I interpreted was based on my impressions at that time. I never was satisfied with that interpretation," she testified.

In a telephone interview with me later that week, Rudolph expressed disgust with the judicial system for granting Cook a new trial. "What I feel now is anger. Anger because I don't like the way the justice system is going has anything to do with the truth," she said. "It's an injustice to Linda Jo Edwards and an insult to the jury which originally ruled."

Rudolph, however, said she was not angry at the defense team for challenging her testimony because "they have to do what they have to do." Still, she stood by her testimony.

The court also revisited Collard's previous testimony in which he claimed the fingerprint found at the murder scene was six to twelve hours old. He testified during the evidentiary hearing that he knew aging the prints (which placed Cook at the scene about the time of the murder) could not be scientifically supported. Collard said his previous testimony was a "personal opinion based on experience." Within weeks of that testimony, prosecutors announced that an expert in Chicago recently had matched a thumbprint found at the murder scene in 1977 to Cook and determined it was left on the patio door edge that is "only accessible when the door is open." The expert was able to make the identification with forensic technology that didn't exist in 1977.

After hearing nearly two hours of arguing, Tunnell took a thirty-minute recess before returning to court and declined to quash the indictment against Cook, saying the trial was the proper forum for the defense to challenge the evidence. "He's going to get a fair trial, but is he entitled to anything more?" Tunnell asked. "We can't have a fair trial by testing the falsity or truthfulness of testimony of the indictment."

The judge's ruling made the double jeopardy issue moot, but the defense didn't give up. They filed a writ of habeas corpus petition reiterating the same allegations of prosecutorial misconduct. It was an approach from a different legal angle. This challenge allowed the defense the opportunity to finally get some testimony and evidence on the record during a required evidentiary hearing. This procedure served to ensure prosecutors had disclosed all required evidence.

The hearing brought Hanners to Tyler, where I would meet him for the first time. It was only a matter of time before we would meet, and it was a day I dreaded. I certainly admired his writing; however, it always is an uncomfortable situation when a journalist from a metro daily newspaper comes into a smaller market, especially when that reporter has been scooping the local newspaper for years.

Based upon my experiences, I figured our meeting could go one of several ways: Hanners could stick his nose in the air and ignore me, he could take on the role as a mentor, or he would be somewhat polite but mostly ignore me.

Besides being journalists, Hanners and I had one other thing in common: We both grew up in small Central Illinois towns within forty miles of each other. Years later I happened to drive through his home-town of Casey and was surprised to see a sign posted at the city limits declaring, "Home of David Hanners: Pulitzer Prize Winner." The town's only other claim to fame is being the home of the world's largest wind chime and other objects. Hanners appeared rather folksy. He rarely wore a suit and tie, preferring more casual wear instead, although as I recall, he did keep a well-worn, brown corduroy jacket on hand. His hair was straight, almost stringy, and swept over the top of his head.

Hanners didn't wait long to put my journalistic integrity to the test. We had discussed the case only briefly before one of the numerous pretrial hearings in the 241st District Courtroom. But during a break one day, Hanners turned to me and asked in a brusque tone, "When are you going to get on board?"

I asked him what he meant, and he bluntly declared Cook innocent and suggested I wasn't a very good journalist for not revealing that truth to my readers. His comments left me speechless. My face flushed from anger as I prepared to launch into a debate about the role of journalism, but I was cut short when the judge ordered the court back into session. We never got another opportunity to discuss that issue and our subsequent meetings were cordial but brief.

Hanners's statement troubled me and not just because he chastised my reporting. With that one sentence, I believe Hanners aligned himself with the defense and me and the *Tyler Morning Telegraph* with the prosecution. Hanners doesn't recall conversing with me in the courtroom and refutes my account of the conversation. For me, it was a defining moment—the moment I believe Hanners breached the line from investigative reporting to advocacy journalism.

It is against the tenets of journalism to take on that role without properly informing the readers.

Hanners obviously had a direct pipeline to Cook, who later, in his book, described the Dallas reporter to be one of his "strongest advocates." It was not uncommon for his news articles to include direct quotes despite the fact Cook was behind bars. I can't really blame Cook for favoring Hanners since, as I said before, it is natural to feel more comfortable with those who support you or your way of thinking. Cook didn't completely shut me out but it was much more difficult for me to get an interview. I was at his mercy. He could decide if and when he wanted to talk to me. In all fairness, I shared a much better relationship with Jimmy Edwards than Hanners did. Edwards didn't hide the fact he disliked Hanners and, in his opinion, the reporter's support for Cook. Edwards always returned my calls and often dropped by my office to talk but I tried to keep his openness in perspective. I continued to be very conscientious about avoiding the appearance of favoring either side in my reporting.

My opinions are not based just on what somewhat said but also on how they made me feel. That brief courtroom conversation with Hanners and subsequent comments compounded a growing feeling that he and the defense team considered Tyler and everyone who lived there as ignorant, small-town folks who refused to embrace a progressive way of living.

It wasn't enough that I reported developments in the Cook case; I apparently was too naïve, inexperienced, or dim to accept their viewpoint. Considering both Hanners and I came from true small towns—less than 2,500 people—I considered his position hypocritical. But it was a classic scenario—professionals from the likes of modern Dallas, Houston, and Princeton, New Jersey, looking down their noses at poor, Podunk Tyler, population 100,000, as full of some sort of backward, ultraconservative country folk who were too stubborn to accept the truth.

"We can't have a fair trial by testing the falsity or truthfulness of testimony of the indictment."

—241st District Court Judge Joe Tunnell

PART III

New Trials

Cook Lied About Fingerprints

Cook Jury Finds 'Lost' Evidence

1992

March 4, 1992
Cook is transported back to Smith County Jail on a bench warrant.

May 8, 1992
Judge Tunnell sets an October 5 trial date, although date would later change.

August 7, 1992
Judge Tunnell moves retrial to Georgetown, Texas, on his own change of venue motion.

August through November 1992
Pretrial hearings conducted in Smith County's 241st District Court in Tyler.

1993

November 2–18, 1992
Jury selection conducted in Georgetown. A panel of seven men and five women is seated.

November 30–December 14, 1992
Testimony heard in Williams County auxiliary courtroom in Georgetown. During deliberations, jurors report finding a "missing" nylon stocking.

December 18, 1992
Mistrial declared after jurors deadlock 6–6. Tunnell schedules new trial for March in Georgetown.

1994

Third Trial Begins

Again Convicted

Sentenced to Die

January 29, 1993
Judge Tunnell releases findings involving prosecutorial misconduct in 1977–1978. Tunnell withdraws from presiding over second retrial but continues to make rulings on other issues in the case.

February 24, 1993
Tunnell announces that Judge Robert D. Jones of Austin is assigned to preside over second retrial.

March 11, 1993
Judge Jones sets July 19 trial in Georgetown.

August 1993
Judge Jones reschedules trial for October 11 in Fredericksburg, Texas.

October 1993
Trial rescheduled for January 10 in Georgetown.

January 10–11, 1994
Judge Jones rules that attempt should be made to seat jury in Georgetown before ruling on prosecutor's change of venue request. Jury selection begins.

January 31, 1994
Testimony begins with six men and six women seated on jury in Georgetown.

February 17, 1994
Deliberations begin in guilt/ innocence phase.

February 23, 1994
Cook convicted of capital murder.

March 3, 1994
Cook receives death sentence.

CHAPTER 23

Retrial No. 1

Georgetown, located about thirty miles north of the bustling Texas capital of Austin, is home of the state's oldest institute of higher education. Southwestern University is a small private college sandwiched between its better-known Interstate 35 neighbors of Baylor University to the north in Waco and The University of Texas in Austin to the south.

During a regular school term, Southwestern students add only about 1,500 to the city's population that hovers just below 50,000 as the Williamson County seat.

Georgetown has a hometown atmosphere much like Tyler, but unlike Smith County,[47] residents have preserved its historic domed courthouse on the downtown square and built modern accommodations just blocks away.

On the square, the stately pillars lead the eye upward to the stone statue of Lady Justice thrusting her balanced scales into the sky.[48] The manicured lawn below features a giant pecan tree,

---

47 On November 8, 2022, Smith County voters approved $179 million in bonds to finance construction of a new courthouse.

48 Smith County's supposed statue of Lady Justice was removed from inside the front entrance of the courthouse once people began to comment that this statue did not include a blindfold—thereby suggesting justice was not blind. That statue had been inside the courthouse for decades before it became an issue.

its exposed roots spreading across the ground where granite markers—one in the shape of a cowboy hat—stand engraved with the names of fallen war heroes and former sheriffs.

The surrounding storefronts reflect an era when this town square was once the center of activity, but it now caters to tourists with its niche coffee shops and antique stores.

From the outside, the nondescript, brick Williamson County Courthouse Annex pales in comparison to its predecessor. But what it lacks in character on the outside, it makes up for in modern convenience and security on the inside.

The interior layout represents a carefully thought-out system to separate spectators from court personnel, attorneys, defendants, and jurors. Limited space in Smith County's courthouse leaves witnesses sharing the same hallway with family members from opposing sides. It also isn't unusual to see a line of jurors snaking its way through the crowded hallway into a Smith County courtroom or sheriff's deputies leading a handcuffed defendant through a gauntlet of judgmental eyes.

The Williamson County annex contains a line of separate courtrooms down the middle of the building. Spectators gain access to public seating in each courtroom through designated double doors on the west or front of each courtroom leading into a common hallway. Doorways on the east or the back of the courtroom lead to courthouse offices, the judge's chambers, the jury room, and a single jail cell for the criminal defendant—all connected by a separate hallway with restricted public access. The arrangement allows jurors, the judge, and court personnel to leave outside public view.

Exits and walkways on the east side of the annex allow deputies to securely transport a defendant to the adjoining county jail that Cook called home for nearly two months in 1992.

The courtroom where Cook would be tried contained four rows of cushioned pews on either side of a short aisle leading to a waist-high wooden wall—known as the bar—separating the business side of the courtroom from the spectators.[49] The jury box occupied the right side of the courtroom. The elevated judge's bench located at the back of the courtroom faced the spectator area and two separate tables for opposing attorneys. The bench was flanked by a witness stand and the court administrator. A court reporter sat in front of the witness stand. Attorneys, court staff, jurors, and journalists spent nearly eight hours a day, five days a week for the next five weeks in this courtroom.

My day quickly became routine. I usually ate breakfast in my room at the hotel where I kept a stock of groceries in a dorm-size refrigerator. I got out of bed about 6:30 a.m. every day, showered, ate while watching or reading the morning news, and then was out the door by 7:30. The drive to the courthouse wasn't very far—a few blocks down the frontage road, across the highway overpass to Austin Street where a mesh of converging roads, stoplights, and fast-food restaurants created a traffic bottleneck every morning and evening. Austin Street, crossed the San Gabriel River, and after a few blocks a right turn on 4th Street led right to the courthouse annex parking lot.

It wasn't unusual to see some familiar faces in other vehicles along the way since prosecutors, some court personnel, and witnesses also were staying at the same hotel, courtesy of Smith County taxpayers.

Every day a handful of news reporters sat in the courtroom pews on the spectators' side of the bar, listening, scribbling notes, and keeping an eye on the clock—a constant reminder of a looming deadline. For the most part, my job consisted of writing about testimony presented that day, pertinent observations, or any new developments in the case. The gag order prevented me from interviewing witnesses, attorneys, court personnel, and Cook. I

---

49 The word bar is a derivative of the word barrister—a fifteenth-century term used to describe a legal professional allowed to make presentations in the higher courts of England—and in reference to a bar association, an organization of legal professionals who license its members. Attorneys must pass a "bar" exam in order to be licensed to practice law. Therefore only those attorneys who pass can "enter the bar" or pass to the other side of the physical barrier in a courtroom.

watched day after day as Cook watched and listened intently to the court proceedings while wishing I could hear his thoughts. Except for a few occasions when Cook was allowed to visit with his mother during a recess, his conversations were limited in the courtroom to consulting with his attorneys or McCloskey.

I rarely had time for lunch because of the deadline for the afternoon edition. Filing a story involved a process a little more difficult in the pre-internet and cell phone era. My "laptop" computer was more or less an electronic word processor. During the one-hour lunch break, I typed a story and filed it via a payphone located in a cubbyhole just inside the courthouse's north entrance. A set of couplers linked the computer to each end of the telephone receiver. Sending the story required entering a computer code, punching the send button, and crossing my fingers in hopes it would go through on the first try. In the event there was a hiccup in the system—which was most of the time—I simply dictated my story over the phone to an editor back in Tyler. Usually, I had a few minutes to gobble down a sandwich and take a few swallows of soda before I hurried back into the courtroom for the afternoon session.

As soon as court was recessed for the day—usually about 5:00 p.m.—I headed back to the motel through the same traffic bottleneck to write and repeat the sending process from the telephone in my room. If I was lucky, I had a few hours to eat dinner and relax before bedtime.

The days weren't any easier for prosecutors, defense attorneys, and court personnel, who had just as much work to do behind the scenes as they did in front of the jury. Travel and lodging arrangements had to be made for witnesses, meals planned for jurors, transcripts produced and copied, and testimony analyzed to prepare for the next day.

My weekends were spent doing laundry, grocery shopping, and writing a story for the Sunday edition about what could be expected during the trial in the coming week. Sometimes I went home for the weekend to spend time with friends, to talk about anything except the trial. I just needed to get away—physically and mentally—from a trial that consumed my entire day, day after day, with very little interaction with anyone. It helped to get my mind off the trial even just for two days before I returned to my routine the next week. On those weekends I stayed in Georgetown, I visited a few local attractions—a candle factory and Inner Space Cavern—and caught up on my sleep.

No matter how hard I tried to distract myself, though, I couldn't completely stop my mind from reevaluating courtroom testimony over and over again in an attempt to make sense of it all.

CHAPTER 24

Settling In

Justice is supposed to be about truth and fairness, but if discerning the truth were easy, there wouldn't be a need for trials. The justice system in criminal cases places the burden of proof squarely on the state's shoulders—a duty to present evidence proving each element of the offense required for a conviction. Defense attorneys are there to protect their client's legal rights—a duty that requires challenging state's evidence through cross-examination and calling their own witnesses if need be. Ideally, the defense wants to convince a jury that the evidence doesn't support a conviction or, at the very least, shows reasonable doubt. A judge's duty is to maintain order and resolve disputes between attorneys based on the law. A jury, arguably, has the most difficult task of all—determining the credibility of witnesses, the sufficiency of evidence, and ultimately the culpability of the defendant. Ideally, the justice system convicts the guilty and exonerates the innocent. But it's not always that simple: Innocent people sometimes are convicted, or guilty people are set free for lack of convincing evidence. The circumstances of Cook's first conviction challenged the common premise of justice and set the stage for an epic courtroom battle in a retrial that presented jurors with two plausible scenarios. Prosecuting and defending Cook, however, turned out to be more than teams of lawyers doing their jobs. It was a clash of passions and egos, of law and the lawless, with life-and-death consequences.

Skeen and Dobbs faced the difficult task of recreating a fifteen-year-old case without a crucial witness—Hoehn—and with lost evidence, changing testimony, and a stronger defense. Nugent and McCloskey had worked equally hard in preparing for what they hoped would right a wrong, exposing the investigation as a travesty of justice and placing suspicion on the victim's married lover and his daughter.

It's often difficult for the average person to fathom the true experience of a criminal trial since most of their exposure to court proceedings comes from television shows or movies that must compress the event into a series of highlights to fit time or space constraints. As a result, media accounts tend to create a sense of constant drama that rarely exists in real life. Not to say there weren't numerous incidents of courtroom surprises in my dozen years of covering trials—including Cook's—but never once did someone jump up in the middle of proceedings to confess. Steven Brill's Court TV—live televised gavel-to-gavel coverage of a trial—was still in its infancy in 1992 and had yet to enlighten a large-scale audience on overall mundane court proceedings.

Every witness who takes the stand must be introduced to the jury in steps to establish their credentials, credibility, and connection to the case before getting to their pertinent testimony. Witnesses usually cannot testify in the narrative, so the attorneys ask a string of questions in which the witness is asked to answer without elaborating. It usually goes something like this.

Dobbs: State your name for the record, please.

Witness: David Hanners.

Dobbs: How are you currently employed?

Witness: I am currently a reporter for *The Dallas Morning News*.

Dobbs: Mr. Hanners, you are appearing here under a subpoena from the state of Texas, an out-of-state subpoena through the state of Michigan, is that correct?[50]

---

50 At the time Hanners was in Michigan to attend law school on a fellowship.

Witness: That's correct.

Dobbs: And a hearing before the Michigan Court of Appeals has resulted in you being up here and testifying?

Witness: That is correct.

Dobbs: And you are here. Let me ask you, do you know a person by the name of Kerry Max Cook?

Witness: I do.

Dobbs: Could you point to him, please?

Witness: He's seated over at the defense counsel's table.

Dobbs: Would you please describe the items of clothing?

Witness: He has on a tan coat.[51]

And so on and so on, the line of questioning slowly draws the witness and the jury to the events surrounding the crime.

A journalist's job is to write an accurate account of the day's newsworthy events within the constraints of a news hole—the amount of space allotted for news on a newspaper page or time allotted in a broadcast. It's the journalist's job to discern what information reflects the most important aspects of the day's proceedings. Performing this duty requires paying close attention, listening carefully, and analyzing hours and hours of testimony before assembling that information into a news story. It is not an easy task to do properly, especially if the reporter doesn't have a lot of experience covering such events. Unfortunately, readers or viewers rarely consider the fact that they are not experiencing the totality of the evidence, rulings, and trial proceedings and tend to form an opinion based solely on the media coverage. Opposing attorneys know this and sometimes play to the court of public opinion as well as to the jury.

It helps to know a little something about how trials work before tackling a deeper understanding of the legal issues and strategies involved. Although I previously had covered three high-profile murder cases—including two capital murder trials—in Smith County, Cook's retrial was my first involving a change of

---

51 Court transcript of testimony recorded on December 4, 1992.

venue and the first in which I faced competition from a metro daily newspaper.

Fortunately for me, Hanners couldn't cover the trial since he was on the list of potential witnesses and therefore could not be in the courtroom to hear the testimony of other witnesses. *The Dallas Morning News* sent Todd J. Gillman instead.

Since I didn't know much about Gillman, I was somewhat skeptical at first. After a few days of talking with him during the many breaks in testimony, I relaxed a little, realizing that this Dallas news reporter was just as astute as Hanners, but without the ego. Sometimes Gillman and I would have dinner together after deadline, and although we tried to stay away from talking about the trial, we usually ended up discussing the testimony anyway. We did not see eye to eye on many issues, but I respected Gillman's opinions and felt he respected mine. We got along.

Transcript of David Hanners testimony.

CHAPTER 25

Battle Stations

Cook endured fourteen years behind bars before getting a second chance to prove his innocence in a courtroom, where such a declaration mattered the most considering his life and liberty were at stake. From the time Cook's conviction was overturned to the start of the retrial, Skeen and Dobbs, on the other hand, only had fourteen months to reconstruct a case burdened by legal baggage and the lingering cloud of doubt created by *The Dallas Morning News* investigation. The gritty determination expressed on both sides served as ample notice that the restrained tension between them was about to become unleashed. Their battle began on the morning of November 30, 1992, before a Williamson County jury of seven men and five women selected after thirteen days of individual questioning.

So much had changed since that day in 1978 when a scared, slightly cocky twenty-one-year-old defendant sat in a packed Smith County courtroom. Now 36, Cook appeared subdued, his deep, dark set eyes reflecting a stark contrast to his pale face. His once full, wild hair was short, tamed, and frosted by age. He sat at the defense table flanked by defense attorney Nugent, Centurion Ministries McCloskey, and attorney Chris Flood, Nugent's brother-in-law. Skeen, Dobbs, and Eddie Clark sat at the other table representing the prosecution.

Except for a handful of reporters, a few family members, and a couple of local attorneys drawn to a sensational trial, the public side of the bar was nearly empty. Curious East Texans could ill afford to observe proceedings after the trial was moved five hours away from Tyler, although a few would make the journey. Most would have to follow the case through the media. As for the Georgetown locals, most showed very little interest in a case that didn't involve familiar names or faces.

A trial presentation—especially one given by the state—tends to follow a simple approach developed by rhetoric master Aristotle: "Tell them what you are going to tell them, tell them and then tell them what you told them." Attorneys give opening statements to tell jurors what testimony they are about to hear, they present that testimony, and then they wrap up with a persuasive summation. Per the doctrine of fairness, the state must disclose all its evidence and witnesses to the defense before the trial. The same doesn't necessarily apply to the defense, however, so there is the potential surprise factor, at least for courtroom observers.

In outlining the state's case, Dobbs told jurors there were three key pieces of evidence that would convict Cook: the defendant's fingerprints, Rudolph identifying Cook as the man she saw in the apartment that night, and Hoehn's testimony about Cook's activities the night of the murder.

Dobbs admitted the fingerprints were the only physical evidence linking Cook to the murder scene, but the positioning of those prints told jurors just about everything they needed to know, he said. What jurors didn't know about was Cook's repeated contention that he only had been window peeping—a problematic issue for the defense since that story didn't match forensic evidence showing Cook had to have been inside the apartment when he left his fingerprints. I recognized another problem with Cook's previous statements. Walking behind the apartments, it's possible to see the victim's bedroom window but not the sliding glass door. The fenced patio prevents seeing into the apartment unless the gate is open. To peer inside (and leave prints on the sliding glass door) a person has to be on the patio inside the fence. Knowing that made Cook's previous statements even more suspect. Did he watch Linda undress in her living room?

Nugent tackled that issue immediately, telling jurors Cook's fingerprints were found at the murder scene because he had been a "guest" inside the victim's apartment. Cook didn't flinch. I did. Time and time again Cook denied he knew Edwards and insisted he had never been inside her apartment. Now I knew for sure there was a lie, but whether Cook was lying before or lying now I just didn't know. I had so many questions. From the beginning of the case, Cook initially told everyone, even his attorneys and McCloskey, he didn't know Linda and had never been inside her apartment. McCloskey had told me that lying was one thing he would not tolerate when taking a case, and yet, here he was sitting next to Cook at the defense table. To this day, I have never had the opportunity to ask McCloskey how he rectified that contradiction. A decade later, McCloskey wrote his own account of Cook's lie, saying only that Cook appeared sincerely apologetic when he finally confessed to lying.[52]

In retrospect, Nugent's new claim shouldn't have been much of a surprise. The defense already felt confident they could prove Rudolph's identification had changed over time and that Hoehn's testimony posed a clear contradiction to the time element. It was imperative for the defense to explain Cook's fingerprints, especially since physical evidence shattered his window peeping story. Finding a way to present evidence of the "guest" scenario without Cook testifying, however, was going to be problematic.

---

52 Jim McCloskey with Philip Lerner, *"When the Truth Is All You Have": A Memoir of Faith, and Freedom for the Wrongly Convicted,* (New York: Anchor Books, 2020).

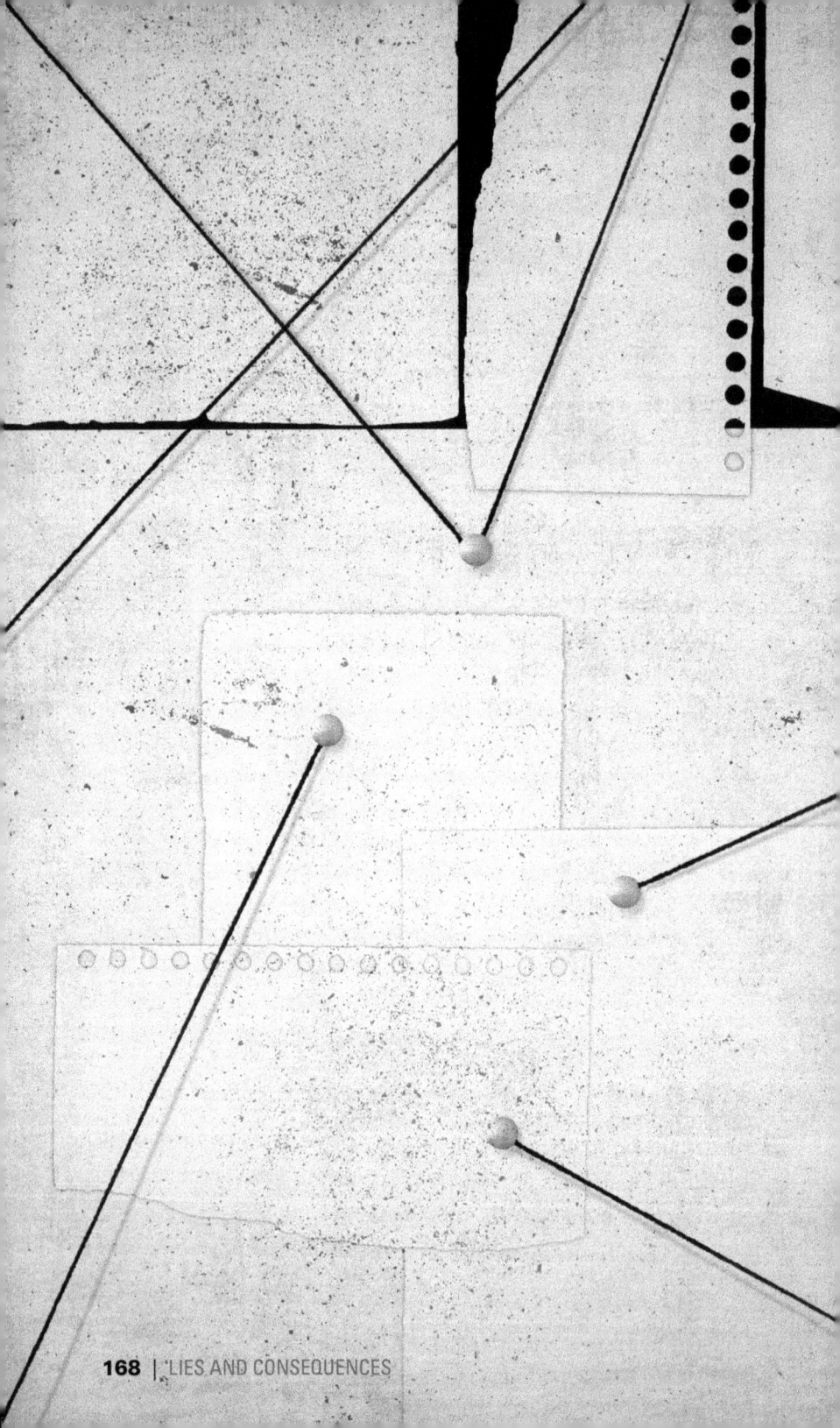

CHAPTER 26

The Fingerprints

Prosecutors opened their case with the intent of quickly establishing two critical points: One, Cook's fingerprints could only have been left while he was standing inside the apartment; and two, he had given contradictory statements about why he had been to the apartment.

Their first group of witnesses—including Tyler crime scene investigator Collard, Rudolph's 1977 neighbor Taylor, and Cook's acquaintance Hoehn (from 1978 trial transcripts)—addressed those points.

Collard, now a police captain, already had taken jurors on a pictorial tour of the crime scene before prosecutors brought in a life-sized, wooded-framed reproduction of the patio doors from Rudolph's apartment. They wanted to be sure jurors understood the significance of the positioning, and the prop provided visual support. Collard explained that although three of Cook's fingerprints were found on the door's exterior, their placement indicated the door was open. "There is no physical way to make contact . . . leave the flat impressions we have . . . with the door closed," he testified. "The only way is from the inside of the apartment." He demonstrated the position he described using the prop.

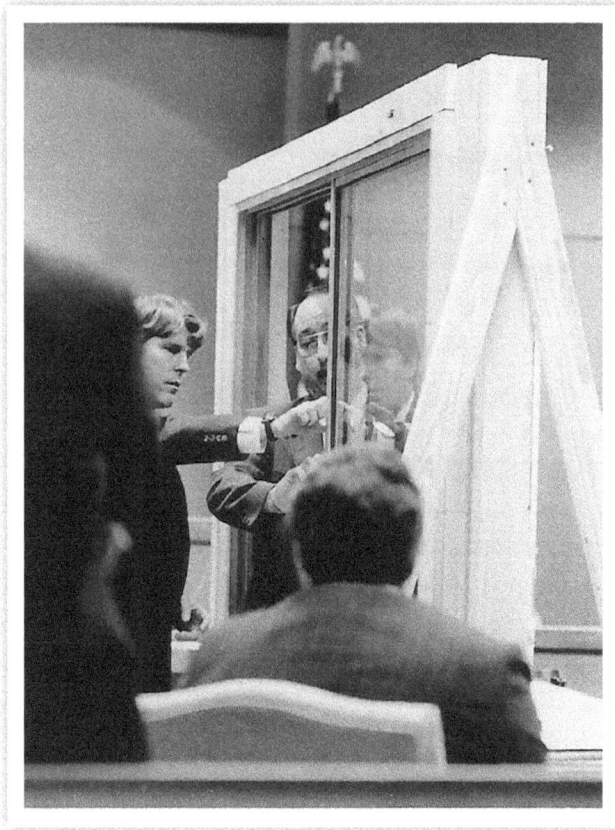

Defense attorney Paul Nugent, left, cross-examines state's witness Doug Collard about his discovery of fingerprints on a sliding glass door prop. Prosecutors were allowed to present the fingerprint evidence using a replica of the door at the murder scene.

Collard's finding was verified by a Department of Public Safety lab supervisor who also identified two more prints found on the edge of door as belonging to Cook. Although those prints had been lifted from the apartment's door in 1977, they had not been identified until before the retrial using a digital enhancement system unavailable during the 1970s.

Prosecutors had to tread lightly to debunk defense contentions that Cook had been invited into the apartment. It was important to establish a prior connection between the defendant and the victim, but the state also needed to lay the groundwork in challenging a suggested personal relationship.

Taylor testified he had been out of town the night of the murder, but, he said, in a later discussion with Cook, the defendant denied knowing the victim. Taylor said he later learned Cook had lied. His two nephews told him the defendant had pointed out Edwards's apartment to them as the one where he "used to watch that girl in," he said.

Submitting Hoehn's previous testimony presented another complication. Any mention of the 1978 trial and its conclusion would bias the jury and surely lead to a mistrial. Prosecutors intended to read aloud Hoehn's testimony from transcripts. The jury would be informed only that Hoehn had testified in a previous proceeding and had since died.

Nugent, on the other hand, saw an opportunity to establish an alternative explanation for Cook's fingerprints through Collard's and Hoehn's testimony. Under cross-examination, he asked Collard if he had received information from "numerous sources" that the defendant had met Linda at the complex swimming pool, and that she had invited him to her apartment. Dobbs objected before Collard could answer. The question prompted the first of many heated debates Judge Tunnell would have to referee outside the jury's presence. A decision about the admissibility of certain evidence usually is handled during pretrial hearings to prevent interrupting the proceedings and to avoid the possibility of tainting the jury. Hearings on admissibility of evidence and other sensitive issues also can be conducted during trial. In that case, the hearing remains public, but the jurors are kept outside the courtroom.

The defense needed the jury to hear testimony about a possible meeting between Cook and Linda at the pool, but Tunnell would first have to hear about it before deciding if such evidence was admissible.

Collard told the judge he may have had information about two such pool meetings but never about an invitation. In a second hearing outside the presence of the jury, Nugent also argued that the jury should be read part of Hoehn's grand jury testimony in which he quoted Cook as saying the apartment belonged to a woman he met at the swimming pool and that she later invited him inside. That statement, Nugent argued, contradicted trial testimony in which Hoehn said that on the night of the murder Cook pointed out the victim's apartment as the one where he had looked at a girl through the window. The defense wanted to consider Hoehn's grand jury testimony as a way to challenge the completeness or accuracy of his trial testimony—a procedure known as impeachment.

Tunnell didn't allow the defense to pursue either line of questioning before the jury, ruling information from Collard constituted "rank hearsay" and that Hoehn's grand jury testimony was not contradictory, only expanded. The latter opinion meant it did not qualify as proper impeachment (evidence that contradicted other testimony) material.

In general, a witness is not allowed to testify about what someone else said. For Collard to say what he was told by someone else who was told by yet someone else constitutes double hearsay. The remedy is to simply question the person who originated the information on the witness stand—a difficult task if the witness is dead or the defendant himself. One exception to the hearsay rule is evidence of inconsistent statements—Nugent's contention as it pertained to Hoehn's statements—but Tunnell's ruling meant jurors could not hear it.

Collard returned to the stand only briefly to tell jurors he believed Cook's fingerprints were "relatively fresh," although he was not allowed to elaborate on the definition of the word fresh.

"There is no physical way to make contact...leave the flat impressions we have... with the door closed. The only way is from the inside of the apartment."

—Doug Collard,
the crime scene investigator

CHAPTER 27

What She Saw

Taking the witness stand and answering questions under oath can be intimidating. As a journalist, I occasionally testified during hearings outside the presence of a jury. Most of these occasions involved verifying articles I had written, although during one capital murder trial the defense subpoenaed me because I had interviewed a codefendant.[53] Based on my experience, attorneys on both sides can carefully craft their questions in an attempt to solicit a specific answer. I mentally fought hard to prevent this, listening carefully to a question and giving simple answers. It wasn't unusual for me to ask an attorney to repeat the question because it was too confusing. Police officers and expert witnesses generally seem to be comfortable testifying, but I can image the angst the average person—especially one who has witnessed a crime—must feel when testifying before a judge, jury, attorneys, a defendant, and trial observers.

---

53 Defense attorneys for Napoleon Beazley wanted access to my notes of an interview with codefendant Coleman. I initially refused to turn over my notes, citing my First Amendment right, despite the threat of being found in contempt. My managing editor also warned me that he couldn't guarantee my job if I didn't comply. In the end, we reached an agreement in which the judge reviewed my notes and turned over one sentence she determined may help the defense. I was never called to testify during the trial.

Edwards's roommate and friend Rudolph testified again and again during the course of this case, each time facing more probing questions from the defense.

From her outward appearance, Paula Rudolph fit the librarian stereotype—slight build, neat, and prim. She often carried a book with her and read between breaks or while she sat in the hallway waiting to be called as a witness. She spoke clearly, with a sense of precision with every word as if determined to protect it from being misconstrued. Her approach could be interpreted as being intentionally evasive or just overly cautious. Either way, she visibly frustrated attorneys, who struggled to avoid telltale facial expressions or to control the tone of their voice during questioning. Sometimes their heavy sighs spoke volumes.

Rudolph's testimony consumed four hours as she recounted her friendship with the victim and the events leading up to finding her body sprawled on the floor of her apartment. Rudolph said that upon arriving home that night, the man she saw whirled to face her after she walked through the front door. "For a split second we stood face to face, then he stepped forward and closed the door to her bedroom," she said.

She described the man as sleek, broad-faced, and tan with medium-length hair framing the face and a "wreath of silver around the head" caused by light reflecting off his hair. She also believed the man was wearing white shorts, but she said she couldn't determine if he was wearing a shirt. She said she first thought the man was Mayfield because there was no other reason for a man to be in the apartment. "Then it went through my mind that this isn't right. That didn't look like Jim," she said. She said she eventually identified Cook as the man she saw because she recognized the shape of his body. She said she didn't make the connection until seeing Cook standing up for the first time in a Smith County courthouse elevator. "I recognized him on the fact I saw him that night in Linda's bedroom," she explained. "I have always maintained that I assumed the person was Jim Mayfield. I have never specifically said otherwise."

Nugent grilled her about what he described as inconsistent statements she previously made about the man's identity and suggested her testimony changed over time. "I'm not certain I saw the hair," Nugent read from a transcript. "I will not swear under oath who it was . . ." He also referred to descriptions of Cook and Mayfield as they appeared in 1977, noting her initial description better fit the victim's married lover. Cook had dark hair, while Mayfield had silver or gray hair, he noted.

Judge Tunnell challenged Nugent's assertions outside the jury's presence, telling the defense he saw "no substantial inconsistencies" between Rudolph's statements in 1977 and her most recent testimony. "This is simply a memory test and does not address proper impeachment procedures," said Tunnell, who admonished Nugent for being too "picky."

"I feel like my testimony has been consistent," Rudolph replied curtly. She also said she was convinced the man she saw wasn't Mayfield because he was hard of hearing. "Had it been James Mayfield, he never would have heard me when I came in the door or when I spoke," she said. The interchange between Rudolph and prosecutor Dobbs and Rudolph and Nugent was exhaustingly arduous. One of the state's next witnesses had a more dramatic effect.

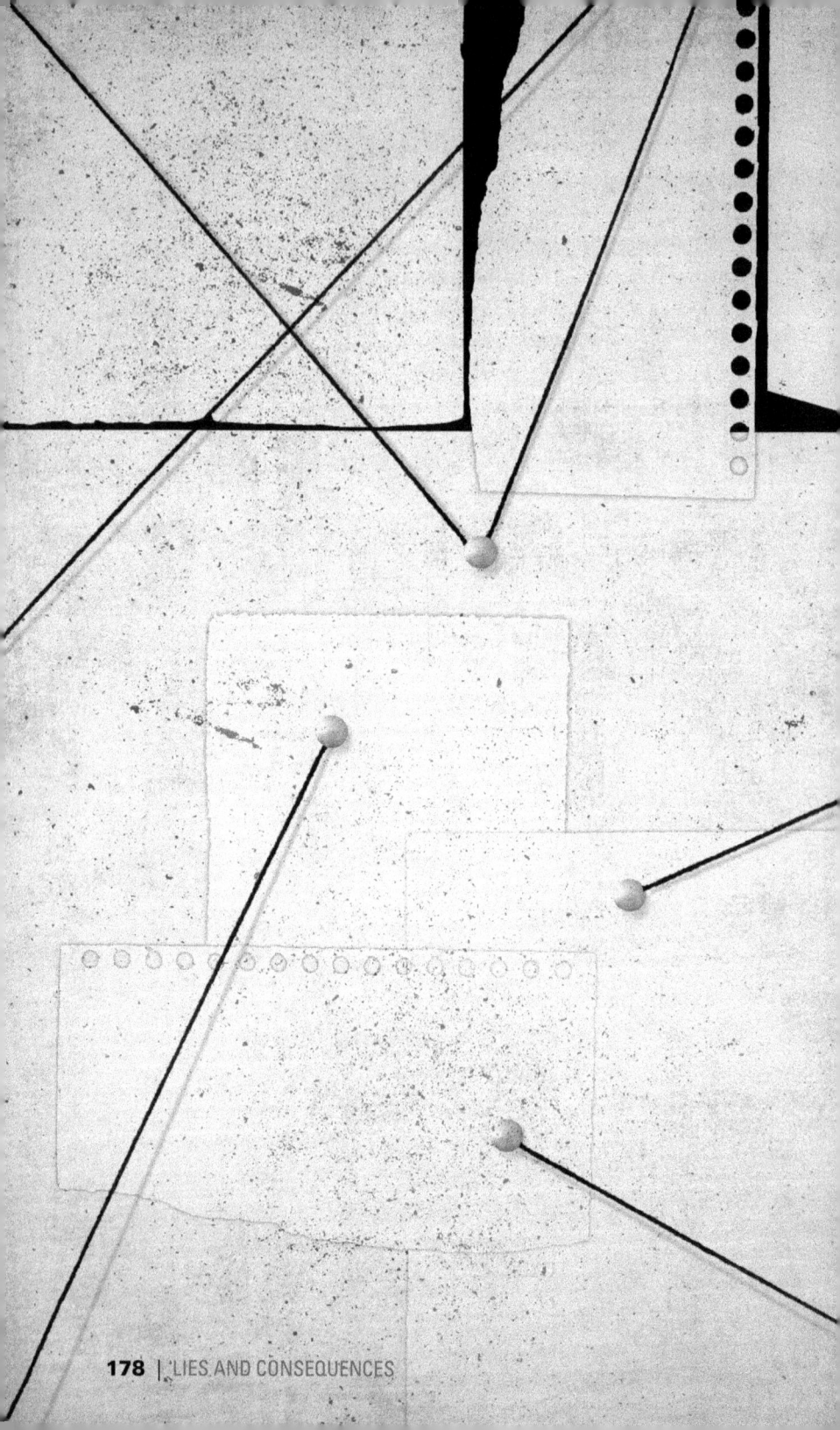

CHAPTER 28

What He Said

Bob Wickham had been a reserve deputy in 1978 when he was called upon to escort Cook from the second-floor courtroom to the upstairs jail. He recounted a conversation he said took place as they stood in the elevator. Wickham recalled Cook starting a conversation.

"Do you think I killed that woman?" Cook asked.

"That's something for the jury to decide," Wickham replied.

"I killed her, and I don't give a shit what they do to me," Cook remarked, according to Wickham.

The alleged conversation went unreported for thirteen years, Wickham testified, because he didn't believe the comment was relevant at the time. Former state trooper Glenn Miller testified Wickham did tell him of the incident, but he, too, "saw no reason to report it."

Wickham first recounted the conversation in a pretrial hearing in Smith County. It was a rare instance when Cook took the stand to testify. The defendant claimed the conversation never happened. "That's such bizarre testimony. I've never seen Mr. Wickham in my entire life, and I have maintained my innocence since the day I was arrested," Cook testified. The defense argued jurors should not be allowed to hear Wickham's testimony because Cook was in custody at the time without his lawyer present. Judge Tunnell denied the objection. Evidence that Cook made the statement without provocation likely proved to be a factor in that decision.

Now in Georgetown, Wickham repeated the story, this time to a jury. He said he didn't report Cook's confession until 1991 because "it would be his word against mine."

"Isn't it still just your word against him?" Nugent asked.

"Yes," the witness replied.

Wickham's testimony filled the void left by Shyster Jackson's recantation but with what prosecutors hoped was more credibility.

"I killed her, and I don't give a shit what they do to me."

—Bob Wickham quoting Kerry Max Cook

CHAPTER 29

Stepping Lightly

If the prosecution and defense attorneys could have agreed on anything, it likely would have been their desire to have Hoehn alive and on the witness stand. The ability to subject him to more in-depth questioning could have changed the course of the entire trial either way.

But both sides had to deal with the hand that was dealt them. Hoehn was dead and had left only his previous testimony for attorneys to interpret for the jury.

The state needed Hoehn's testimony for two reasons: to place Cook at the apartments the night of the murder and to attempt to establish his state of mind. But, again, the state had to tread lightly about the homosexuality issue broached by Hoehn's testimony. Tunnell ruled in a pretrial hearing that jurors could not hear testimony about reported homosexual acts between Hoehn and Cook because it was too prejudicial. The exclusion of that evidence left prosecutors without a key part of the puzzle they believed explained why Cook went on a murderous rampage that night. Under their theory, Cook's inability to sexually perform with Hoehn ignited years of suppressed sexual frustration—a conclusion not clearly established in 1978.

The prosecution found another way to present jurors with a possible motive through the testimony of Austin Police Sgt. Dusty Hesskew, a specialist in reconstructing violent crime. Hesskew said he reviewed all the evidence in the case and believed Linda's murder was a "sexual-oriented crime," committed by someone who hated women. The murderer, he said, posed the victim's body "the way he wanted her to be found."

Jurors heard excerpts of Hoehn's prior trial testimony (read from transcripts) and viewed an approved copy of the 105-minute movie *The Sailor Who Fell from Grace with the Sea*. The original videotape used in Cook's first trial had been inexplicably lost. Establishing the authenticity of a copy required a pretrial hearing.

Once again, a jury heard Hoehn contend Cook pointed out the victim's bedroom window the night of the murder. The defense jumped on the statement and approached the judge's bench to object. The jury was once again ordered to leave the courtroom while Nugent argued that testimony contradicted statements Hoehn made to a grand jury, ones in which Cook reportedly told Hoehn the apartment belonged to a woman he met at the swimming pool and that she had invited him into her apartment. Tunnell again ruled the grand jury statements did not qualify as proper impeachment material and ordered the jury to return.

The ruling helped the prosecution's case, no doubt, but the state wasn't satisfied with leaving the relationship question just hanging for the jurors to contemplate. Dobbs and Skeen needed to attack Nugent's claim to the jury that Linda had invited Cook into the apartment. Their ammunition, however, included a hostile witness named Hanners.

The Dallas Morning News reporter Hanners had unsuccessfully fought a subpoena compelling him to appear in the Williamson County courtroom. Prosecutors took issue with Hanners's approach to the case since they strongly believed evidence supported retrying Cook, a stance that put them on the defensive with Hanners.

Given this adversarial relationship, I wasn't surprised Hanners didn't make it easy for the state when he took the witness stand. He declined to authenticate a state's diagram of his articles because he had not compared each entry with certified copies of his articles. His stance forced another recess for the jury. Hanners also found fault with the state's use of quotation marks around excerpts from newspaper reports about conversations he had with Cook. The state had reprinted the excerpts on poster board to present before the jury, but Hanners refused to attest to the accuracy of the excerpts if the quotation marks were included.

It was an epic hairsplitting argument outside the presence of the jury. Dobbs contended the punctuation was necessary to establish that material on the poster board was taken word by word from Hanners's newspaper article. Hanners, however, contended the quotation marks were not part of the original news article and therefore made the jury exhibit inaccurate. Hanners's testimony also sparked a match of wills between Flood and Dobbs as to who could get in the final word. Tunnell chastised the men for being childish, comparing their complaints to an argument between his grandsons. He sternly warned both sides that he was tiring of the "ping-pong match."

Eventually Hanners testified before the jury that in a 1988 interview, Cook denied knowing the victim and being inside her apartment. He claimed he left his fingerprints while peeping inside the window. Outside the presence of the jury, Hanners testified that in a subsequent interview—conducted within months of the first retrial—the defendant claimed he had lied about how his fingerprints were left at the scene. The hearsay rule again prevented the jury from hearing about that statement.

For good measure, Dobbs also presented former *Tyler Morning Telegraph* reporter David Barron as a state's witness. He testified Cook told him during a 1978 interview that he did not know Linda Jo Edwards or who had killed her.

The prosecution provided other witnesses to bolster the state's contention that Cook had not been a guest in the apartment. James Taylor told jurors the defendant denied knowing the victim but later learned from his two nephews that Cook had pointed out Edwards's apartment as the one where he "used to watch that girl in."

Taylor's nephews—Rodney and Randy Dykes—confirmed that conversation during their own testimony. Rodney Dykes also testified he and Cook had spent some time at the complex swimming pool, where they once met two women whom the defendant described as attractive. Dykes said the women appeared disinterested in Cook. A

Photo by Vanessa E. Curry/*Tyler Morning Telegraph*

James "Jim" Mayfield sitting in a Williamson County
courtroom during a break in testimony.

few days before the murder, Cook came home with some "passion
marks" on his neck, the brothers said.

The defense wanted to question the Dykes brothers about their
testimony to a grand jury in 1978 in which they claimed Cook said
Edwards had left the marks, but Tunnell again ruled the testimony fell
under the hearsay rule and jurors would not hear it.

So far in presenting the state's case, prosecutors had addressed the
elements of the indictment and the issue of whether Cook had known
the victim. Now they turned their attention to disproving defense
contentions that someone else killed Linda Jo Edwards.

Prosecutors wanted to score points with the jury by being the
first to call Linda's lover Mayfield and his daughter to the witness
stand, presumably to preempt any defense claims that the state was
attempting to ignore other potentially viable suspects.

Mayfield's testimony consumed four hours as attorneys—first
Dobbs and then Flood—questioned him about his relationship with
the murder victim. The witness, now nearly sixty, still appeared athletic
for his age—slim and tan yet supporting a full head of white hair. His
shoulders sagged slightly as he recounted his long-ago affair in a matter-

of-fact tone as emotionless as the expression on his face.

Although he had returned to his wife, Mayfield admitted he continued being intimate with a woman—Linda—he considered a good friend.

"I knew it was wrong to continue the sexual relationship," he testified. "She had to make a life for herself, and we [Mayfield and his wife] were trying to help her do that."

Mayfield told jurors he saw Linda at least four times on the day of her death, the last time around 7:00 p.m., at least three hours before he returned home. He said he knew his daughter had threatened to kill Linda, but he arrived home between 10:00 and 10:30 p.m. the night of the murder and was in the home with his wife and daughter the rest of the night. Mrs. Mayfield and Ms. Raitano supported that statement in their own testimony before the jury.

Raitano also testified she once considered Linda "like a sister," but their relationship changed after she learned about the affair. She admitted she threatened Linda during a face-to-face confrontation, but she denied that she intended to carry out that threat.

Dobbs ended his direct examination, asking Mayfield if he had killed Linda.

"No, I did not," he replied.

During cross-examination, Flood questioned Mayfield at length about the details of his affair and his daughter's threat. He asked the witness if he had been aware his daughter had posed as a police officer investigating a murder involving him and Linda before the actual slaying.

"I was not aware of that," he testified.

Asked the same question, Raitano testified she didn't remember.

Prosecutors wrapped up their case with the presentation of the autopsy report—the gruesome details of Linda's murder. Skeen had questioned Tyler pathologist Dr. V. V. Gonzalez so many times during his career that Gonzalez's testimony was almost routine—only the names and circumstances of death changed.

It was a standard closing for Skeen, who wanted jurors to have those visual details in their minds as the defense began its case.

CHAPTER 30

Another Suspect?

So far in the trial, the defense's strategy was twofold: to challenge state's witnesses before the jury and to protect the record for appeal if Cook was again convicted.

Nugent and Flood worked to discredit the state's key witnesses, attempting to raise reasonable doubt in the mind of at least one juror, if not all. Preparing for a possible appeal required objections and timely hearings outside the jury's presence.

But now it was the defense's turn to put on witnesses—many of whom had not been called to testify during the 1978 trial. Nugent turned to Mayfield's former coworkers to discredit the former dean and to add substance to a case against other viable suspects.

Former Texas Eastern University library staff member Olene Harned of Tyler told jurors she remembered Rudolph calling to tell her Linda had been attacked.

"She told she me thought she had seen Jim Mayfield jump back and close the door when she entered the apartment earlier that night," Harned said. "She was unsure, but she assumed it was Jim."

Harned said Mayfield blamed Linda for losing his job and had expressed concern that she would follow him to another city and continue to impede his career.

History professor Dr. Andrew Szarka testified that hours before the murder, the victim told him Mayfield was upset when she told him she wanted to see other men.

Ann White, also a former Texas Eastern University library staff member, told jurors Mayfield cried when it was confirmed Linda was dead but also appeared angry because "she had ruined him." Harned, White, and at least two other defense witnesses testified they didn't believe Mayfield was a truthful person.

"I would sometimes doubt his statements," Harned said. "He certainly didn't tell the whole truth."

The defense also followed up on its contention that the description of the man Rudolph saw that night better fit Mayfield than Cook. Through the testimony of Cook's sister-in-law, defense attorneys presented a photograph reportedly taken of the defendant on July 4, 1977. Cook appeared in the photo with dark black hair that reached below his ears. The photo, however, was not dated.

Nugent also wanted jurors to hear testimony about the book *The Sexual Criminal* found in the university's library. The defense claimed the murder scenes appeared the same as some depicted in the book.

Dr. Frederick Mears testified outside the presence of the jury that he called police about the book after he learned of the slaying. Although Mayfield supervised library book purchases, Mears said he didn't know who had ordered that specific book.

Judge Tunnell barred the defense from presenting that testimony, ruling it had "no relevance on the contested issue" since Mayfield denied having any knowledge of that specific book.

The final group of defense witnesses to testify consisted of experts who challenged state's witnesses' opinions about key elements of the murder.

Fingerprint expert George Bonebrake of Maryland contended an investigator improperly characterized Cook's fingerprints as being "fresh."

"The term 'fresh' is too general because we can't say it means one hour or one week," he said. "So that's a term we never use because there is no way to determine how long a print was on a surface."

Defense witness Dr. Linda Norton, a Dallas forensic pathologist, expressed surprise that the initial autopsy report did not note that any body parts were missing—a glaring omission that pointed to incompetence.

And finally, the defense called Dr. Richard Coons, a forensic psychiatrist from Austin, who told jurors his review of the evidence in the case suggested not an act of violence against women in general but against a particular woman. He disagreed with Hesskew's analysis that Linda was killed by a stranger, not a "jealous lover."

On that note, the defense rested its case. Cook, not surprisingly, did not take the stand. Although defense attorneys rarely discuss their reasoning for such a move, I'm almost certain Cook's notorious lack of restraint (i.e., previous courtroom outbursts) was a factor in the final decision.

To be fair, defendants often find themselves in a no-win situation. For some observers a defendant who appears calm and collected reflects innocence and yet others consider the same characteristics as being dispassionate or even cool and calculating. The same contradiction occurs when a defendant chooses not to testify, with some people interpreting that as guilt, while others simply recognize that a defendant has nothing to prove.

Cook had spent more than a decade in a jail cell thinking and rethinking every detail of his case. With his previous courtroom outburst, the defendant already had proven he couldn't control himself. He was too excitable and too willing to throw caution to the wind to face questioning by prosecutors Dobbs or Skeen. No matter how much Cook wanted to tell the jury his side of the story, putting him on the witness stand was just too risky.

CHAPTER 31

Final Arguments

Closing arguments in a trial consist mainly of attorneys giving the jury a summation of the evidence, basically weaving testimony together in a neat package in support of their argument of guilt or innocence. It's a time when persuasive speaking skills are put to the test—a matter of appealing to a juror using logic, emotion, or ethics, one or all. Ideally a juror can filter the information—focusing on the facts while deflecting the fluff. Determining just how much fluff gets left behind or if, and how, it influences a particular juror in any case offers fodder for endless research.

One of the most time-consuming tasks before a jury hears closing arguments requires a judge to compile formal instructions for jurors to follow in their attempt to reach a verdict. The judge does this by considering suggested submissions from opposing sides before carefully wording a final document that gives general instructions about deliberations, lists the specific charges against the defendant, and lists possible verdicts. In some circumstances, the judge may include more specific information to assist in explaining the legal language, but jurors are strictly forbidden from using dictionaries, other legal references, or any other sources during deliberations. If an issue arises, the jury's foreman must communicate in writing to the judge asking for assistance. The

Photo by Vanessa E. Curry/*Tyler Morning Telegraph*

Smith County District Attorney Jack Skeen displays an
enlargement of murder victim Linda Jo Edwards before
the jury during closing arguments. Skeen wanted to ensure
jurors would not forget Linda during deliberations.

judge may receive input from opposing attorneys and then decides
if or how the question can be answered. The subject of these notes
could be a request to review certain testimony, to define a term, or
to tell the judge the jury is ready for lunch.

It is not uncommon for the jury instruction in complicated cases
to be more than ten pages long and require thirty minutes or more
to be read aloud in court before opposing attorneys address the jury.
Explaining the factors involved in the capital murder charge against
Cook consumed an inordinate amount of time. The indictment
attempted to "cover all the bases" by alleging the defendant killed

Linda during aggravated rape or intent to commit aggravate rape, burglary with the intent to commit aggravated sexual abuse, theft of a stocking, or aggravated assault. To convict Cook, jurors had to determine he committed murder while committing at least one of the other offenses.

Nugent and Flood characterized the wordy charges as a "shotgun approach" by prosecutors who had "overstated their case." Cook's fingerprints proved he had been to the apartment, but did not prove when since there is no scientific method for aging a print, Nugent argued to the jury.

He suggested Mayfield could have killed Linda in a jealous rage after their affair ended and, he reminded jurors, a police officer once characterized Mayfield's daughter as a "pathological liar." She could have killed Linda, he added in reminding the jury she had admitted threatening the victim during an angry confrontation.

He also contended Rudolph's testimony gradually changed over time to conform more to Cook's appearance, leaving her final identification in doubt, he said.

"Fingerprints on the door do not prove a murder. Paula Rudolph's identification does not prove a murder," Nugent said. "If you do not believe the state has proven its case, please have the courage to say that."

In his arguments, prosecutor Dobbs summed up the defense's case as nothing more than a "character attack" on the victim's lover and police investigators. To believe the defense, he said, jurors would have to believe the state's presentation of twenty-two witnesses was nothing more than a "parade of liars."

The prosecution criticized the defense for failing to provide any evidence supporting its claim that Cook had been invited into the apartment. As for Rudolph's identification, Dobbs and Skeen contended it was a "natural assumption" for her to initially believe the man she saw was Mayfield. They explained away her description of silvery hair simply as an appearance caused by the bright room lights in the background.

Photo by Vanessa E. Curry/ *Tyler Morning Telegraph*

Defense attorney Paul Nugent makes his closing
arguments, urging jurors to consider evidence
pointing to other possible suspects.

The defense couldn't explain away Cook's fingerprints, they
claimed, because Cook was the killer who attacked Linda and stole
her nylon stocking—a missing piece of evidence that was more than
a coincidence. The stocking, Dobbs said, was linked to the movie
the defendant watched that night.

"This movie is a lot more probative than you first thought," the
prosecutor said. "The part where the boy is holding the stocking
is an innocuous little scene unless you look at the facts in this case.
Linda Jo Edward stocking was missing. Interesting, isn't it?"

Interesting indeed. Nearly seven hours into deliberations,
a shocking discovery would leave Dobbs regretting he ever
emphasized that alleged connection.

"The part where the boy is holding the stocking is an innocuous little scene unless you look at the facts in this case. Linda Jo Edwards' stocking was missing. Interesting, isn't it?"

—Prosecutor David Dobbs

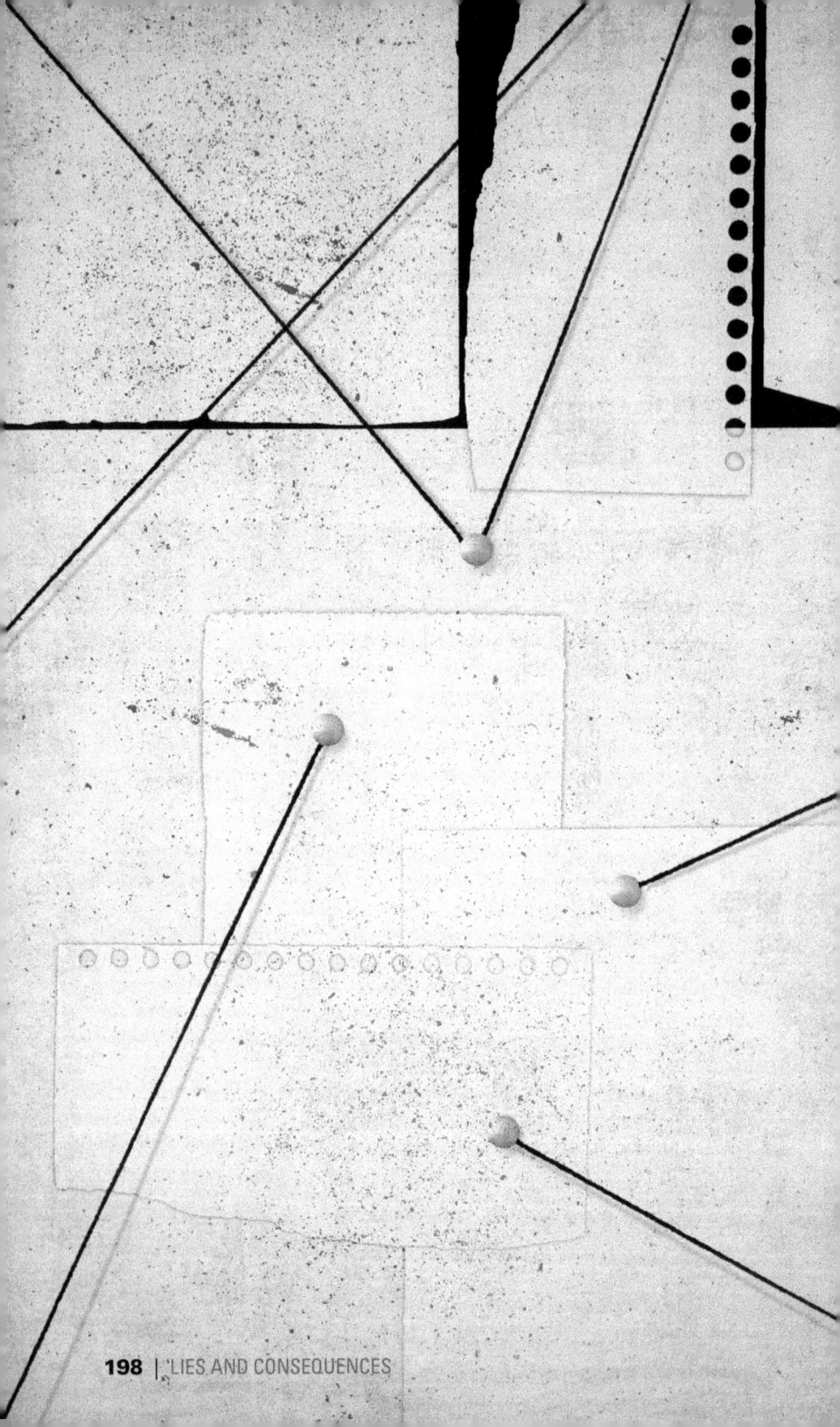

CHAPTER 32

Waiting Game

After hearing two weeks of testimony and nearly two-and-a-half hours of final summations, the jury retired to deliberate while everyone else began the waiting game—an excruciating test of patience. How long a jury will take to reach a decision, if any, is a question that can only be answered in hindsight. In the meantime, the judge, attorneys, court personnel, family members, and reporters must find a way to occupy their time without straying too far from the courtroom since the jury could send out written requests or return a verdict at any moment.

For reporters, the wait usually played out while sitting in the courtroom or hallway, passing the time by predicting the verdict, sharing stories, reading, or dozing. As I recall, one of the television reporters had brought a handheld video game—Tetris—that we passed around to play so many times we all eventually couldn't stand the sight of it.

What goes on during deliberations is a mystery to those of us waiting on the other side of the closed door. If the jury room is close, sometimes I might hear an occasional raised voice or maybe even laughter, but nothing is discernable. The bailiff posted at the door sometimes will share general information—off the record, of course—but usually all they can tell is whether the discussion inside is getting heated. Being a juror is another role I always wished to have experienced because I wanted to study the dynamics of the decision-making process from the inside. Despite being called to appear for jury selection throughout my years in Tyler, I was never selected for a criminal case, likely because of my profession. I usually already knew too much about the case. I did serve once on a civil jury, but the case settled just moments before we were to begin deliberations.

Deliberations in Cook's case began late on a Monday afternoon, giving jurors only about three hours together before Judge Tunnell decided to sequester them for the night at Smith County's expense. The seven men and five women were bused to a nearby hotel under the watchful eyes of sheriff's deputies.

The change of venue Tunnell ordered hadn't sat well with Smith County commissioners who had to find the funds to pay travel and trial expenses. Tunnell, who was aware of the financial discontent, stayed in the motel, but also utilized a camping trailer the district clerk parked at a Williamson County campground.

The judge couldn't refrain from responding to the occasional grumbles that filtered down from Smith County, especially when County Commissioner Andrew Melontree questioned the expenditures. Tunnell addressed Melontree's concerns and the county's allocations for meals in a handwritten November 20 note served with a generous portion of sarcasm.

"I want you to know that I am being very frugal. I tried the first day to eat $5.00 worth of breakfast, $8.00 worth of lunch, and $12 worth of dinner, but just couldn't do it," Tunnell wrote.

The judge went on to say he brought a toaster, a coffee pot, and some strawberry preserves for breakfast in a motel room he shared with his wife.

"That does not cost the county anything and we enjoy it more," he added.

He also reported that he sometimes skipped lunch to save money and consumed a lunch meat sandwich and a glass of milk in his room for dinner.

"We pay that ourselves," Tunnell wrote. "Just wanted to give this report."

On one occasion, the judge and his wife invited The *Dallas Morning News* reporter Gillman and me to the camper for a bowl of Tunnell's famous homemade chili. The chili was thick and tasty, the host and hostess, charming, but the conversation was a bit thin since we could not discuss the trial. Gillman and I also spent another evening bowling with a group of Smith County deputies, a welcome break from the courtroom.

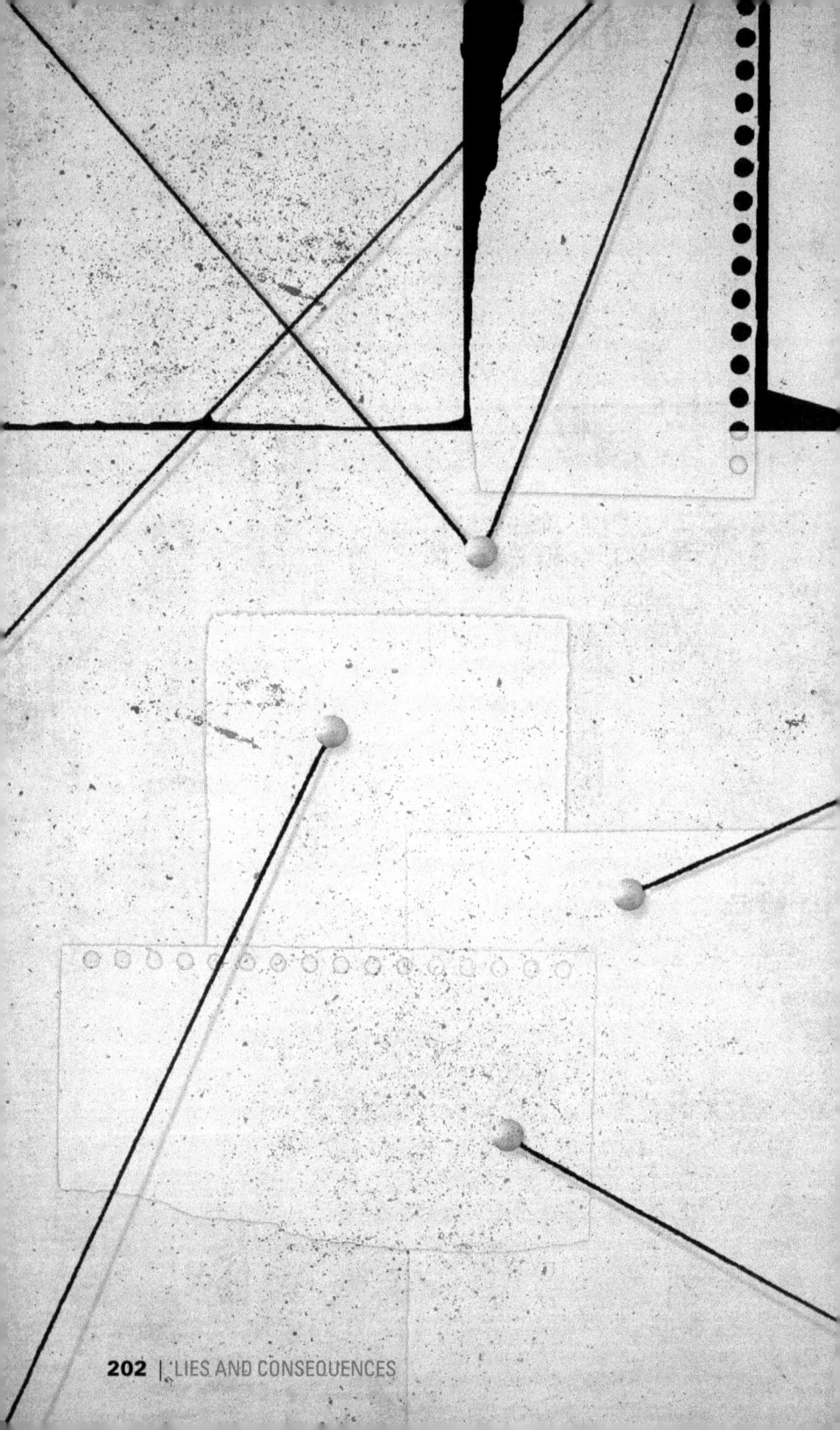

CHAPTER 33

Surprise Inside

Everyone returned to the courtroom on Tuesday to begin the second verse of the same song. Jurors resumed discussions and within two hours decided to begin their day inspecting the physical evidence brought into the deliberating room.

That evidence included the victim's pair of blue jeans found discarded on the bedroom floor. The jeans had been folded and placed in a clear plastic bag and sealed. At some point during deliberations juror Marilyne Rowland held the jeans up at arm's length, gently shook them to straighten the folds, and unknowingly dislodged part of the state's case.

"It just fell out the bottom," the juror later told Judge Tunnell.

I was contemplating writing a news story for the afternoon edition when word spread that Tunnell had received a jury note. The courtroom came alive as everyone scrambled to take their places (jurors remained in the deliberating room), expecting a verdict was about to be read. Instead, Tunnell assembled the attorneys before the bench.

"I daresay no judge in Texas has ever been confronted with a situation like it, but come and read the note," he told attorneys, handing them a yellow legal-size piece of folded paper.

"Bring to the judge's attention that we have found the . . . a nylon stocking in the jeans of Linda Jo Edwards," the jury foreman wrote in the note.

I can only imagine the cold, sinking feeling or the pure euphoria the respective attorneys must have felt at that very moment. My reaction was a mixture of disbelief and slight panic as I realized my deadline was just an hour away. Why does it always seem that major news happens just before deadline? On the bright side, I broke the story before the Tyler television stations and *The Dallas Morning News*.

Skeen, who obviously was trying to hide his embarrassment, regained enough composure to request permission to inspect the stocking. The defense countered with a request for a mistrial or at least an instructed verdict for acquittal on that one count alleged in the indictment.

Tunnell denied both requests, allowing deliberations to continue.

I sprinted toward the pay phone in the hallway and breathlessly broke the news to the editor. "You're not going to believe this," I told him. He took my dictation as I scribbled sentences on my notepad, the telephone receiver tucked precariously between my clavicle and jawbone. It was a Perry Mason moment like I had never experienced before, or since.

The mystery surrounding the jury's discovery continued throughout the rest of the week, heightened by comments from the jury foreman in Cook's 1978 trial.

In an interview with the *Tyler Morning Telegraph*, 1978 jury foreman Charles Reasoner of Tyler insisted the stocking was not in Linda's jeans when jurors inspected them during that first trial.

"I remember it as if it was yesterday. Every member of the jury looked at those jeans," he said. "There was no nylon stocking."[54]

---

54 Vanessa Curry and staff, "Cook Jury Finds 'Lost' Evidence," *Tyler Morning Telegraph*, December 16, 1992.

"I daresay no judge in Texas
has ever been confronted
with a situation like it..."

−241st District Judge Joe Tunnell

CHAPTER 34

Indecision

Tuesday and Wednesday came and went with the only news from jurors coming from notes asking to review testimony from witnesses Rudolph and Hoehn. They asked for smoke breaks, sodas, supplies, and copies of parts of the charge that defined murder and reasonable doubt.

On Thursday, the jury ended the day by informing Judge Tunnell it was deadlocked 8–4 on a verdict. The foreman's note said the jury had taken three separate votes—beginning with a 10–2 count on Monday—on each charge and remained split. "We...can not [sic] come to a unanimous decision," he wrote. He underlined the words "can not" for added emphasis.

Tunnell urged the jury to continue, telling them in open court that there was no reason to believe another jury would find the questions in the charge any easier to resolve. Deputies escorted the group back to awaiting vans and took them back to their motel.

They returned Friday and began the arduous task of reconsidering the evidence once again. Jurors took turns expressing their opinion. The process took several turns around the table until it became apparent there was nothing more to say, juror Mahlon Arnett of Round Rock later told reporters.

A note to the judge shortly after 1:30 p.m. reported a 6–6 split. Tunnell urged them to continue, but the vote remained unchanged in another note sent out just before 3:00 p.m. Tunnell studied the note through his dark-rimmed glasses perched on the end of his nose. After a brief pause, the judge again announced a deadlock before declaring a mistrial on December 18, 1992, thanking jury members for their service, and dismissing them from the courtroom. Jurors had deliberated a total of twenty-nine hours in five days. The courtroom door had barely closed when Tunnell set another retrial for March 29, 1993.

The media feeding frenzy that followed was something I had experienced before, but this time it rattled me a bit because of the change of venue. I alone had to interview the attorneys, Cook, and hopefully at least one juror for my story with only a short window of opportunity before everyone left town. I would have preferred private interviews that would have allowed me to write a story different than other reports, but that wasn't possible under the circumstances. The interviews produced expected results. Undeterred by the 6–6 split, Skeen expressed his disappointment but did not waver in vowing to retry Cook on a capital murder charge and to seek a death sentence. Flood characterized the jury's indecision as "encouraging . . . the first step on the road to freedom for Kerry Max Cook." Reporters were allowed into the inner sanctum of the courthouse—a small room located on the other side of the back courtroom wall. There Cook sat misty-eyed in a court holding cell, telling reporters he would never give up his battle to prove his innocence.

"Six jurors said Kerry Max Cook is innocent. All I need is six more," Cook said.

"We...can not [*sic*] come to
a unanimous decision."

—Note from jury

CHAPTER 35

Tunnell's Findings

Finding the stocking likely was the death knell for the state's case—giving credence to defense claims that prosecutors bungled the investigation from the beginning. During testimony, jurors had learned crime scene investigators didn't find the vegetable knife stashed in the victim's closet despite searching the apartment. At the very least finding the stocking created reasonable doubt. If investigators failed in the simple task of examining the jeans, what other mistakes could they have made in the case? Three months after the trial ended, a forensic report determined the nylon stocking that fell out of Linda's jeans was similar in design, construction, approximate color, and age as the one found on the victim's body. In other words, the stocking likely belonged to Linda.

Under their breath prosecutors considered the possibility the stocking had been planted. Former jury foreman Reasoner insisted the stocking was not there in 1978. McCloskey told reporters he had viewed the evidence before trial but did not believe anyone on the defense touched the evidence. It did seem unlikely that someone could have planted a stocking that appeared to match perfectly. The most likely culprit was static electricity.

Fighting such a tough court battle without a verdict is like a wrestling match that ends in a tie. Both sides are disappointed, exhausted, and not looking forward to starting all over again. In the eyes of the law, a mistrial sends everyone back to square one. It's as if the trial never happened. Although he had set another trial date, Judge Tunnell had no intention of hearing all that testimony again. In an unexpected announcement a month after the trial, Tunnell withdrew from the case, saying he needed to concentrate on clearing his docket before reaching the mandatory retirement age of seventy-five in June. Although he would clean up any issues pertaining to the Georgetown mistrial, any future issues for the next retrial would be handled by a different judge.

In the same announcement, Tunnell ruled, Smith County prosecutors in 1978 had withheld evidence that from the defense—namely, Luella Mayfield's (Raitano) threat and a police account that she had presented herself as a law officer investigating a murder at several apartment complexes weeks before Linda's death. Tunnell also addressed the lack of transparency about the "tacit" plea agreement with Shyster Jackson and statements about the age of Cook's fingerprints knowing the testimony could not be scientifically substantiated. Prosecutors did not present testimony aging the fingerprints or the alleged jailhouse confession during the 1992 Georgetown retrial. However, since that trial ended in a mistrial, it was as if it never happened, and the defense was free to argue that prosecutorial misconduct should prevent another retrial.

Although these acts constituted misconduct, Tunnell concluded they were "not so egregious" as to bar another retrial.

In his written findings, Tunnell chastised Dobbs for contacting Cook in jail in 1992, saying his actions were "improper and misguided" but did not rise to the level of prosecutorial misconduct. The ruling brought a glimmer of hope for the defense attorneys who had fought so hard for the system to recognize instances of prosecutorial misconduct in Cook's case, although they adamantly believed it should prevent continued prosecution.

I didn't realize it at the time, but Tunnell's findings would complicate the case even more, renewing defense challenges that would require more hearings and appeals similar to those filed before.

Nugent planned to revisit the double jeopardy issue, but he needed time to prepare and file an appeal to Tunnell's ruling. With Cook's third trial set to begin in less than a month, Nugent requested a postponement. Tunnell denied the request, contending the defendant waived his right to a stay pending a final ruling by filing it too late.

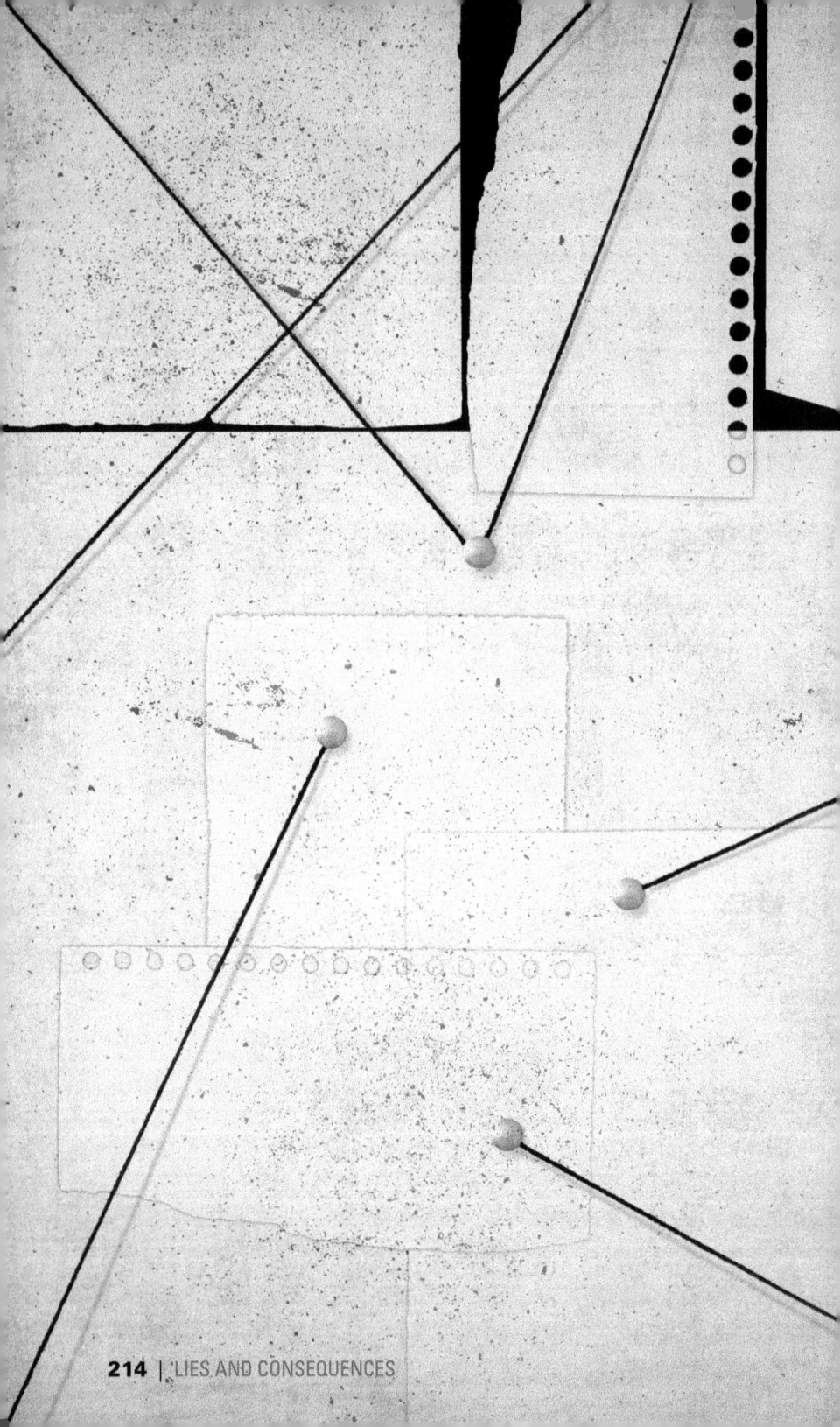

CHAPTER 36

Funding Issues

Cook's second retrial never materialized in 1993. It isn't unusual for a trial date to be changed. I got used to it in Cook's case. Despite being scheduled and rescheduled three times, a renewed defense strategy, jurisdictional issues, and the logistics of accommodating a new judge encumbered any attempt at any progress. Skeen's continued belief that the evidence warranted another trial deepened the rift between the prosecution and Cook's supporters, who began to ramp up their public campaign to pressure the state into abandoning prosecution.

McCloskey's battle plan included a not-so-subtle appeal to taxpayers, who, in his opinion, were footing the bill to fuel Skeen's ego, not justice.

Smith County spent nearly $71,500 to try Cook in Williamson County in 1992 without a conclusion to the case—an expenditure Skeen defended as immaterial in the search for justice. "I've always said I don't think you can put a price on obtaining justice for victims of capital murder," he told me. "When we make a decision to try a case, it's based on facts; and under the facts, justice is only being served if Kerry Max Cook is found guilty by a jury." Despite the change of venue, Cook's case wasn't the most expensive capital murder case for Smith County. In fact, two other capital murder cases that had been tried in Tyler cost more than twice as much.

But the defense took the prosecutor to task, publicly denouncing the continued prosecution of a man they believed to be innocent. "It's unbelievable they're even spending a dime or a minute in this effort," McCloskey told reporters. "It's a negative effort based on the district attorney's stubborn, stiff-necked decision to try this case." McCloskey's organization—Centurion Ministries—spent about $57,600 to defend Cook. That figure did not include paying defense attorneys.

Whether out of a true need or an attempt to pressure the prosecution, the defense appealed to Judge Tunnell, asking him to order Smith County to pay Cook's outstanding debts for expert witnesses, compensation for representing Cook in his third trial, and the cost of trial transcripts. Defense attorney Nugent contended Cook could not receive a fair trial or effective assistance of counsel unless, defense attorneys were fairly and adequately compensated. Reading between the lines, the request suggested possible dissension within the defense's ranks. McCloskey vowed to go into debt defending Cook, but were Nugent's continued services contingent upon guaranteed funding? Nugent brushed off the question. "We'll have to cross that bridge when we come to it," he told me.

Tunnell denied the request, noting that Nugent accepted financial responsibility when he agreed to represent an indigent defendant for free. The judge said taxpayers shouldn't now have to pay defense costs just because the case turned out to be a "bad bargain."

Nugent renewed his plea months later before Judge Robert D. Jones, a former district judge in Austin who had been assigned to preside in the next retrial. The defense specifically asked that Cook be declared indigent and ultimately require Smith County to pay for his defense. The only catch: Nugent and Flood wanted to be appointed to represent Cook—a logical but audacious request since the constitutional right to an attorney doesn't include the privilege of choosing one.

Jones called their bluff, declaring Cook indigent but appointing Bill Wright of Tyler and Jim Brookshire of Williamson County to take over the defense. The decision brought mixed emotions from prosecutor Dobbs, who said it was a "shame" taxpayers would have to foot the bill but agreed that, in that case, Cook shouldn't be allowed to choose his own attorneys.

Nugent, however, said he was surprised by the decision to appoint new attorneys since he was most familiar with the case. He said the decision disappointed, surprised, and perplexed his client. Cook now faced a put up or shut up decision: Accept the new attorneys and the funding that comes with it or ask Nugent and Flood to remain with limited or no funds. Dobbs relished Cook's conundrum. "I don't know if that's the intention of Judge Jones's ruling, but if that's the result . . . we certainly are in favor of it," he told me.

CHAPTER 37

Another Appeal

The defense's second multifaceted battle of the year revisited the double jeopardy issue. Although pleased Judge Tunnell had found that previous prosecutors didn't follow the rules, Nugent wanted to appeal the judge's determination that the misconduct didn't bar the state from retrying the case. To do that, the defense needed time. They couldn't file the appeal and hope for a decision before the scheduled March 29 retrial in Georgetown. Besides, the defense team also had to have time to prepare for trial, too, in the case of an unsuccessful appeal. Tunnell did conclude that the misconduct "standing alone" or its "cumulative effect" likely would have won Cook a new trial if known by his attorneys and raised on direct appeal in 1978. However, he also noted that Cook was granted a new trial—albeit for a different reason—and none of the instances of prosecutorial misconduct were repeated during that retrial. So, for Tunnell, at least, the misconduct issue was now moot.

The legal wrangling during the first part of the year added to the confusion. Tunnell continued to rule on issues pertaining to the defense's habeas corpus writ involving the prosecutorial misconduct claims, while Judge Jones presided over issues involving the upcoming retrial—a rather unusual situation. Although intended to operate independently of one another, the two paths often crossed, adding to the confusion. Tunnell refused to entertain a second writ of habeas corpus because, he said, "it raises nothing this court hasn't already ruled on." The 12th Court of Appeals in Tyler claimed it did not have jurisdiction to hear an appeal because of the change of venue. The 3rd Court of Appeals, which includes Georgetown, also refused to hear the appeal, leaving the defense to seek relief from the Texas Court of Criminal Appeals.

Jones eventually agreed to tentatively reschedule Cook's trial for July 1993 to allow time for court officials to transcribe the 1992 trial testimony and give the transcription to the defense. That trial date was later rescheduled for October 11 in Fredericksburg, the county seat of Gillespie County west of Austin, despite warnings from Jones that he would not accept any more delays. A delay in finishing the transcripts from the previous trial, however, forced the retrial to be moved into 1994.

In the meantime, Nugent—who decided to remain as counsel to "finish what I started"—attempted to secure Cook's release on bond. Cook's aunt, Joyce McElyea of Jacksonville, testified in an August bond hearing that she planned to help raise funds if a bond was set and to allow the defendant to live in her home if he was released. She characterized her nephew as a "good boy" who was raised with the right morals. Jones denied bond in a ruling released three months later, prompting the defense to vow yet again to appeal.

"It raises nothing this court hasn't already ruled on."

—24st District Judge Joe Tunnell

CHAPTER 38

Keeping Busy

The legal challenges kept prosecutors on the defensive throughout most of 1993, although Skeen and Dobbs had five other Smith County capital murder cases to contend with throughout the year.[55] I covered all those cases too.

Prosecutors also faced a public opinion campaign launched by Phyllis Salter, a Henderson woman who had taken up Cook's cause. She sent out letters containing pre-addressed postcards, directing recipients to mail them to newspapers in Austin, Tyler, and Williamson County to "express concern" that Cook was being tried unfairly. The *Tyler Morning Telegraph* received a handwritten letter from a Jacksonville woman dated December 7, 1993, along with a flier outlining his plea of innocence. "He has never been proven guilty and as you read this you can see how he got railroaded to his death [*sic*]," she wrote. "Luckily a

---

55 In February, the Texas Court of Criminal Appeals granted Andrew Lee Mitchell a new trial based on a finding of prosecutorial misconduct. In July, Dobbs served as lead prosecutor in the capital murder trial of Stacey Lawton, who was convicted and sentenced to die. Three months later a Smith County jury returned James Joseph Wilkens Jr. to death row after his retrial. And by the end of the year, the Smith County prosecutors secured a conviction—but not a death sentence—against Lawton's codefendant, Karlos Fields, and crafted a plea agreement that returned Edward Eldon Corley to prison for life.

lot of people are trying to help him by publishing these fliers." In a postscript, the woman wrote, "I do believe Cook is innocent or I would not do this for him. It is so awful to keep a boy locked up 12 years [*sic*] for nothing."

Skeen set out to evaluate the news coverage in those areas to determine whether the information may have tainted potential jurors—giving the state a taste of what the defense faced in Smith County.

"He has never been proven guilty and as you read this you can see how he got railroaded..."

—Jacksonville woman writing in support of Kerry Max Cook

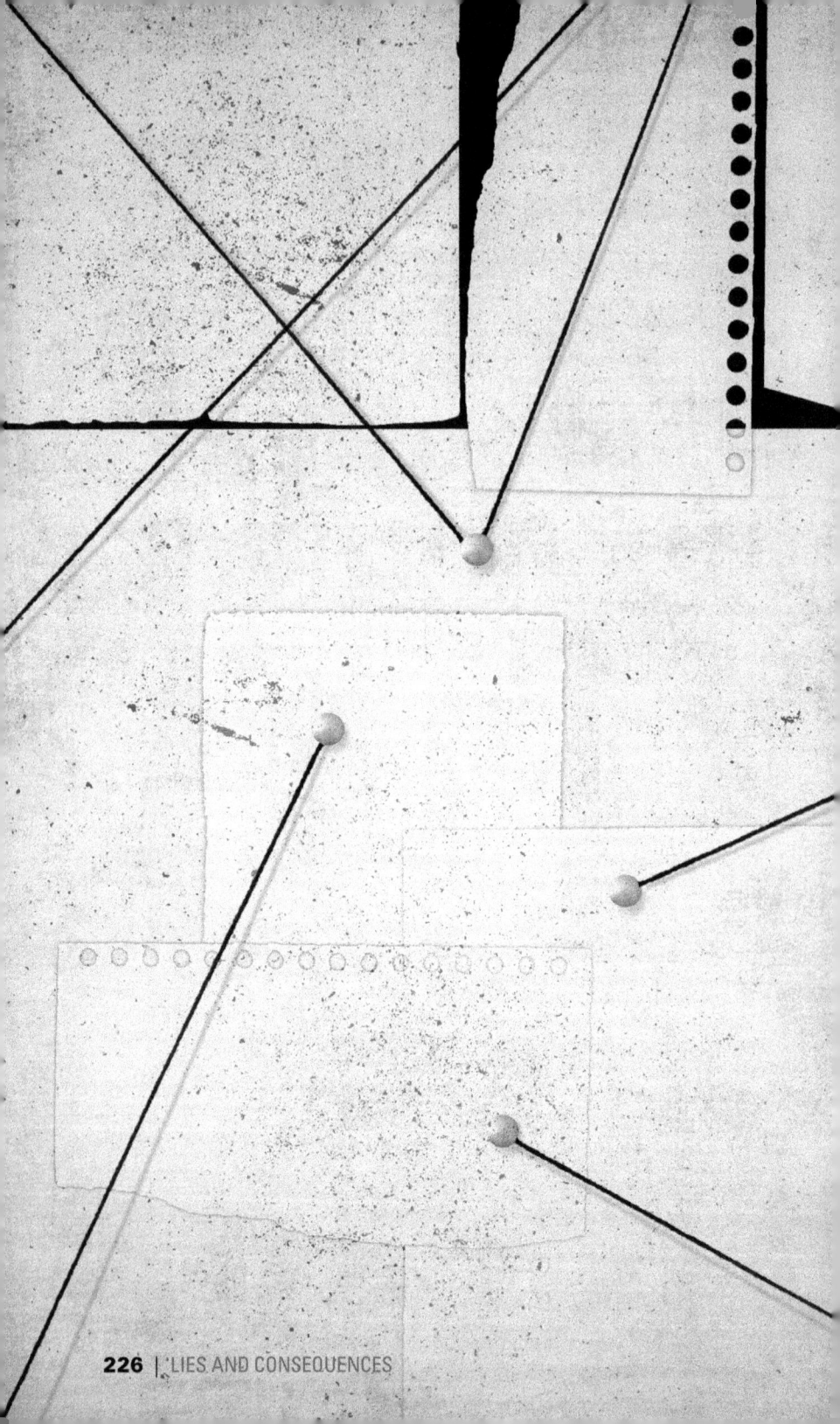

CHAPTER 39

Media Weighs In

Now it was the state's turn to claim they couldn't receive a fair trial because of extensive publicity. Newspapers with significant circulation figures in Williamson County—more specifically *The Dallas Morning News* and the *Austin American Statesman*—had saturated the county with stories "very prejudicial" against the state, Dobbs argued in the state's motion. He presented Judge Jones with stacks of newspaper articles written about Cook's case as well as seventy of Salter's postcards the district attorney's office received in Tyler.

Dobbs asked Jones to move the trial to an available courtroom in Fredericksburg—a suggestion Nugent characterized as "jury shopping." The state, the defense attorney argued, simply was searching for a county where they thought the citizens would be more favorable to the prosecution.

Jones agreed to take the change of venue motion under advisement while going ahead with the jury selection. How best to determine whether extensive publicity tainted the jury pool than to carefully question the citizens during individual voir dire, he reasoned.

Jury selection began in Georgetown the second week of January 1994, just days after an Austin appeals court refused to stay the retrial and dismissed a defense complaint that the retrial constituted double jeopardy. Now opposing attorneys turned their focus on questioning potential jurors one by one to seat a twelve-member jury and two alternates. The individual voir dire process began with all potential jurors completing a lengthy written questionnaire designed to give attorneys some insight about a prospective juror. Attorneys are supposed to want jurors who haven't yet formed an opinion about the case—who can listen to the evidence, follow the law, and remain fair and unbiased to reach a verdict. Attorneys, however, really want jurors who appear to lean toward their respective side or at least not lean toward the opposition.

Although the jury selection process can be fodder for interesting news stories, it's a gamble for a journalist who must sit through hours of questioning day after day without garnering enough information for a meaty story. Generally, journalists don't have the luxury of spending an entire day in court only to report the selected juror's gender and possibly their occupation. In capital murder cases, I usually just call the district clerk in charge to get the tally at the end of the day.

Although there is no Texas law forbidding the media from publishing the names of jurors, it usually does not. I've always maintained a list of jury names just in case I need to attempt an interview at the conclusion of the trial.

But Jones threw the media a curve ball—refusing to allow court personnel to release the names of selected jurors. He intended to maintain some control of the public opinion frenzy by issuing an order prohibiting all parties involved in the case from speaking to the media. That didn't sit well with *The Dallas Morning News*'s Gillman or me, who believed the public had a right to know who had been selected to make a life-or-death decision during a public trial.

The bosses at the family-owned *Tyler Morning Telegraph* didn't like the order, but they weren't about to spend money to launch a legal battle. Officials at *The Dallas Morning News*, however, didn't bat an eye and immediately called an attorney. In the meantime, Gillman submitted a handwritten motion, challenging the judge's decision. I cosigned Gillman's motion. Jones rejected the request for information, saying his order did not violate constitutional rights to freedom of the press because reporters were welcome to attend the jury selection in open court to obtain information. Although we huffed and puffed about it, the issue basically was moot once testimony began.

But the incident did give the media some insight into Jones, an unknown factor since he had served in Austin until he lost a reelection bid. In Texas, retired judges and even those voted out of office may revive their careers on the bench as a visiting judge. An administrative judge may appoint these former elected judges to preside over civil and criminal matters—the state's relief valve plan for an overcrowded court system with a backlog of trials. Until challenging Jones in court, I'd had only a few opportunities to speak with him on the telephone. He came across as somewhat hesitant in speaking with the media, but he certainly didn't appear to be holding some grudge.

One thing was clear: Gillman and I would not be eating homemade chili at Jones's place during the trial. Despite concerns that news coverage of Cook's case had tainted the jury pool, attorneys were able to select a jury, and Jones ordered the trial to continue in Georgetown.

CHAPTER 40

Back to Georgetown

The 6–6 jury split in 1992 forced opposing attorneys back to the drawing board to rebuild their respective cases. Another retrial gave each side a "do-over"—a rare opportunity to piece together a theory based on their own strengths and the weaknesses of their opponents. Attorneys reread and reevaluated the previous testimony like coaches studying game tapes.

The placement of Cook's fingerprints at the murder scene and the defendant's repeated lies about how they got on the sliding glass door remained the foundation of the state's case. Witness Hoehn's testimony—although censored dramatically by previous judicial rulings—and witness Rudolph's testimony about seeing Cook in the apartment that night, provided the mortar. But the third trial would show that prosecutors had to come up with a better way to explain Rudolph's first impression—testimony the defense eagerly attacked. And, although prosecutors are not legally required to provide one to convict in Texas, they desperately needed, and did not yet have, a motive to help jurors understand the "why" of the crime.

The defense believed it could provide the "why" of the crime. Evidence of the affair between the victim and her married lover provided a legitimate theory to support reasonable doubt, but for the most part the defense had to play defense, chipping away at the state's evidence to build on that doubt while protecting the record for possible appeal. Defense attorney Nugent—keenly aware of the state's lack of a clear motive—also needed to provide an alternative theory, one that would likely throw suspicion toward Mayfield or his daughter. The defense also wasn't about to give up attacking Rudolph's testimony, especially since Nugent and McCloskey adamantly believed she had changed her description to better fit Cook.

No doubt the second retrial was going to be another epic but arduous battle. The jury and judge were fresh to the case, but everyone else certainly was not looking forward to hearing weeks of the same testimony and the same arguments. Taxpayers would not be funding Cook's defense. Nugent would defend Cook during trial again. Wright was out, but Brookshire was appointed to continue to assist, though he would have little or no role in this retrial.

For reporters who covered the 1992 retrial, the challenge was attempting to provide news coverage that didn't reflect our boredom with the same material. The only difference for me in 1994 was that I would be writing three stories a day instead of two. In addition to writing for the morning and afternoon editions of the Tyler paper, I also had agreed to write a separate daily article for the Associated Press, which maintained a bureau just down the road in Austin.

What I couldn't have known at the time was the ethical decisions I would face as each side's desire to win spilled out of the courtroom and into the court of public opinion once again.

"No doubt the second retrial
was going to be another
epic but arduous battle."

—Author

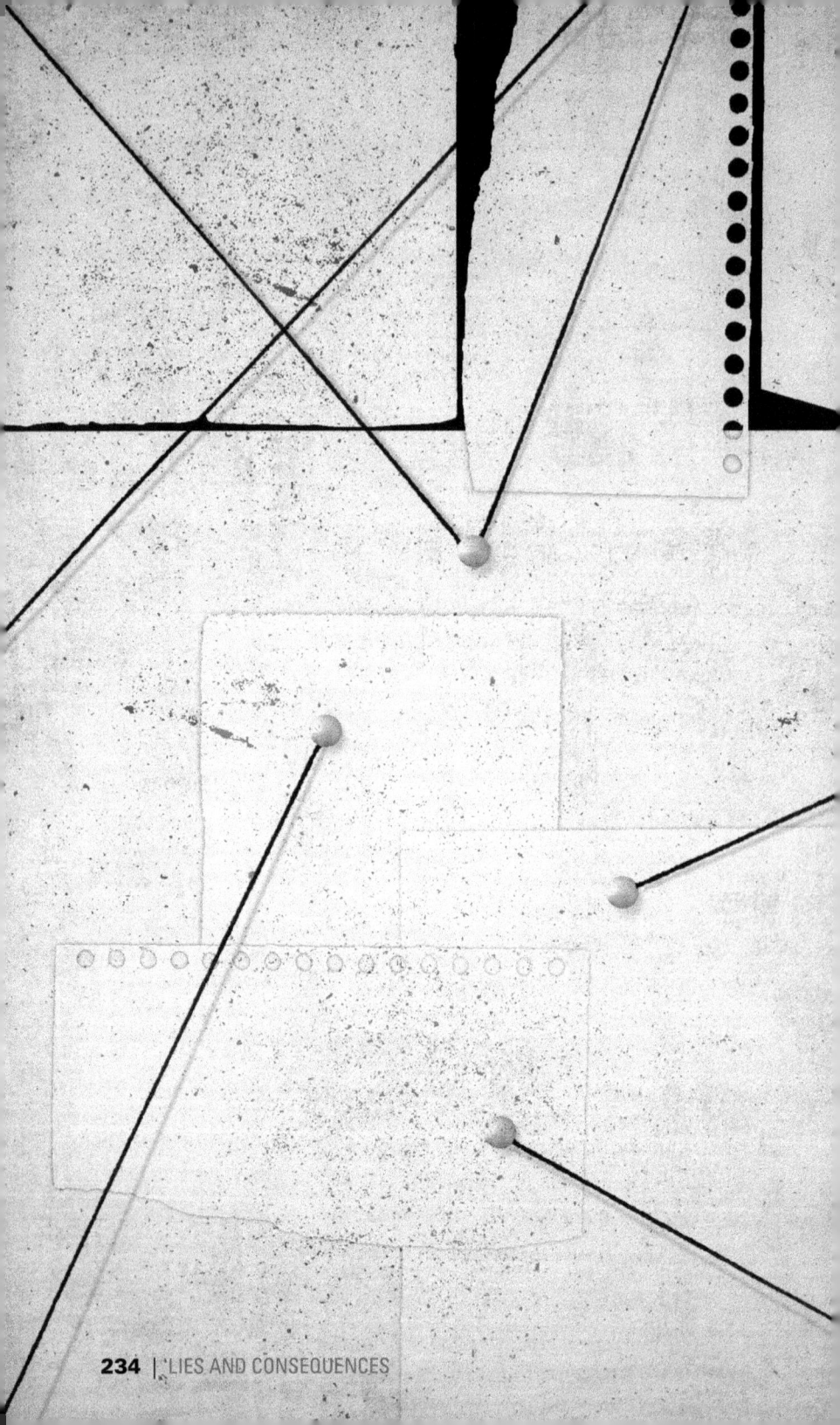

CHAPTER 41

Retrial No. 2

Back in Georgetown, residents returned to their day-to-day routine after a Christmas holiday devoid of snow. Winters in central Texas generally are mild, and only once did icy road conditions delay Cook's proceedings.

The court system cranked up again in January 1994, beginning another chapter of a sensational murder case that jurors failed to resolve in the same courthouse just thirteen months earlier. With few exceptions, all the players in Cook's case returned to the same courthouse, motels, restaurants, and traffic patterns they had become accustomed to during the first retrial.

Judge Jones seated a fourteen-member jury—seven men and seven women—that included two alternates as a precaution in case circumstances required replacements. Alternate jurors often are selected in case a regular juror must be dismissed for some legal reason. The alternates in Cook's case were never needed and were not involved in the deliberations.

Opposing sides ended the month wrangling over familiar pretrial motions challenging the admissibility of certain evidence. Nothing new about the arguments, but Jones muzzled attorneys concerning any discussions with the media about his rulings.

Case No. 1-77-179 *The State of Texas v. Kerry Max Cook* reopened in a Williamson County Courthouse Annex courtroom for a second time without much fanfare. Those involved had high hopes this trial would lead to legal finality, although realizing that no jury verdict—whether for conviction or acquittal—would ever change entrenched personal opinions.

Skeen, Dobbs, and Clark took their seats behind the prosecution's table. Nugent and McCloskey joined Cook at the defense table. Notably absent was second-chair defense attorney Flood—a sign that the defense quite likely was financially strapped.

The courtroom arrangement this time situated all the attorneys directly across the room, facing the jury box—a position that allowed me to photograph parts of the trial without obstruction. At the time allowing cameras in the courtroom was a controversial topic throughout the nation.[56] Those who opposed the practice argued cameras—especially television cameras—created a "circus-like atmosphere" and prevented defendants from receiving a fair trial by pandering to public opinion. Those who supported it contended openness promotes education about the judicial system and keeps the process honest.

Journalists in Texas do not have an automatic legal right to have cameras in the courtroom. For that matter, no one is allowed to bring a camera into a courtroom without permission. That decision is generally left up to the presiding judge. Judges Tunnell and Jones both allowed the media to visually record some courtroom proceedings with stipulations. For example, the media could not photograph jurors under any circumstances. Doing so could bring a contempt charge.

---

56 The 7th District Court in Smith County played a historic role in the courtroom cameras issue. In 1963, West Texas businessman Billie Sol Estes was tried in Smith County on a change of venue. His conviction on fraud charges was later overturned by the US Supreme Court, which ruled television cameras allowed in the courtroom contributed to him receiving an unfair trial. The case set the standard for banning cameras in the courtroom for decades.

"… Jones muzzled attorneys concerning any discussions with media about his rulings."

—Author

CHAPTER 42

Head-to-Head

Cook's second retrial opened on the last day of January 1994, a Monday. The courtroom was quiet, although it seemed as if everyone took a collective sigh as if to say, "Here we go again," before deputies escorted the jury into the room and opening statements began.

As predicted, Dobbs focused on the fingerprint evidence, witness Rudolph's identification—a "crucial point" he told jurors—and evidence that explained why she initially described the man in her apartment as having "silvery hair." Dobbs also told jurors three news reporters would testify about interviews in which Cook claimed he did not know Linda and had never been inside her apartment.

"The evidence will be absolutely clear . . . he is lying," Dobbs said.

Nugent focused his opening statements on Mayfield and his daughter as possible suspects, telling jurors that testimony would show both expressed anger toward the victim before she died. He asked jurors not to consider that testimony in determining their guilt or innocence but as evidence as to the veracity of the state's case.

"I believe you will be left with one conclusion: that this is an unsolved crime," he said.

The defense addressed the "why" question, but prosecutors did not, apparently saving their answer to wrap up their case.

Jurors spent the first day of testimony hearing Collard describe how Cook's "fresh" fingerprints were placed in such a manner that it would have been impossible for him to have been on the outside when he touched the sliding glass door.

"You'd have to bend your fingers ninety degrees to get them in this position from the outside. There's no way possible for the prints to be left while the door was closed," he explained.

Jurors were allowed to leave their seats to examine the same life-sized reproduction of the door used during the first retrial. Two other fingerprint experts also identified Cook's fingerprints, but under cross-examination didn't agree on whether the prints were "fresh."

Collard's testimony also introduced jurors to the crime scene through the photograph slides as he described the victim's multiple wounds and the alleged murder weapons. Nugent took the opportunity to again assail the witness for failing to find the vegetable knife during a supposed "thorough" crime scene investigation and the fact that a nylon stocking believed to have been stolen was found in 1992 in the pant leg of the victim's jeans.

"Not finding the stocking was one of my mistakes," Collard admitted during cross-examination.

Collard also admitted he didn't have the victim's underwear tested for semen because it appeared the garment had been cut off the victim's body.

No one would realize the significance of that decision for another five years.

"I believe you will be left
with one conclusion: that this
is an unsolved crime."

–Defense attorney Paul Nugent

CHAPTER 43

Running Interference

Barely two days into testimony, Judge Jones announced he might ask for a federal investigation into a petition he received, apparently by one of Cook's supporters. The petition, he said, "distresses" the court. The document contained the names of fourteen South Carolina residents who claimed Cook's constitutional rights were violated in his previous two trials. The petitioners wanted to "remind" the judge of his duties during the trial. "Your role . . . is to serve as an unbiased party with the grave responsibility of ensuring the defendant receives a fair trial. We sincerely urge you to make every effort to guarantee that pattern of abuse stops in your courtroom." The petition showed just how far public opinion reached in the case. Jones never explained his reaction to the petition, but I can imagine he was perplexed about how it would be perceived. Did the petitioners believe Jones needed to be reminded of his responsibilities as a judge? Their wording could have been considered a poorly written threat or an example of emotions dominating intellectual reasoning. Following the petitioners' way of thinking, any judicial decision they didn't agree with suggested a judge was a party to the "pattern of abuse." I can't help but be a little sarcastic here. Apparently, they knew better than a licensed attorney sworn to uphold the law whose decisions were subject to review by an appellate court.

The situation posed the first of many dilemmas for me in this retrial. A reporter decides what is important and what is not. Certainly, a judge feeling "distressed" is newsworthy, but I also had to consider the possibility that the petitioners simply wanted publicity. Writing too much about the incident risked blowing it out of proportion and giving the public the wrong impression about its newsworthiness. Not mentioning it could suggest intentional suppression to downplay support for Cook. I didn't appreciate the attempt to control the media in that way. I covered the event in a few paragraphs at the end of the day's article and decided to take any further developments on a case-by-case basis.

"Your role...is to serve as an unbiased party with the grave responsibility of ensuring the defendant receives a fair trial."

–Petition received by Judge Robert Jones

CHAPTER 44

Lust Attack vs. Jealous Lover

The prosecution didn't waste any time in introducing to jurors their theory that Linda was the victim of a "lust-type attack" committed by a stranger. Dobbs finished out the first week of testimony with expert witnesses Sgt. Dusty Hesskew of the Austin Police Department and David Gomez, an FBI special agent who worked for the National Center of Analysis for Violent Crimes in Virginia. Hesskew told jurors his analysis of the crime scene indicated the victim had been "totally surprised" by someone she did not know.

"The pattern at this scene is of a disorganized crime . . . [because] weapons of opportunity are used, the victim's body is left there and the [attacker's] inability to hide particular evidence," he said. The witness also said body parts were apparently taken from the scene as a souvenir so the murderer could fantasize later about what he had done.

Hesskew also said wounds to the victim's sexual organs fit a "lust-type attack," a point defense attorney Nugent challenged under cross-examination. Nugent suggested the wounds to the victim's head and face indicated an attack by a jealous lover. Hesskew disagreed, saying total disfigurement of the face is a better indicator of a domestic-type crime.

Gomez testified that lust-type murderers often have prior fantasies stemming from sexual inadequacies, immaturity, or ambivalence about sexual performance—"precipitating factors that can trigger violent sexual attacks." The defendant, he said, exhibited those characteristics when he went window peeping at the victim's apartment.

The expert testimony gave prosecutors what they thought they needed, the "why" of the case, but not all they wanted. Jurors would not be allowed to hear evidence that Cook reportedly engaged in a homosexual relationship hours before the murder in an apartment near the victim. That part of witness Hoehn's 1978 testimony was redacted from the transcript when Judge Tunnell ruled it irrelevant, prejudicial, and therefore inadmissible. Dobbs attempted to have that part of Hoehn's testimony reinstated, much to the chagrin of Judge Jones, who denied his request and admonished the prosecutor for continuing to argue the point.

"I have ruled. That's it. If I'm wrong, I'm wrong," Jones said.

Surprisingly, Nugent's cross-examination of both expert witnesses didn't take long, suggesting he had his own expert testimony planned for later in the trial. He saved his tougher questioning tactics for the next state's witness—the woman who identified his client as the killer.

"I have ruled. That's it. If I'm wrong, I'm wrong."

—Judge Robert Jones

CHAPTER 45

Rudolph's Return

Rudolph's return to the witness stand at the end of the first week marked the seventh time she had testified about what she had seen the night of the murder. After briefing the jury about her friendship with Linda and the events of that night, Rudolph appeared to brace herself for another verbal boxing match with Nugent. The defense attorney hammered her description, insisting it initially matched Linda's lover Mayfield rather than Cook.

The witness didn't falter, insisting again she had assumed it was Mayfield because it made sense at the time. Rudolph adamantly denied ever changing her description, admitting only she had used different words in previous testimony. Rudolph again insisted it was not Mayfield she saw that night because the man was not wearing glasses and had not heard her come through the door. Mayfield, she noted, always wore glasses and had difficulty hearing.

The state's next witness explained to the jury how the ceiling light in the victim's bedroom likely created a "halo effect" on the man's hair, making it appear different on the top of the head. Alan Weckerling of Weckerling Laboratory in Dallas said he photographed a male model with black hair in a series of photographs in an apartment like Rudolph's. The photographs showed how a light over the back of the head reflected on the hair, making it appear a different color. Despite the debate over the color and length of Cook's hair at the time of the murder, it wasn't difficult to see the irony jurors faced. Across the room sat the defendant, seventeen years after the crime, with short hair, grayed by age.

The remainder of the state's case nearly repeated previous testimony from Mayfield, his wife and daughter, and other state's witnesses. Mayfield testified that he saw the victim four times the day of the murder and insisted he and his wife, as well as their daughter, were home asleep that night and did not learn about the murder until the next day. Elfriede Mayfield backed her husband's alibi.

"That's the only thing I have always remembered through all these years," she said about her husband being home that night.

Following up on his opening remarks, prosecutor Dobbs called three news reporters, who recalled Cook telling them he did not know the victim and had never been inside her apartment. This time, however, the state entered a videotaped interview by former KETK-TV Channel 56 reporter Nita Wilson. In that interview the jury heard Cook admit the fingerprints were his but say, "I never entered that woman's apartment. I looked through the window."

The state also presented former Reserve Deputy Wickham, whose account of Cook's alleged confession in a courthouse elevator drew an outburst from the defendant and a reprimand from Judge Jones. Finally, pathologist Dr. Charles Petty supported findings that parts of Linda's body were missing from the scene, although the initial autopsy report didn't specifically reflect that finding.

Before closing, the state revisited the motive angle, calling witnesses who testified Cook was "confused" about his sexual preference. Since Hoehn's testimony about a homosexual encounter with Cook could not be used as evidence, prosecutors had to work around that issue. Tommy Wilbanks's relationship with the defendant filled in the gaps for the jury without ever using the words gay or homosexual.

Wilbanks said he met Cook at a Dallas club in 1976 and that he believed the defendant was sexually ambivalent, a term he defined as a person who is confused about being effeminate or masculine. In his testimony, Taylor described Cook as sexually ambivalent and recalled a conversation in which the defendant denied knowing the apartment where the murder occurred or knowing the victim.

Jurors also heard part of Hoehn's testimony read from the 1978 trial transcripts and watched the movie *The Sailor Who Fell from Grace with the Sea*. In his testimony, Hoehn described Cook's hair as dark, shoulder-length, and full. He also said Cook was wearing blue shorts trimmed in red the night of the murder. Taylor contended Cook's hair was full but flared back over the ears. Rudolph had described the man she saw as wearing white shorts and as having full, medium-length, silvery hair.

Nugent's attempt to submit evidence explaining Cook's fingerprints at the scene—testimony that he told others of meeting Linda at the pool and going to her apartment—failed again, as Jones ruled it inadmissible hearsay.

CHAPTER 46

Defense Mistake

Nugent opened his case on Friday during the second week of testimony and immediately crippled the defense's plan of attack. The admissibility of his expert witness—Robert Ressler, a former FBI crime scene analyst—quickly came into question when prosecutors learned the witness had read the transcript testimony of an expert state's witness who had testified earlier in the trial. Ressler was expected to challenge the state's contention that Linda was the victim of a "lust-type attack." Judge Jones ruled Ressler's testimony inadmissible because the defense had violated the rule that forbids witnesses from listening to or reading the testimony of other witnesses—a major blunder for the defense. The rule is designed to keep the testimony from one witness from influencing another's.

Nugent had no choice but to turn the focus to the victim's former lover and his family. He called two former coworkers and a colleague, who recounted Mayfield's behavior before and after the murder. Harned testified Rudolph thought Mayfield was the man she saw inside the apartment, and Dr. Szarka testified that the night of the murder Linda told him Mayfield was "very upset" about her wanting to date other men. White recalled how Mayfield's mood changed when he learned Linda was dead.

"He said she had ruined him," White testified.

Nugent also submitted two undated photographs[57] purportedly showing Cook as he appeared in 1977, with hair reaching below his ears.

The defense attempted to rebound on the motive issue through the testimony of Dr. Richard Coons, a forensic psychiatrist from Austin. He testified he believed the murder was committed by an "enraged attacker" who knew the victim. "More is done than is necessary to kill this individual and then with the mutilation . . . that describes to me anger, very powerful anger," he said. Evidence that the victim's face was mutilated, he continued, is characteristic of a homicide committed by someone the victim knew personally. Coons also did not believe any body tissue was taken, an opinion echoed by Dallas forensic pathologist Dr. Linda Norton, who also noted the autopsy report did not include any notation of missing parts.

Nugent wrapped up the defense's case with testimony from fingerprint expert Dr. George Bonebrake, who confirmed Cook's fingerprints but stated it was improper for other experts to characterize them as "fresh." "It is not a scientific term. What does fresh mean? An hour? A day? A week or a month? It's a term that doesn't describe anything to me," he said.

The defense also attacked Ms. Raitano's credibility through the testimony of former Tyler police officer Gerald Hayden. He told jurors he knew Ms. Raitano in 1977 and had characterized her in a police report as being "mentally and emotionally unstable" and a "pathological liar."

---

57 The defense dropped attempts to present Cook's driver's license photo as evidence after prosecutors claimed they had evidence the document had been doctored.

"It is not a scientific term. What does fresh mean? An hour? A day? A week or a month? It's a term that doesn't describe anything to me."

—Fingerprint expert Dr. George Bonebrake

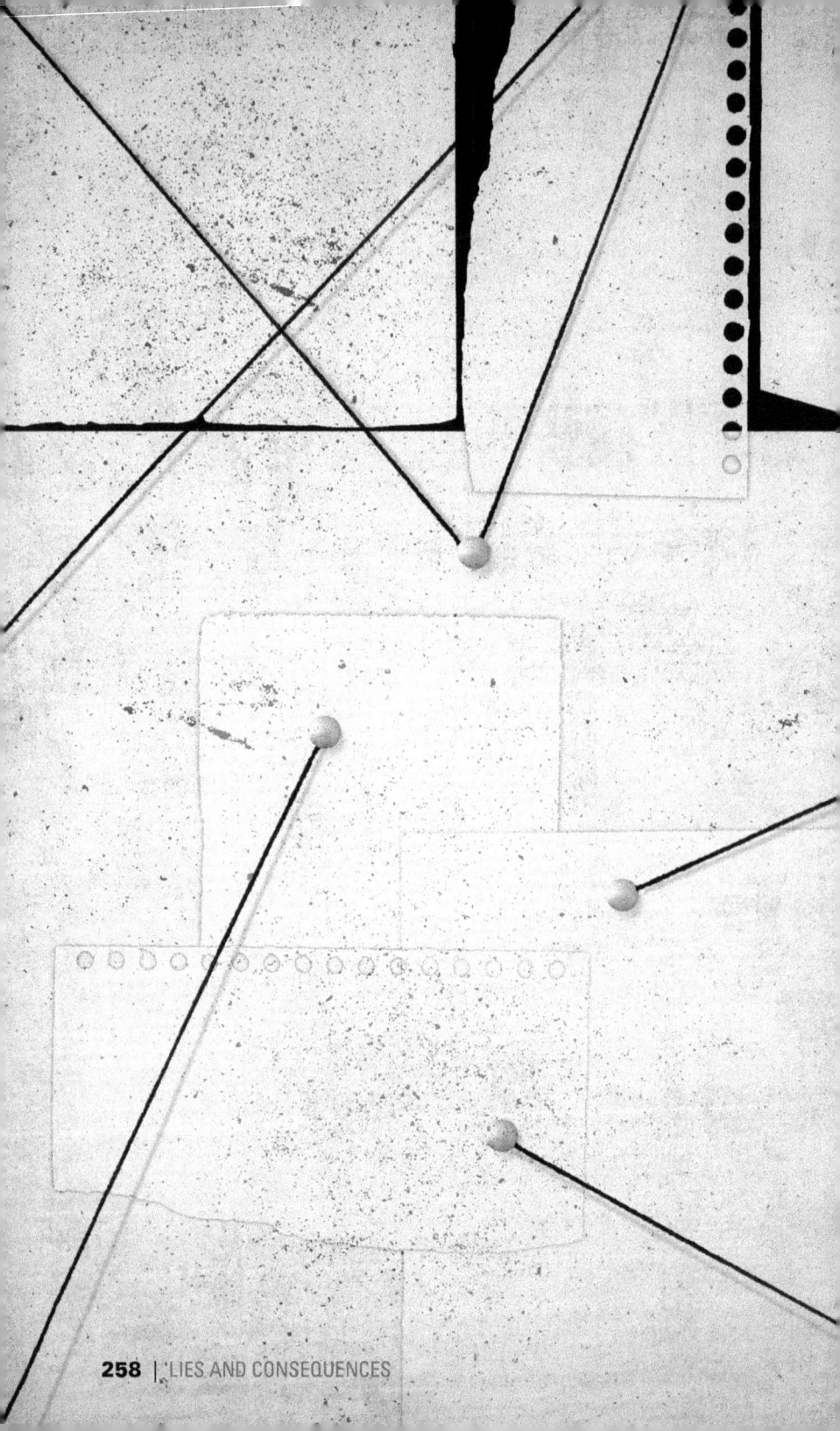

CHAPTER 47

Final Arguments

After ten days of testimony, opposing attorneys prepared to argue their case for three hours before a jury.

Skeen and Dobbs summed it up for the jurors as simply as they could: Evidence proved, they said, the murder was a lust-type attack committed by the defendant—a sexually ambivalent man who bragged about peeping through the victim's window, was seen inside the apartment the night of the murder, removed body parts from the scene, and repeatedly lied about why his fingerprints were found on the apartment door. "He's a liar. Why lie? Use your common sense," Dobbs told jurors. "Because he knows what he did in there."

Nugent finally addressed the elephant in the room—Cook's sexuality—by assailing the state's theory as "outrageous" and accusing prosecutors of using innuendo instead of facts to label his client as a homosexual to play upon their fears. "They want you to think [that] . . . so you'll decide this case based on prejudice and fear and not on the facts," Nugent argued. Finding Cook's fingerprints, he said, only proved the defendant had been to the apartment, not when, and Rudolph's description of the man she saw matched

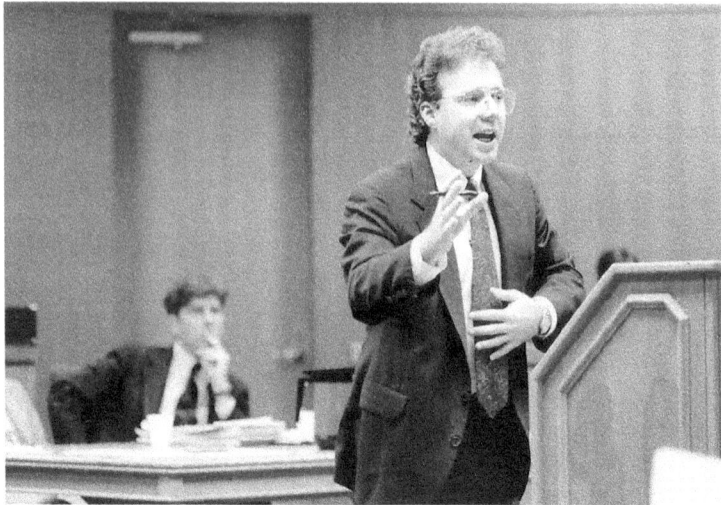

Chief Felony Prosecutor David Dobbs addresses a Williamson County jury while defense attorney Paul Nugent (in background) awaits his turn at the podium.

Mayfield, not his client. "She's trying to justify what she saw by saying it was a halo effect. She came up with the halo theory when Cook was arrested and realized he had dark hair, not silver," Nugent said. Defense experts, he reminded jurors, believed the wounds to the victim's face were inflicted by someone she knew who was intensely angry with her.

"You have the hardest job of your life. Make the state prove its case," he concluded. "Our system is in sorry shape if you convict on innuendoes."

"He's a liar. Why lie?...Because
he knows what he did in there."

–Assistant District Attorney David Dobbs

CHAPTER 48

Breaking a Deadlock

The waiting game started about noon on a Thursday when jurors began deliberating. But it didn't take long.

Five hours later, jury foreman Thomas Winn Jr. sent out a note: "The jurors are divided on the issue of guilt/not guilty" and asked that the court recess until the next day. A promising sign for the defense, but the collective sigh that started the trial turned into a silent groan as if to say, "Here we go again."

Jurors spent the night sequestered in a hotel. During seven-and-a-half hours of deliberating the next day, Winn sent out about ten more notes including requests to review certain testimony. Jurors wanted to hear witnesses Rudolph's and Hoehn's testimony again—clues that at least some of the panel members appeared to have doubts. Still no word by the end of the day. Judge Jones lifted the sequestration, allowing jurors a three-day weekend for Presidents' Day.

Deliberations the following Tuesday produced more notes and a continued deadlock, although there was no indication of a numerical split. In one note, Winn told the judge there were individuals on both sides of the issue who "are not inclined to change their viewpoint in the absence of additional evidence." Three notes that day reported the jury could not reach a unanimous decision. It would take another day and about six

Photo by Vanessa E. Curry/*Tyler Morning Telegraph*

Defendant Kerry Max Cook, center, seeks support from defense attorney Paul Nugent, right, and Jim McCloskey, left, of Centurion Ministries just moments before a guilty verdict is read.

more hours of deliberations to break the deadlock. That day, a Wednesday, began with bad news for the prosecution.

"We took a vote this morning . . . A very small number of jurors do not believe that the prosecution proved the case to their satisfaction," Winn wrote. About thirty minutes later, the foreman asked to review the testimony of FBI Special Agent Gomez. After lunch, the message everyone was waiting for arrived. They had reached a verdict.

Members of the media, Evelyn Cook, Jimmy and Ray Edwards, Clark, and a handful of others quickly returned to their seats, their faces reflecting the angst of uncertainty. Across the bar Skeen and Dobbs filled the void behind their table. Deputies escorted Cook back to the defense table where he sat flanked by McCloskey and Nugent.

The mood was tense but quiet. I lifted my camera and focused on the defense table, preparing to get a reaction shot when the verdict was read. Just for a moment Cook reached out and grasped

Nugent's hand on his left and McCloskey's hand on the right and quietly spoke to them.

I snapped the shot—one of the most dramatic courtroom photographs I had ever taken. One single frame captured that moment just before Cook stood before the jury to hear the words he hoped he never would hear again.

"We, the jury, find the defendant Kerry Max Cook guilty of capital murder."

Cook took several deep breaths, turned his head, and locked eyes with his mother. There was no other sign of the emotions he must have felt. Evelyn Cook left the courtroom and cried.

Relief crept across Jimmy and Ray Edward's faces as they hardily shook hands with the prosecutors. I didn't realize until then that in all the years I had known them, I had never seen them smile.

Jimmy Edwards and his father, Ray Edwards, react to the jury's guilty verdict against Kerry Max Cook for the murder of Linda Jo Edwards.

Photo by Vanessa E. Curry/ *Tyler Morning Telegraph*

CHAPTER 49

A Question of Dangerousness

I recall feeling indifferent about the verdict. I really didn't have time to think about it much since I had to rush to report the verdict by telephone. I also took my film to the Associated Press bureau office in Austin to be developed. At that time, I wasn't certain I had captured what I had seen through the lens. The moment had come and gone in such a flash. Unlike the digital world of today, I simply couldn't review my shots on a small screen on the back of the camera. Once the film was developed, the scene I was looking for was on one single frame. Relief. The Associated Press sent the photo out over the wire. Not only did it appear on the front page of the *Tyler Morning Telegraph*, but it also appeared in *The Dallas Morning News*.

In the criminal justice system, trials are bifurcated, meaning there is one phase to determine guilt or innocence and another phase to determine punishment if the defendant is found guilty.

Certain testimony not allowed in the first phase now became relevant when jurors deliberated whether Cook deserved to die. Before a death sentence can be applied, however, the jury must unanimously find that the defendant's actions were deliberate, that he constitutes a continuing threat to society, and that no mitigating circumstances exist to warrant a life sentence. In most capital murder cases, the second question proves to be the key focus for prosecutors. By its verdict alone, the jury obviously believed Cook beat, stabbed, and mutilated his victim on purpose. All the questions were difficult for the defense to address since the jury already disagreed with Cook's plea of innocence. That left them to challenge the state's evidence concerning the future danger posed by the defendant and tread softly around any mitigating evidence. It would only take one juror to decide if Cook didn't deserve to die. Deadlocking the jury again would mean an automatic life sentence.

There was no rest for jurors. They returned to the same Williamson County courtroom one day after the verdict and began hearing testimony from state's witnesses.

One of the state's most common arguments in capital murder cases is that a defendant's past behavior is a good indication of his future behavior. Skeen and Dobbs had plenty of ammunition to support that theory.

They called ten witnesses—a majority of whom were former or current Cherokee County law enforcement officers—who testified that in the mid-1970s Cook had a bad reputation and was not a peaceful or law-abiding citizen. Jurors heard evidence of Cook's prior arrests and convictions, prison sentence, and commitments to Rusk State Hospital. The state also was allowed to present evidence of separate incidents of Cook mutilating himself—including a gruesome videotape of one incident—and testimony from a woman who claimed the defendant sexually assaulted her. Judge Jones ruled the state could not present the latter evidence during the first phase of the trial because it was too prejudicial.

Nugent had argued against allowing the jury to see the videotape because he said it was "outrageously inflammatory" and it had nothing to do with the murder. But prosecutors successfully argued that Cook's willingness to mutilate himself was relevant to the case. The forty-five-minute videotape of a bloody 1990 incident is so graphic, Jones forewarned the courtroom audience they might want to wait outside until the viewing was over.

I certainly could attest to his characterization of the videotape. Long before the trial began, I stopped by the district attorney's office at the Smith County Courthouse on my regular rounds, and somehow a discussion with Dobbs led to references to that incident. I was allowed to have a private viewing on a television monitor and chair set up in a closet. The video was taken by a prison official as officers responded to a medical call in Cook's cell. Blood was everywhere, but the most gruesome sight was a picture of Cook's penis, which appeared to be cut; his testicles were not only black and blue but hideously swollen. My stomach churned and I nearly became physically ill.

I stayed in the courtroom during the viewing at Cook's trial, not to see it again but to watch for any reaction from members of the jury. They all appeared to maintain their composure during the viewing, but they also appeared uncomfortable. They watched intently but avoided making eye contact with anyone else in the room.

It was Cook's turn to look uncomfortable when Amber Norris, a Port Arthur woman, took the stand and testified Cook raped her in 1977 after she drove to pick him up from a club where he worked as a bartender. Cook's body language—adjusting in his seat, avoiding making eye contact or showing any emotion—suggested controlled contempt for Norris, although he refrained from verbally expressing it. She said she had been living with Cook shortly before his arrest. That night, Cook had been drinking and began beating and kicking her before stopping the car and forcing her to have sex, she testified. Under cross-examination, the witness admitted she never reported the incident to police and said she might have been using drugs the day of the incident.

Prosecutors wrapped up their case with testimony from Jerry Landrum and Tom Allen, Tyler psychologists who testified they reviewed Cook's mental health records and criminal and prison records, as well as evidence and photographs taken from the crime scene. Based upon those reviews, both said they believed the defendant was prone to violence and posed a continuing threat to society.

Landrum, a supervisor in correctional psychology for the state prison system, said he stood by his 1973 diagnosis that Cook has an antisocial personality disorder even though he hadn't interviewed the defendant in decades. "Absolutely, [he's] a continuing threat—when on the streets, in prison or on death row," Landrum said.

CHAPTER 50

Using the Media

The challenge of this trial wasn't in writing about what was going on inside the courtroom, it was deciding how to handle what was going on in the hallways outside Judge Jones's view. Jones had issued what is commonly called a gag order that prohibited parties from speaking to anyone, especially the media, about the case. As the battle got more intense in the courtroom, the urge for opposing attorneys to vent their frustrations, through the media, about one another and Jones's ruling became irresistible.

Of course, the gag order didn't apply to members of the media. We could interview just about anyone, but they were the ones who had to decide whether it was appropriate or safe to respond. It seemed to me the attorneys loved to hide behind the gag order when they didn't want to answer a question, but when they wanted to vent, they expected the media to pick it up and run with it.

Huddles outside the courtroom—attorneys whispering to a reporter, usually *The Dallas Morning News*'s Gillman or myself since the attorneys didn't want to appear on television openly violating the gag order—weren't unusual. The hushed conferences happened more and more often as the trial proceeded. My stomach churned every time I saw Gillman with the defense team. If Dobbs saw the same scene, he would bend my ear with an opposing point of view. Sure, I could get a story this way, but did I really want to be used like that?

Right or wrong, I decided not to play the game. I might have listened, but I used my best judgment to decide whether what I was being told was important for the public to know or simply an attempt to try the case through the media. This only created a problem when Gillman's story for the day contained information that mine didn't. It was then my boss would ask me why. I tried to explain, but I don't think he quite got my point.

The out-of-court conferences finally became a serious issue in the punishment phase of the trial when Evelyn Cook, who had been subpoenaed to testify, gave *The Dallas Morning News* an exclusive interview. I was disappointed, of course, but already had become accustomed to being snubbed. Jones apparently monitored the media coverage every day and was not too happy to read her comments about the justice system in a newspaper with a statewide circulation. Jones called her before the bench and admonished her, threatening to find her in contempt and bar her from testifying if she violated the rule again. It didn't matter much; she got her say and Jones couldn't take it back.

What would I have done if Evelyn Cook had come to me instead? I'm grateful I never had to make that decision.

"Right or wrong, I decided not to play the game."

—Author

CHAPTER 51

To Save a Life

Nugent tackled the future danger issue with mental experts of his own who testified Cook was a "passive" individual—a term psychologist Landrum later called "ludicrous"—and unlikely to commit acts of violence in the future. And, they said, his behavior while in prison was not uncommon considering his circumstances and living conditions. "He does not display, and never has displayed, behavior consistent with antisocial disorder," former prison psychologist Dr. Jo Anne Johnson said.

Cook's aunt, Joyce McElyea, told jurors the defendant was a "loving child, kind and considerate." Dr. Arlo Hendrickson, a college math instructor who ministered to Cook in the Smith County Jail, used similar adjectives, calling the defendant "warm, caring, intelligent and fun loving."

One of the most interesting witnesses called to testify on Cook's behalf was former death row inmate Clarence Lee Brandley[58]—the Conroe school janitor sentenced to die for the 1980 rape-slaying of a teenage girl. A judge later ruled Brandley was innocent and set him free. Brandley testified Cook was a model prisoner—a nonviolent person who was quiet and "easy to get along with."

---

58 Brandley died September 2, 2018, from pneumonia.

Former death row inmate Clarence Brandley describes life on death row as a defense witness during the punishment phase of Cook's trial.

Photo by Vanessa E. Curry/*Tyler Morning Telegraph*

That female witness who McCloskey had once told me could verify Cook is "very normal and had no sexual inadequacies" never materialized.

If not for the attributes of the murder itself, testimony in the punishment phase simply came down to a difference between Cook's record and testimony from people who knew him personally.

But prosecutors Skeen and Dobbs weren't about to let the jury forget the gruesome details of Linda's death. The defendant was a high school dropout with a criminal record who twice committed himself to a mental hospital years before the murder. While in prison, disciplinary records reflected an attack on another inmate, acts of self-mutilation, possession of marijuana and homemade knives, and threatening a guard, prosecutors reminded the jury.

Nugent argued that his client had "fessed up to and took his punishment" for previous indiscretions. And, he countered, Cook's trouble while imprisoned was the product of his environment, not his character. He asked jurors to make their decision based on facts, not emotions, and to have the courage to "stick to your guns" if any member did not believe the state had proven its case—an apparent appeal to the juror or jurors who initially had held out for acquittal in the first phase of the trial. "It's easy to be cynical," he argued. "It takes more courage to rise above that."

Skeen, however, didn't allow jurors to forget the gruesomeness of Linda's last moments on earth. As per his style, Skeen worked himself up into a red-faced frenzy in arguing for the death penalty. At one point, he held up an enlarged photograph of the victim's bloodied body and the fourteen-inch vegetable knife used to kill her. "What type of person does it take to commit that type of crime in that manner?" he asked. "I don't think you need an expert to come in here and tell you . . . [and] the deliberate nature of the crime says a whole lot about the probability of future dangerousness."

And with that final statement, the jury retired to deliberate Cook's fate.

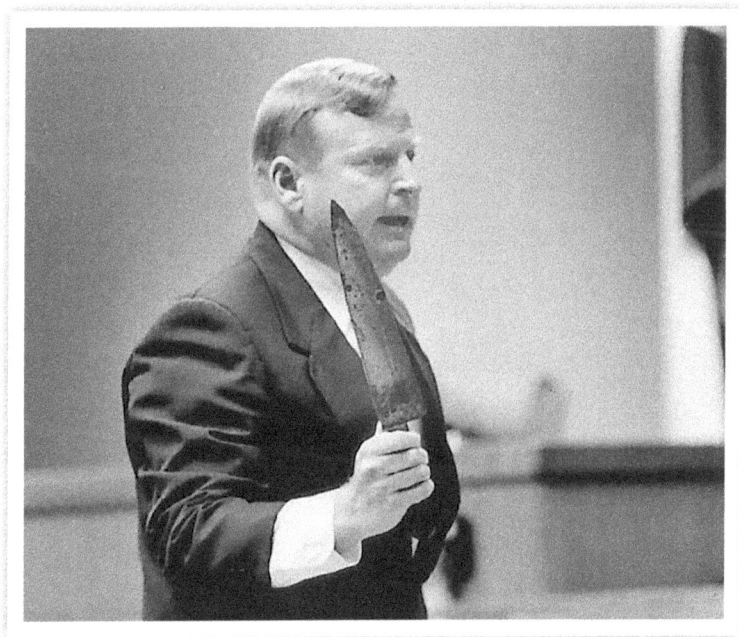

Photo by Vanessa E. Curry/*Tyler Morning Telegraph*

Smith County District Attorney Jack Skeen makes a point to jurors about the brutality of Linda Jo's murder.

CHAPTER 52

Last Word

The decision to return Cook to death row on March 3, 1994, came after nine hours of deliberations over a period of two days. I don't think it came as a surprise to anyone, but it was emotional just the same. Cook stood calmly before Judge Jones, who officially pronounced the sentence. He responded by saying, "I am an innocent man. Lord forgive them, for they know not what they do." He was returned to his cell after declining media interviews.

His mother broke into tears, comforted by her sister-in-law, while the Edwards family congratulated the prosecutors once again.

In interviews with reporters, Evelyn Cook, Nugent, and McCloskey vowed to continue their fight to prove Evelyn's son's innocence. Jimmy Edwards said he and his family could not rest until Cook was finally executed. Skeen and Dobbs reportedly celebrated by sharing a high five in the parking lot of their motel, a gesture *The Dallas Morning News* reporter Gillman made special note of in his written report.

During earlier testimony, Jimmy Edwards said his sister's death and the trials had taken a tremendous toll on him and his father. "It's caused me lots and lots of grief. It nearly killed my father. My father has not been the same father I knew years ago," he said.

Deputies escorted members of the jury to their vehicles. There would be no juror interviews. Jurors had requested the judge "shield" them from the media in a note sent out during the first phase of the trial. Instead, they would send a message to the victim, in a unique gesture no one expected.

Linda Jo Edwards gravesite in Bullard, Texas.

CHAPTER 53

Graveside

"It was a small thing to do," jury foreman Thomas Winn Jr. told me, "but something we felt was right."

Acting upon an impulse, he said, the six men and six women decided to pool their money and buy flowers for the victim's grave. "We felt very close to Linda Jo after spending weeks on this issue," Winn explained. "All of us thought 'That could have been my sister or my daughter.'"

The $48 they collected paid for an arrangement featuring white and purple irises, pink carnations, and small yellow flowers nestled in lush greenery. Skeen and Dobbs joined Jimmy and Ray Edwards at the Bullard cemetery to place them on Linda's grave. "If she was here today, I know she would be happy. Linda loved flowers," her brother said. "I think we can have some rest . . . and I thank them very much for that."

CHAPTER 54

Back to Death Row

Cook returned to J-23 cellblock at Ellis I Unit to find it not much different than when he left it—a grimy, depressing, threatening world within walls. The roller coaster of feelings he had experienced since winning his appeal three years earlier had come to a crashing end. And worst of all he said he felt alone despite McCloskey's vow to continue fighting for his freedom and Nugent already working on an appeal. Two months into his new sentence, guards found Cook bleeding in his cell with a one-quarter- to one-half-inch self-inflicted cut on his penis.

PART IV

A Possible Ending?

TIMELINE:

Cook Goes Free on $100,000 bond

November 15, 1995
Oral arguments heard on appeal before Texas Court of Criminal Appeals.

4th Cook Trial Likely

November 11, 1997
Cook released from Smith County Jail on bond.

February 16, 1999
Cook enters a no contest plea to a reduced charge of murder in exchange for time served.

Cook Accepts Plea Deal Without Admitting Guilt

2003
Skeen appointed to 241st District Court Bench.

2007
Cook releases book.

1995

1996

November 6, 1996
Texas Court of Criminal Appeals grants Cook a new trial.

Judge Jones sets Cook's bond at $100,000.

1997

1998

September 15, 1998
Scheduled retrial date.

1999

Court Awards Cook New Trial

2000

New Lawyers

2001

2002

2002
Dobbs leaves district attorney's office to private practice.

2003

2004

2004
Bingham appointed as district attorney.

2005

2006

2007

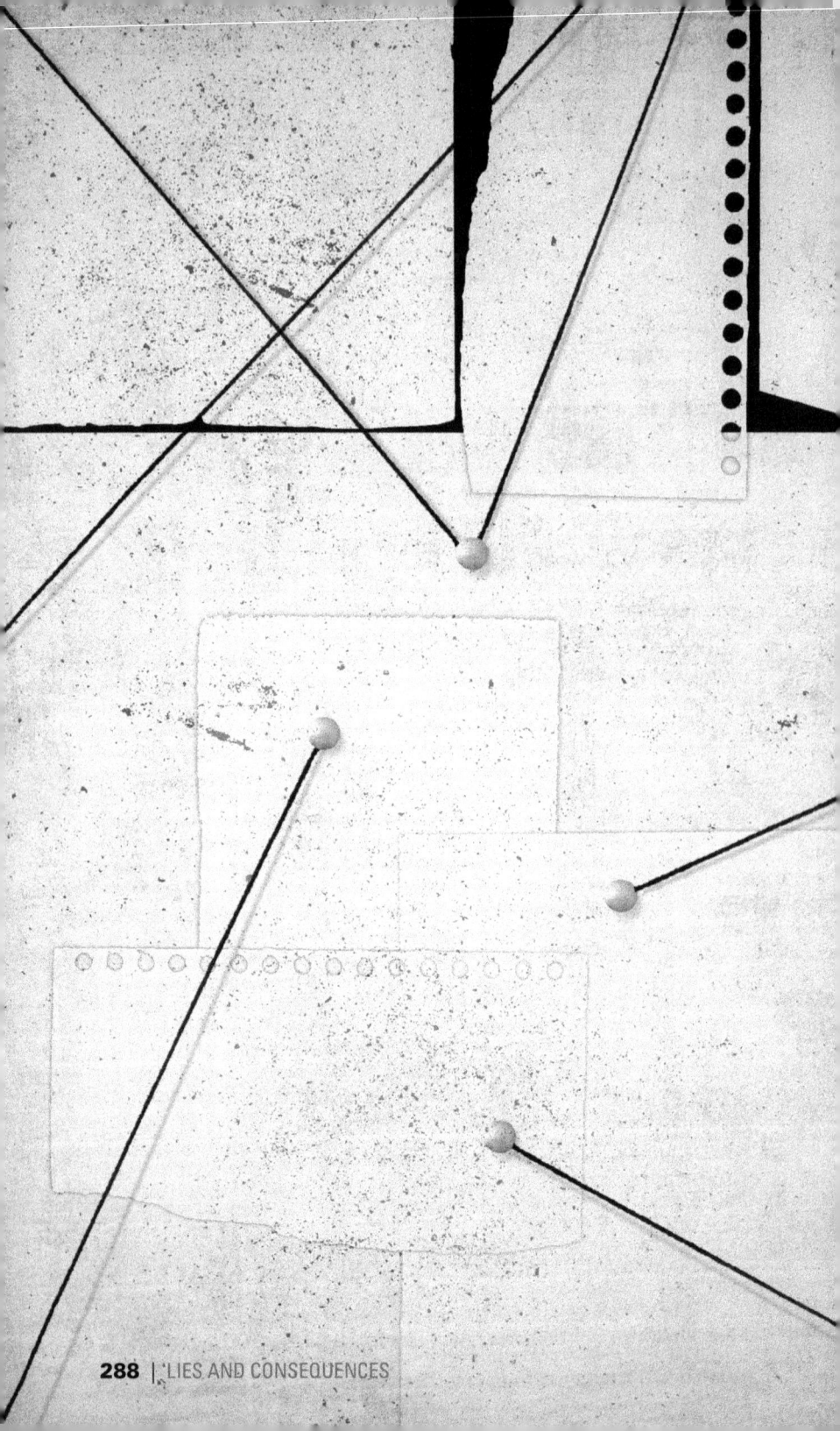

CHAPTER 55

Capital Offenses

For Nugent, the process started all over again, but this time he had issues from the second retrial to add to his list of reasons why the court should throw out Cook's new conviction and death sentence.

Smith County prosecutors, however, barely had time to rest before starting on a series of three capital murder cases that would consume their time the rest of the year.[59] That year I spent nearly five months covering capital murder or murder trials moved out of Tyler because of extensive publicity.

Cook's case was relatively dormant during 1995, except for a hearing before the Texas Court of Criminal Appeals in Austin in November. Nugent argued prosecutorial misconduct should have barred prosecutors from retrying Cook a third time, or at the very least, jurors should have been allowed to consider misconduct claims. Assistant District Attorney Ed Marty argued that what Nugent termed misconduct were simple mistakes that had been corrected via a new trial. "People—conservative or liberal—do

---

59 In April 1994 Skeen and Dobbs won a conviction and death sentence for Rickey Lynn Lewis. In August, the prosecuting team spent weeks in Kerrville, Texas, trying Donald Aldrich, who also received a death sentence. They then would spend two months retrying Baker Steven Lucas on a murder charge in Dallas on a change of venue.

not like lies. People—conservative or liberal—are disgusted by prosecutors and elected officials lying and cheating," Nugent said after the hour-long arguments.

The major trial schedule continued for prosecutors at a hectic pace in 1995—three other capital murder cases, although those trials remained in Smith County.[60] In the meantime, Cook's defense once again prepared and submitted an appeal.

---

60 In March, Napoleon Beazley was convicted and sentenced to die for killing the father of a federal judge. Skeen and Dobbs also won convictions against Henry Dunn and Christopher Wells in separate capital murder charges.

"People—conservative or liberal—are disgusted by prosecutors and elected officials lying and cheating."

—Defense attorney Paul Nugent

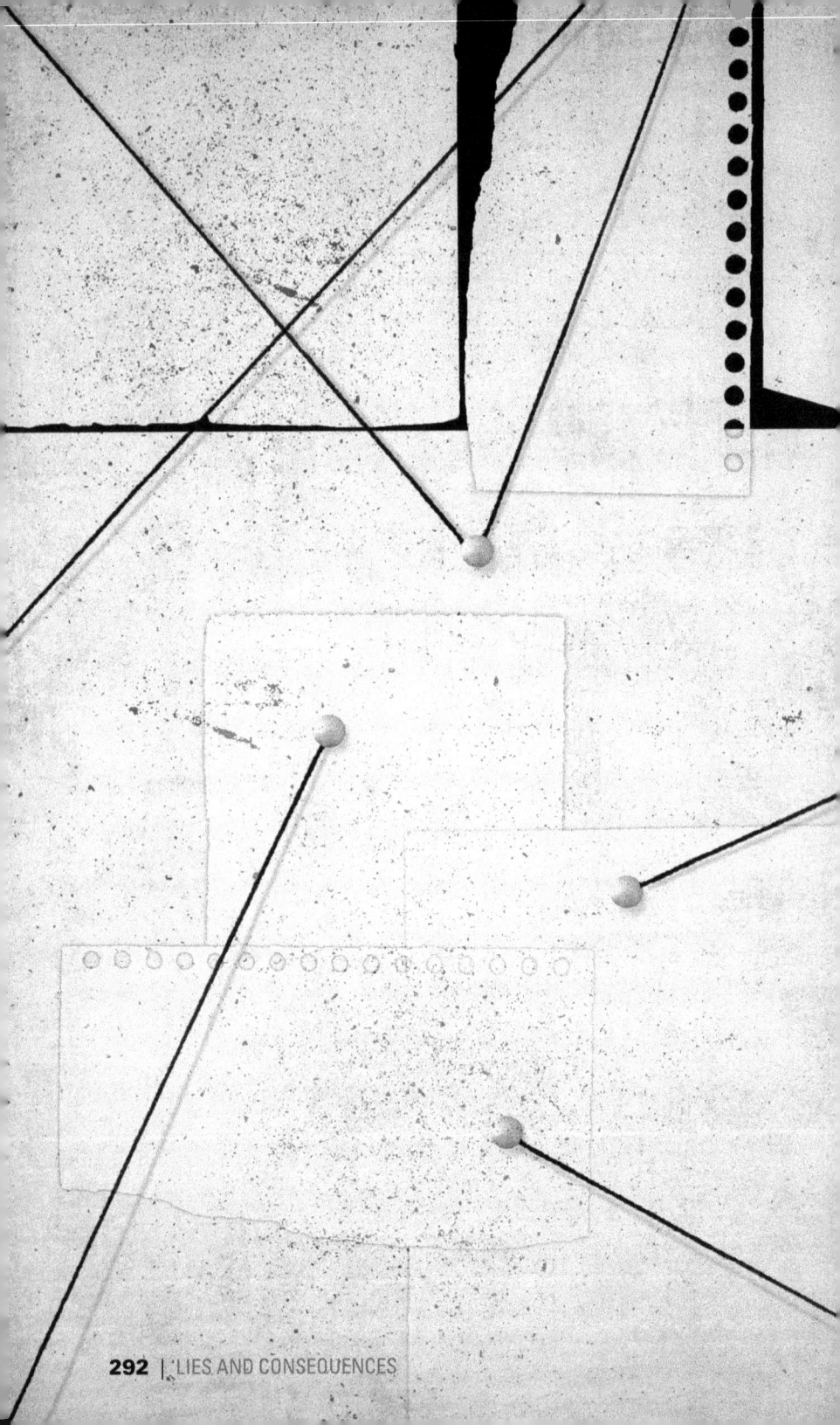

CHAPTER 56

Another Strike

Although I have no proof, I suspect Nugent knew for sure the Texas Court of Criminal Appeals would overturn Cook's second conviction before it was publicly announced on November 6, 1996. Either that or he was just extremely confident. The news hit with nearly the same punch in the Tyler community as the previous reversal. Those who believed in Cook's guilt responded with disbelief that the appellate court continued to give the prosecution a failing grade despite all their work to correct the missteps of the past. Those who supported Cook's innocence saw the decision as the strongest confirmation yet of prosecutorial misconduct. They were cautiously optimistic that Skeen would finally see the light and concede defeat.

The decision, however, was more divisive than the 5–3 final vote appeared. Although five justices agreed prosecutorial misconduct tainted the case from the beginning, they didn't agree on whether the state could have another bite of the apple. Justice Steve Mansfield wrote for the majority, focusing on just a handful of the defense's claims of fifty-five points of trial error.[61]

---

61 Mansfield was a political unknown before winning a seat on the Texas Court of Criminal Appeals in 1994 on the coattails of a Republican tide and admittedly with very little criminal law experience. During his term, he was arrested for allegedly

No doubt the prosecution had not played fair, he said, but the real question was "whether prosecutorial misconduct, magnified by the passage of fourteen years and the death of a key witness, can so degrade the normal workings of justice that a fair trial becomes impossible and thus retrial is forbidden under due process and due course of law principles."

He outlined a laundry list of misconduct:

- failure to disclose information that Luella Raitano had "investigated" her father and his lover at the apartment complex two weeks before the murder,
- failure to reveal grand jury testimony that the defendant and victim may have known each other,
- misrepresentation of Shyster Jackson's deal to testify during the 1978 trial,
- inconsistent statements made by Hoehn about the type of relationship he had with Cook the night of the murder,
- misleading information about the age of Cook's fingerprints found at the murder scene, and
- Dobbs' encounter with Cook in 1992.

Under the law, prosecutors must disclose to the defense all the evidence they have collected even if it favors the defendant. Most of the evidence not disclosed to Cook's attorneys until 1991 involved grand jury testimony from witnesses Rodney and Randy Dykes (Taylor's nephews) and Hoehn recorded in 1977. At trial, Rodney Dykes testified Cook sent him over to two females at the pool in hopes of getting acquainted, one of whom matched Linda's description; however, in his grand jury testimony, the witness said Cook told him he got hickeys on his neck from the girl at the pool who invited him to her apartment. The opinion also noted inconsistencies from Hoehn, who gave contradictory statements about having sexual intercourse with Cook.

---

trying to scalp complimentary tickets to the Texas–Texas A&M football game. He did not seek reelection. The *Texas Observer* once referred to Mansfield as "a poster boy" for judicial election reform. "A Poster Boy for Reform," *Texas Observer*, December 9, 1994, 3.

The defense especially applauded Mansfield's sweeping opinion of the prosecution in the case—presenting the statement repeatedly as a broad "I told you so" denouncement of the state's representatives, including Skeen and his staff. "Prosecutorial and police misconduct have tainted this entire matter from the outset. Little confidence can be placed in the outcome of appellant's first two trials as a result, and the taint, it seems clear, persisted until the revelation of the State's misconduct in 1992," according to the ruling.

Mansfield, however, put the misconduct in perspective in a footnote that Cook and his supporters often forget to disclose: "We note the acts of misconduct on the part of the Smith County District Attorney's Office and the Tyler Police Department took place nearly twenty years ago and we do not imply any complicity in said act on the part of the current District Attorney or current members of the Tyler Police Department."

With that said, it seemed odd that the state's highest court was now reevaluating Cook's first trial even though the same court—albeit with a different slate of justices—already had overturned that conviction. But this court noted the residue of the misconduct—some of which was not discovered until much later—continued to give the state an unfair advantage. Most of the misconduct was corrected prior to the third trial, Mansfield wrote, since inmate witness Jackson didn't testify, Collard's testimony was corrected, and the Dykes brothers had testified at trial, giving the defense an opportunity to cross-examine them. Luella Mayfield Raitano also was available to be called as a witness.

The suppression of Hoehn's testimony, however, was a much more serious issue since his account of the night of the murder put the defendant near the scene in an alleged aroused emotional state. However, Hoehn's death precluded Cook's team from investigating the contradictions of his testimony. Did they or did they not have sexual relations that night? Did Cook watch all of the suggestive movie or only part of it? "Use of Hoehn's testimony at appellant's third trial, under these circumstances, casts serious doubts as to the fairness of appellant's third trial and the reliability of the proceedings against him," according to the opinion. Mansfield and two of his colleagues therefore agreed: A retrial was possible, but prosecutors would have to do it without Hoehn's testimony.

In his concurring but dissenting opinion, Justice Charlie Beard addressed the same examples of prosecutorial misconduct but strongly disagreed that another trial could be fair. He chastised the trial court for treating allegations regarding the Dykes brothers and Hoehn in a "cursory manner." He also made a special point to note that the residual and cumulative effects of the misconduct over fourteen years—not the misconduct during the first trial—were the key issue needing to be addressed. "The state's suppression of the evidence until after Hoehn's death has denied appellant the opportunity to investigate, clarify and perhaps impeach Hoehn's testimony in the same manner as the state had developed evidence like Rudolph's testimony, through repeated clarification and investigation," Beard said. "Hoehn's death prior to the discovery of the state's misconduct has made it impossible to access the full impact of the misconduct on appellant's ability to defend himself."

Although Beard said he didn't necessarily believe Cook's attorneys could have built a successful defense if they had knowledge of all of Hoehn's statements, the fact is they were denied the opportunity to fully investigate and develop a case in the same manner as the state. "In the instant case, the State's misconduct has ripened with the passage of years into a situation where the State cannot demonstrate that a fair trial, free of the taint of its misconduct, will ever be possible," he said. Beard concluded the state should be barred from retrying the case.

"Under these circumstances appellant's retrial serves no purpose but to subject him to continuing mental, emotional and financial hardship," Beard wrote.

Justice Sharon Keller wrote the dissent, in which she characterized "yet a different account" of the murder.[62] Concerning

---

62 In 1994, Keller, a Republican, became the first woman elected to the Texas Court of Criminal Appeals. She became the court's presiding judge in 2000. She earned

Hoehn's statements, Keller said the justices had missed a critical point. What was not disclosed, she noted, was the fact that Hoehn testified, not the fact that Cook had made statements about being with a woman in her apartment. And since Cook knew he'd made the statement—and knew Hoehn knew—it had not been suppressed. The defense could not now argue that they had been denied information when the defendant knew about it all along. In other words, Cook created his own dilemma because he initially denied knowing the victim and claimed he had never been in her apartment.

Even if Cook had been in Linda's apartment making out, "that fact does not in any way show or tend to show that appellant did not murder Edwards," she wrote while also noting that other testimony indicated Linda would not have been attracted to someone like Cook.

Keller also downplayed the importance of testimony involving Luella Raitano, noting that it was insignificant because she did not match the description of the person Rudolph saw that night—a man, not a woman. "Reversal is not required simply because one can speculate that a stronger defense might have been devised," she said, "especially if that defense is inconsistent with undisputed eye-witness testimony or physical evidence. Such is the case here."

To bar prosecutors from using any of Hoehn's statements, she said, "encroaches upon the authority of the trial judge."

Keller concluded her opinion, writing that the suppressed evidence "does not put the whole case in such a different light as to undermine confidence in the verdict."

---

the nicknames "Killer Keller" and "Sharon Killer" in 2007 after an incident involving the last-minute appeal of death row inmate Michael Richard. Richard's attorneys notified a court official they were having computer problems and asked if someone would be available to accept the appeal request later that night. Keller reportedly told the court officer, "We close at five." The attorneys missed the deadline and Richard was executed.

CHAPTER 57

Witness to the Execution

By the end of 1995, I had covered more than a half-dozen capital murder trials involving kidnapping, rape, robbery, or burglary—senseless killings committed by convicted defendants with varied histories and circumstances. Of those victims, most had been fatally shot. Only two had died from being bludgeoned and/or fatally stabbed.

The testimony I heard exposed me to the reality of a part of society I had only seen depicted in movies. The courtroom and courthouse became my classroom, fueling my curiosity about the criminal mind, law, legal strategies, social issues, the media's role, and public perception.

I found myself going beyond just reporting the news: I began writing in-depth, enterprising stories that I hoped would make readers think.

One of those deeper topics came to mind in 1996 when the Texas Board of Criminal Justice adopted a new policy allowing victim witnesses to view executions. A group of victim advocates and survivors had met with board members the previous year, requesting access to executions as part of the healing process.

The new policy allowed an immediate family member or close relative of the deceased victim to watch the execution.

That policy was relaxed in 1998 to also include close friends of surviving relatives.

I asked myself: "Now that they could view an execution, would they?" I posed that question to some survivors and relatives in Smith County cases and received mixed responses. My research also led me to interview Sister Helen Prejean, a Roman Catholic nun associated with the Congregation of the Sisters of Saint Joseph of Medaille in New Orleans, who had written about her experiences as a spiritual adviser to death row inmates. Her book *Dead Man Walking* was published in 1993.[63] She was and still is an anti–death penalty advocate.

In those pre-internet days, it took a little more work to secure an interview with her. I got the telephone number of her parish through the long-distance operator and dialed the number, and surprisingly the person who answered brought Sister Prejean to the phone.

That interview gave me two important issues to think about:

- Although opposed to the death penalty, Sister Prejean advocated for public executions, believing opposition would increase dramatically once capital punishment became more than an abstract idea.
- Given the unlikelihood of lifting the moratorium on public executions, Sister Prejean encouraged more media accounts, believing they also could generate more opposition.

Hoping to open my eyes, she suggested I witness an execution. For me, capital punishment had become more than just a topic for a high school term paper. I not only read more about the topic—both pro and con—but my position as a reporter allowed me to discuss it directly with those involved: lawyers, judges, survivors, and even offenders.

For Texas executions, held in Huntsville, five seats in the witness rooms are reserved for members of the media. Two automatically go to representatives for the Texas bureau of the Associated Press and the Texas bureau of United Press International because they serve a

---

63 The book was made into a movie, *Dead Man Walking*, and starred Susan Sarandon and Sean Penn. It was released in 1995.

long list of member stations and newspapers. Another two usually are reserved for one representative each from print and broadcast outlets located in the city or county where the case was tried. A local reporter from the Huntsville newspaper automatically gets a seat.

All the cases I had covered were still in the appeals process and no execution dates had been set. I had plans to move out of reporting once I earned my graduate degree in interdisciplinary studies (journalism, criminal justice, and political science), so I feared I wouldn't have an opportunity before I left.

It's not that I was excited about seeing an execution, but something rang true to what Sister Prejean and I had discussed. If I was going to write about capital punishment, then I should cover it completely as part of my duty as a public watchdog. If being a member of the media afforded me an opportunity to witness something I write about for the public, then I should take that opportunity. My chance came in 1997, with the scheduled execution of John William Cockrum. He had been convicted and sentenced to die for the 1986 murder of Eva May, a sixty-nine-year-old store owner in Bowie County.

Two factors played roles in my decision to watch him die: One, I didn't know him and didn't cover his trial; two, he intentionally dropped all his appeals. I knew it wasn't going to be easy to watch someone die, but I believed, or at least hoped, those factors would ease any emotional impact for me.

Officials approved my request to witness Cockrum's execution (only because one of the reserved seats had not been claimed), so I headed to Huntsville on the afternoon of September 30, 1997. In hindsight, I should not have worn a skirt and pantyhose since I was surprised to learn I would have to be searched for contraband prior to entering the prison, known as the Walls Unit. The female guard did a thorough job of "patting me down," including running her hands up each leg and around my inner thighs. Wearing a skirt may have made her job easier, but I'm certain I would have felt more comfortable wearing slacks.

I, along with a group of other witnesses, was escorted into two separate viewing rooms to keep those representing the victim or offender apart. I was placed in the designated offender side simply because there wasn't any room available in the other.

Within minutes, curtains covering large picture windows slid open, revealing the death chamber with bright blue colored walls. The color had a calming effect in contrast to an otherwise cold, sterile appearance. Cockrum lay prone on a gurney with padded leather straps restraining both ankles and wrists. His arms lay on supports extending from the gurney, while surgical tubes stretched from both arms into a wall in the back of the room.

Our eyes met for just a second as he scanned the faces on the other side of the glass. As I recall, the warden stood near Cockrum's feet and read the standard statement pronouncing the death sentence and asking Cockrum if he had any final words.

As Cockrum apologized to the victim's family, expressed love for his family, and asked Jesus Christ to forgive him, the deadly combination of drugs began flowing through his veins. I wanted to believe Cockrum was sincere, although there is the possibility he just wanted others to believe he was. Did he deserve credit for dropping his appeals, or did he just give up on life? I don't know.

His breathing slowed, and within seconds he took his final breath, ending with a slight gasp. The next five minutes seemed like an hour to me as we waited for a physician to officially pronounce Cockrum dead.

It seemed impolite to stare at his motionless body, but it was awkward to look away because I didn't want to make eye contact with anyone else in the room. My reaction was more introspective than emotional.

I knew nothing about Cockrum or his past, nor that of his victim. Cockrum just walked into a convenience store one day wanting money and ended up putting a gun to the head of the cashier and pulling the trigger.

A sensation of heat crept up the back of my neck and across my face as I visualized that gruesome scene. I wasn't just angry about that woman's murder—it also angered me that it took a death sentence for Cockrum to recognize the senselessness of his crime. If only he could have contemplated—even just for a second—the consequences of his actions before doing something so unthinkable. Pulling that trigger didn't just take an innocent life, it sealed his own fate.

The crime caused a wave of grief, anger, and fear that reverberated into a larger circle of people, including family members and friends on both sides as well as society.

CHAPTER 58

Return to Square One

Despite the reversal in 1994, Cook spent another year behind bars as prosecutors again asked the US Supreme Court to reverse the Texas Court of Criminal Appeals. In the meantime, Cook, his family, and supporters began to appeal to public opinion once again.

Starting in January 1997, Cook wrote me sixteen letters in nine months. Up until then our relationship had been tentative. I simply could not get him to understand why I refused to take sides. And he simply could not understand why I didn't support his innocence as *The Dallas Morning News* appeared to have done. We attempted to build a better rapport through written correspondence. Cook's approach was an emotional appeal, revealing a great fear of men in the process. His greatest moments of unbearable humiliation and anxiety, he said, came from having other men see his exposed tattooed buttocks in prison. He also feared being alone in the single side cell away from other inmates.

As a journalist, I couldn't allow myself to become emotionally involved even though Cook begged me to possibly intervene on his behalf for better treatment if he returned to the Smith County Jail. I wanted Cook to be more accessible and more open in interviews, but I couldn't afford to jeopardize my journalism integrity by becoming personally involved. My attempts to explain only added to his frustration. My contact with Cook—frequent telephone calls (collect) and letters—apparently worried some of my friends and coworkers, who later told me they came close more than once to confronting me with their concerns.

Final word came in October 1997 when the US Supreme Court returned from its summer break and declined to consider the state's appeal. The decision (or nondecision for that matter) resurrected public debate. "I just want to go home and try to pick up the shattered remnants of a life that has been stolen from me," Cook said in an interview. Nugent seemed reinvigorated by the decision, confidently telling reporters he believed that prosecutorial misconduct would finally force the state to dismiss the charges against Cook.

The thought of yet another trial—which Skeen vowed to pursue—and more appeals shattered the Edwards family, but they resolved to continue the fight for justice for their daughter/sister with as much fervor as Cook continued his fight to prove his innocence. "There ain't no words for it. It just doesn't make sense," a tearful Jimmy Edwards said. And for the first time in years, his oldest sister, Carolyn Edwards Loftin, spoke out, too, vowing to be by his side during the next trial. "Her [Linda Jo's] memory deserves to be at peace, and we deserve to be at peace," she said in a written statement to the media.

Cook's family released a four-page statement expressing their disdain for the district attorney's office. "It is difficult for all of us to watch side-lined as a skillful, professional politician deliberately continues to exploit and manipulate this horrible lie against Cook," the statement read. "As he continues to drum up support for an unprecedented fourth trial to persecute an innocent man. All the while a trusting unsuspecting media condones their continued suppression of the facts, the truth."

McCloskey remained hopeful and vowed never to give up. "We're bound and determined to lead him out of court a free and acquitted man," he said.

At least part of that statement became a reality within a month.

"I just want to go home and try to pick up the shattered remnants of a life that has been stolen from me."

–Kerry Max Cook

CHAPTER 59

Free at Last

Nugent wasted no time in filing an application for bond—arguing that the US Supreme Court's decision had given prosecutors even less evidence to support the charge against his client. During a November 1997 bond hearing before Judge Jones, he suggested a $75,000 bond, noting it was a "benchmark" set in 1993 when former death row inmate Andrew Lee Mitchell was released pending a decision on his retrial. Dobbs argued against setting a bond, reminding Jones of former Reserve Deputy Bob Wickham, who testified Cook confessed to the slaying.

Jones ended the hearing by setting a $100,000 bond—a decision the prosecution asked him to reconsider in a nine-page motion filed days later. The petition argued that the set amount was "woefully inadequate" and urged a new bond amount of at least $500,000. It was a last-ditch effort for the prosecutors, who knew the defense team was likely bankrupt and wouldn't be able to raise enough to secure Cook's release on $100,000. They didn't want to take any chances. But the defense had other plans.

November 11, 1997, was a Tuesday. Word came that Centurion Ministries had secured enough funds from a private donor to post bond. News reporters rushed to the Smith County Jail. The *Tyler Morning Telegraph* sent two photographers, another reporter, and

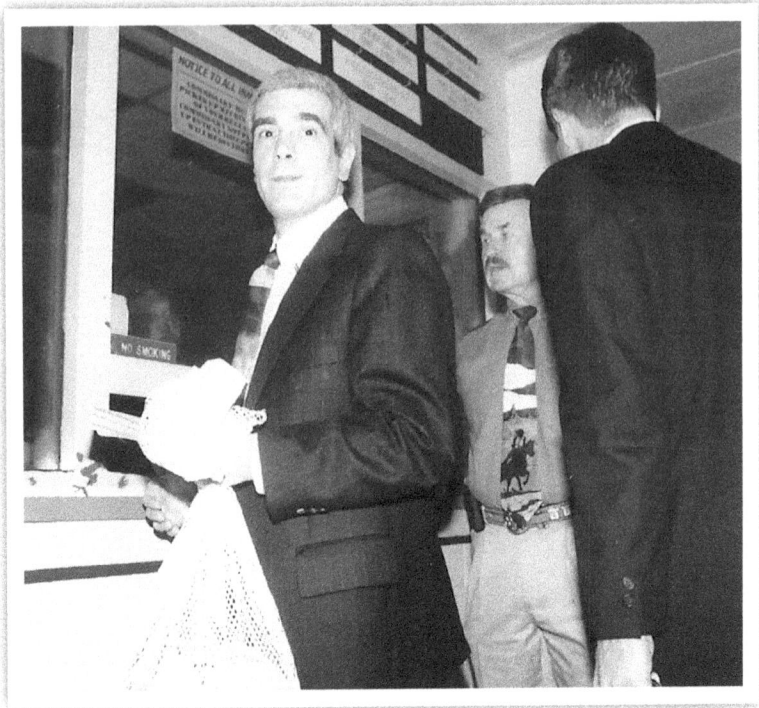

Photo by Vanessa E. Curry/*Tyler Morning Telegraph*

Kerry Max Cook prepares to leave the Smith County
Jail after posting bond.

me. While Cook's mother, family members, and a few friends waited
in the jail lobby, a representative from each media outlet was allowed
to go inside the jail and witness Cook being "processed out."

It was a tight fit in the narrow hallway leading to a small open
area—a T-shaped hallway intersection—where McCloskey and
Nugent waited patiently as Cook signed forms and received two
plastic trash bags and a net mesh bag containing his few belongings.

There would be no interviews until the group passed through the
final outer door into the sunlight. "It's like today is almost a surreal
day," McCloskey said. "I can't believe it's actually happening, but it is."

Cook, now forty-one, was dressed in a suit and tie and
appeared calm and collected. For such an exciting moment, Cook

uncharacteristically remained quiet, letting his attorneys do most of the talking. I could only imagine what it must've felt like, after having fought so many years, to walk out into a world so different from when he went in. For him, it was as if time had stopped. Now, he was walking without shackles or handcuffs, no guards to direct his every movement, and above it all a deep appreciation for what others took for granted—the sky and a fresh breeze.

The first thing Cook did after passing the threshold to freedom was hug his mother.

Kerry Max Cook's mother, Evelyn, waits anxiously with other relatives and friends to greet Cook when he walks out of the Smith County Jail.

Photo by Vanessa E. Curry/*Tyler Morning Telegraph*

Their embrace seemed to instantly erase the underlying tension between them that waxed and waned over the decades. "It was the most wonderful feeling in the world," Mrs. Cook told reporters with tears in her eyes. "I am walking on cloud nine. You just don't have any idea." Her worn, stern face always seemed to reflect the tragedies of her life. She lost her husband to cancer and her oldest son to murder, and her youngest son had been on death row for nearly two decades. Her relationship with Cook was strained, although she supported him in public for appearance's sake. There had been periods of time when she didn't speak to her son, but her face reflected nothing but joy when he was released. She wasn't easy to interview either. Her expression and gruff voice made her position clear to me—she didn't trust the Tyler media. Telephone interviews with her were short. Personal interviews were rare, although I recall the day she marched into the Tyler newsroom to deliver a letter to the editor proclaiming her son's innocence. A brief conversation I had with her was awkward. She apparently didn't appreciate my attempt at a casual conversation.

Cook met with his family and friends in the lobby before exiting the jailhouse hand in hand with Nugent and McCloskey to face a group of television cameras and news reporters. It was the defense's day in the spotlight.

"When you wake up tomorrow, what are you going to do?" a reporter in the crowd asked Cook.

"Praise the Lord for bringing me to this moment. My lawyers, Centurion Ministries. Nothing would be possible without them," he said.

Cook, Nugent, and McCloskey joked about some of the skills Cook now would have to learn—like working with computers and reapplying for a driver's license.

A Smith County prosecutor and at least a dozen other people watched from a nearby street corner. Dobbs and the Edwards family were notably, and expectedly, absent. They later declined interview requests, citing the judge's gag order still in effect.

Former death row inmate Andrew Lee Mitchell—who had been released on bond—drove up in a flashy pickup truck, got out, and spoke privately with Cook. He likely was the only one in the crowd who could relate to what Cook was feeling the moment he walked out into the sunshine. "He's very nervous. Cook's a very paranoid-type person. He's been lied on. He's been abused. He's been mistreated on death row, and I know what it's like to walk out that door after so long of a time," Mitchell said. "I'm here because I believe in his innocence and if there's anything I can do for him, I'm willing to do it . . . within the law."

After seeing the two together, I couldn't help considering that even though two separate juries once considered each man to be

Flanked by Jim McCloskey, left, and defense attorney
Paul Nugent, Kerry Max Cook poses for the media
outside Smith County Jail.

a future danger to society, their personalities were at the opposite
ends of the spectrum. Mitchell, whom I had interviewed both
inside and outside prison, was a brash ladies' man who projected an
intimidating growl of a voice and remained fearless in expressing
strong opinions. Cook, on the other hand, was soft-spoken, even
whiny at times, catered to sympathetic women, and used carefully
crafted comments—often using cliches—as if he were writing a
novel. "There was a lot of doubt along the way," Cook said of his road
to conditional freedom. "Every time the finish line was put up in
front of me, someone came and moved it a little further up the road."

As a reporter it was interesting to be a part of a rare story as it
unfolded there at the Smith County Jail, but I still felt uneasy about
Cook's release as I battled with conflicting thoughts.

CHAPTER 60

Life on the Outside

Cook faced a whole new world outside of prison—a world he had only read about as a convict. When he first went to death row, Jimmy Carter was president, *Rocky* and *Star Wars* first hit the big screen, and football great Earl Campbell, the "Tyler Rose," was a senior running back at The University of Texas. Twenty years later, President Bill Clinton was in office, *Rocky V* had been a rerun for years, *Star Wars* was thrilling a whole new generation, and Campbell had been retired from professional football for more than a decade.

Imagine all the everyday things Cook hadn't done in two decades: pump his own gasoline, eat a pizza, or just sit outside and enjoy nature. It was time for him to catch up to real-world time. He returned to live with his mother in Tecula, a little town near Jacksonville, and, for the most part, avoided media interviews. The main stipulations of his release required him to submit to a monthly test for drugs and alcohol, remain in the state, and avoid all contact with the victim's family. Some Jacksonville residents weren't so certain they were glad to see him return to the area. Random interview responses ranged from uneasiness about a man who had twice been sent to death row living among them to relief that a man they believed to be innocent was finally home.

Jacksonville police officers fielded dozens of telephone calls from citizens asking about their safety and whether Cook would be under surveillance. "I have told them they just need to continue living their own lives. Yes, he is accused of doing some things, but he is not the only person out there who could be a threat to society," Capt. Marvin Acker told a reporter.[64]

Cook would spend Thanksgiving and Christmas with his family that year after Judge Jones rejected the prosecutor's request to increase his bond amount. He would have almost another year before he had to prepare himself for another trial. The date of his fourth trial was scheduled for September 15, 1998.

64 Mary Edwards, "Jacksonville Reactions Vary to Cook's Release," *Tyler Morning Telegraph*, November 13, 1997.

"Yes, he is accused of doing some things, but he is not the only person out there who could be a threat to society."

–Capt. Marvin Acker, Jacksonville police

CHAPTER 61

Light at the End of the Tunnel

With a fourth trial looming, defense attorney Nugent filed a change of venue request contending extensive publicity had tainted potential jurors in Smith County—a request supported by three attorneys in accompanying affidavits. Despite being a slam-dunk motion, prosecutors again challenged the request with twenty-eight affidavits of their own, to no avail. Judge Jones agreed to schedule the trial for October 1998 in Bastrop, Texas—population 7,218—located about thirty miles east of Austin. The town is considered a part of the greater Austin metropolitan area.

After being released on bond, Cook lived briefly with his mother, but he later moved to work as a legal assistant for a Dallas law firm. I, too, changed venues after working nearly ten years for the *Tyler Morning Telegraph*. Although I continued to live in Tyler, I commuted daily to work as the associate editor for the *Jacksonville Daily Progress*. I saw my opportunity to work for an editor I deeply respected and who supported my efforts to write in-depth stories, features, and columns, as well as to expand my passion for photojournalism. I also could still cover developments in Cook's case since Jacksonville was his hometown.

The *Jacksonville Daily Progress* was an afternoon newspaper, so I had to get up before dawn every day and drive about twenty-five miles to the office located just across from the football stadium known locally as the Tomato Bowl. After the paper went to press, I would then drive home, grab dinner, and head off to a night class at The University of Texas at Tyler. I had been working on my master's degree since 1996 and had only two classes left to complete my requirements. Ironically, my daily routine took me to the very places that remain forever a part of the lives of Linda or Cook—the university campus, the former Embarcadero Apartments, Bullard, and Jacksonville.

As 1998 turned into 1999, Cook continued his tirade against Smith County prosecutors, granting an interview with the *Nightline* program in a report titled "Shadow of Doubt." Dobbs complained that the televised report had spoiled the jury pool. Judge Jones gave Cook a stern warning during a pretrial hearing. "This is not going to be tried in the public media," the judge said. "I am not going to stand for it."[65]

Centurion Ministries again sought donations to foot the bill for the fourth trial, and attorneys Steve "Rocket" Rosen of Houston and Cheryl Wattley of Dallas were added to the defense team. But just a month before the scheduled trial date, Cook announced he had fired Nugent. No one—not even McCloskey—would comment on the reason behind the change. It seemed now they wanted to honor Jones's gag order. It's possible Cook didn't believe Nugent had much left to offer after representing him in numerous writs, appeals, and two trials.[66]

Rosen is known for defending a member of the Branch Davidians involved in the group's 1993 standoff with federal authorities near Waco, Texas. Although I had seen Rosen in court appearances, I never had the opportunity to meet him or Wattley. Cook's new defense team immediately contested the trial with a double jeopardy claim, citing misconduct by prosecutors and police. This petition, however, was different. They filed it in federal court, another avenue through which a defendant can seek relief, especially when state appeals have been exhausted.

Two weeks before the trial date, prosecutors reported that experts had found a stain on Linda's underwear—enough of a sample to submit

---

65 Associated Press, "Judge Warns Cook about Media, " *Jacksonville Daily Progress*, December 18, 1998, 1.
66 In his book, *Chasing Justice*, published in 2007, Cook contends Nugent offered to resign after attorneys split on whether to consider a plea agreement or risk another trial.

for DNA analysis. The underwear had never been examined because investigators believed it wasn't necessary since it had been cut from her body. Besides, DNA testing wasn't readily available in 1977. After some posturing, both Cook and Mayfield submitted blood samples for comparison. The results, however, wouldn't be known until sometime after the trial began.

Facing delays, Jones had scheduled jury selection to begin on February 16, 1999, for a trial I would not be able to watch from a courtroom seat. The *Jacksonville Daily Progress* couldn't afford to send me to Bastrop, and we couldn't leave our small staff shorthanded while I covered a trial that could last as long as five weeks. Besides, I couldn't risk missing classes, and I was expected to complete my required assignments and tests. We relied upon reports from the Associated Press. My situation frustrated me. I wanted to be there, but I didn't. The thought of hearing nearly the same evidence for a third time, the same arguments and all the other drama this fourth trial surely would entail, made me cringe. I just didn't know if I could sit patiently though another trial and report it with fresh eyes. Yet, there wasn't another East Texas reporter who knew the case as well as I did.

I didn't get to hear the jaw-dropping announcement the opening day of jury selection: Cook had agreed to plead *nolo contendere*, aka no contest, to the reduced charge of murder in exchange for a twenty-year sentence—a term he already had served. I can appreciate the angst Cook must have felt trying to decide whether to accept the plea. He did so on his own terms. Cook repeatedly rejected the prosecution's attempt to get him to plead guilty. He agreed not to contest the charge but adamantly refused to say he was guilty. Despite the final plea, the judge, by law, found him guilty, meaning Cook would remain a convicted felon for the rest of his life. Anyone could certainly understand the desire to be free and not risk being sent back to prison; however, Cook had one ace in the hole—the DNA sample he knew was not his. What if he had rejected the plea? If the results had been released during the trial, that evidence would give the defense a critical piece of evidence supporting reasonable doubt. If a nylon stocking found by jurors during the first retrial contributed to the 6–6 deadlock, imagine what another man's DNA at the murder scene could do for his case.

I didn't get to experience what I thought would be the final chapter of Cook's long quest for freedom, but I did get to participate in the second-best thing—McCloskey allowed me into his inner circle as he and Cook prepared for an exclusive television interview at KETK–Region 56 in Tyler. Cook, McCloskey, and a few others were meeting at the La Quinta Inn just down the road from the news station. I had a political science class that night, but after I told my professor about my once-in-a-lifetime opportunity, he excused me. McCloskey met me on the walkway that led from the back of the lobby and down a row of rooms that faced the outdoor garden to the far side of the property. "Before I can let you go in," he said, "you need to appear to be a lot happier about this situation than you look right now."

His directive stunned me, even offended me, and I expressed those feelings to McCloskey that night. In the eight years that I had known him I thought I had made my stance perfectly clear—I wasn't on anyone's side. I always intended to cover the case as an unbiased observer. McCloskey let the awkward moment pass. The festive atmosphere was obvious once we entered his motel suite. I can't recall who else was in the room, but it didn't really matter. Cook was so charged he couldn't stand still or stop talking—like a child who had just opened that one special gift he had hoped for so long. It reminded me of deceased Tyler hairdresser Hoehn's testimony about how excitable Cook was, according to Hoehn, when they shared a pizza in the apartment the night of the murder. But Cook's behavior was getting to McCloskey, who had called one of the former librarians to thank her for her support. McCloskey talked with her in between his attempts to quiet Cook. "Kerry! Shut up and sit down," he finally snapped.

Later that night, I watched from the sidelines as McCloskey and Cook gave a live television interview. Cook was calm, cool, and collected. It was, I thought, the final chapter of a long, strange mystery without a conclusive ending.

Uncertainty still clouded my thoughts. Though I understood the reason for Cook's plea, to have it end this way was unsettling given that Cook, his attorneys, and McCloskey were so adamant about his innocence and had made some serious allegations about Smith

Photo by Vanessa E. Curry.

Kerry Max Cook and Jim McCloskey prepare to be
interviewed live at KETK-TV Channel 56 studios
after a plea agreement set Cook free.

County. I was never privy to Cook's discussion with his attorneys and
McCloskey about the plea decision. I can only image how intense it
must have been weighing the pros and cons.

The plea agreement ended the story in a draw. Each side won and
lost. Prosecutors added another mark in their conviction column, but
they lost the death sentence they thought Cook deserved. Cook won
his freedom without admitting guilt, but he couldn't shake the label
society put upon him. The consequences of being a convicted felon
eventually proved to be unbearable.

CHAPTER 62

Unfinished Business

Within weeks after the preemptive plea, test results concluded the DNA in the semen stain on Linda's underwear belonged to her married lover, Mayfield. Initially the news seemed anticlimactic since the plea agreement was final. But it raised more questions than it answered. What if Cook hadn't entered a plea and the results were returned before or during his third retrial? No doubt Mayfield's DNA at the crime scene, at the very least, would have supported reasonable doubt. But it was too late. That didn't sit well with Cook, who believed the discovery finally exonerated him, just not legally. Cook insisted the DNA was proof Mayfield had killed Linda. His argument, however, reeked of hypocrisy. Cook and his attorneys argued for years that his fingerprints only proved that he had been at Linda's apartment, but not when. They cried foul when an expert testified the prints were six to twelve hours old and challenged later testimony that that same evidence was "fresh." And yet, the last time I checked, there is no scientific way to age a semen stain either. In time, the test result would expose yet another lie.

CHAPTER 63

Cheap Shots

Taken at face value, the plea agreement between Cook and Smith County prosecutors appeared to have finally put an end to a long, nasty legal war. But egos and personal beliefs on both sides had taken numerous direct hits during the battles, leaving a residue of animosity that I believe fed an underlying need for revenge.

In 2000, *Houston Chronicle* reporter Evan Moore published a scathing revue of the Smith County District Attorney's office titled "Justice Under Fire: 'Win at all Costs' Is Smith County's Rule, Critics Claim." The news article concluded the "good old boy system" was alive and well in Tyler with prosecutors Skeen and Dobbs at the helm. Moore cited interviews with two local attorneys and unnamed sources in an attempt to prove the prosecutors were corrupt. The article contended prosecutors suppressed or planted evidence, encouraged lying, and practiced selective prosecution, among other shady or illegal practices. Moore also made it a point to note who was related to whom in the Smith County legal community, thereby implying a natural line of collusion.

Cook's case remained the focal point of the story, and Moore quoted McCloskey and Nugent liberally. At one point Nugent made the unsupported claim that "Smith County has got more innocent people in jail than any other county in the state." Moore's article may have been factual in that he was simply reporting the opinions of others, but he failed to be fair—selectively using information to create a flimsy, one-sided view and drawing shaky conclusions. It was a cheap shot and poor journalism—a story I suspect was suggested or supported by someone in Cook's camp.

I'll bet most criminal defendants don't like prosecutors, but let's face it, it's not a popularity contest. The same is true for defense attorneys, who work hard protecting their client's constitutional rights but often face criticism themselves for defending the guilty.

Skeen and Dobbs filed a libel suit against Moore and his employer, the *Houston Chronicle*, and its parent company, The Hearst Corporation.[67] The defendants requested an immediate dismissal (summary judgment made by a judge), claiming the lawsuit was without merit, but their motion was denied by the 43rd District Court.[68] In a decision issued on March 18, 2004, the Second Court of Appeals, Fort Worth, Texas upheld the trial court's decision to deny summary judgment. Among its findings: the complaint filed by Skeen, Dobbs, and Cashell contained "genuine issues" of material fact and "sufficient circumstantial" evidence showing reckless disregard for the truth and "raised a material issue of fact" that Moore's behavior was intentional. The opinion also referred to statements from an expert (not clearly identified) who testified that the standard for adequately reporting information in Moore's article "fell far below that standard."[69] That decision was appealed to the Texas Supreme Court.

---

67 Assistant District Attorney Alicia Cashell joined the suit against Moore and The Hearst Corporation D/B/A *Houston Chronicle* since she also was named in the story.
68 The lawsuit was filed in the 43rd District Court. That court's decision to deny summary judgment was appealed to the Second Court of Appeals, Fort Worth, Texas. That court upheld the lower court's decision. That decision was then appealed to the Texas Supreme Court.
69 *The Hearst Corporation* v. Skeen, 130 S.W.3d 910 (Tex. App. 2004). Second Court of Appeals, Fort Worth, Texas decision, March 18, 2004.

But as public figures, the burden to prove malice was upon Skeen and Dobbs. The Texas Supreme Court determined in 2005 that they failed to establish actual malice—that the article was published with either the knowledge of falsity or reckless disregard for the truth. Apparently, actual malice is as difficult to prove as actual innocence seemed to be.

The libel complaint was dismissed but the damage was done. There was little to no news coverage of the Second District Court of Texas's opinion that the case had merit. So, the illusion of Smith County corruption Moore created still lingers in the public's mind. In fact, writer Catherine Ferguson-Gilbert referenced Moore's article in a 2001 article to support contentions that prosecutors, in general, maintain a "win-loss scorekeeping mentality."[70]

I read the article with disgust while sitting in my office at The University of Texas at Tyler. I had finished my master's degree in the fall of 1999 and accepted an offer to become a journalism lecturer and the student newspaper adviser. I had not intended to leave the daily news business just yet, but I couldn't pass up the opportunity to again work with a supportive journalism professional whom I deeply admired.

It was a difficult career move at first, but I kept up with the daily news and continued to check on all my old contacts. The legal community in Tyler was again changing. Collard—now a captain—retired in 1999. Smith County prosecutor Thomas Dunn took the County Court at Law No. 1 bench in 1996. Dobbs left the district attorney's office in 2002 to go into private practice. Skeen was appointed to the 241st District Court bench in 2003.

Occasionally I caught a news report about another Centurion Ministries case and saw McCloskey being interviewed. I followed Cook and Nugent by occasionally searching the internet. Cook

---

70 Catherine Ferguson-Gilbert, "It Is Not Whether You Win or Lose, It Is How You Play the Game: Is the Win-Loss Scorekeeping Mentality Doing Justice for Prosecutors?," *California Western Law Review* 38, no. 1 (2001): Article 8.

went on to create a new life outside the prison walls. He married and fathered a son, Kerry Justice Cook, and spent time speaking to a variety of different groups and organizations around the country and world about his nightmare on death row.

I would see pictures of him with celebrities—Robin Williams, Aidan Quinn, and Richard Dreyfus to name a few. When I saw his story had been featured in the play *The Exonerated,* that plague of cognitive dissonance flared inside me again. I took issue with Cook claiming to be exonerated. According to state records, he was still a convicted murderer at that time. I began to see Cook's name more and more associated with the term exoneration and frequently referenced in related *Texas Monthly* articles, television shows, and websites as being "wrongly convicted." Cook published a book in 2007 titled *Chasing Justice: My Story of Freeing Myself after Two Decades on Death Row for a Crime I Didn't Commit.*

From reading it myself, I can understand why someone unfamiliar with the case could conclude Cook is innocent. Cook certainly has the right to tell readers his point of view, but in the process his atrocious spin on some facts reinforced my recurring uneasiness about wanting to accept his version of events. Some examples: Within the first 40 pages, Cook claims Rudolph admitted under oath that Cook was not the man she saw that night, and in fact she had positively identified Mayfield; Cook repeatedly fails to present certain events in context, i.e., admissibility of hearsay evidence and prosecutorial misconduct.

I know a lot more about the story than what he wrote about. I still read true crime stories, but based on my experience as a journalist I reserve judgment until I've considered both sides of a story. I did learn one thing from reading the book: For the first time in sixteen years, Cook revealed why he had lied about his fingerprints. In a conversation shortly after his arrest, Cook claims he told his father he knew the woman who had been killed and that he had been inside her apartment. His father, he said, made him promise to never admit what he had just revealed because investigators would use the information to build a case against him.

The references to Cook being "exonerated" and "wrongly convicted" appeared more and more often in print media and even online podcasts. I wrote a letter to the editor of *Texas Monthly* to protest the use of those words in Cook's case. The letter was never printed or addressed in reply.

My indecision about Cook's innocence or guilt began to bother me again. I thought about it over and over, going through all the testimony and evidence. And although I understand Cook's resentment, I couldn't stand the hypocrisies. Cook lied about how his fingerprints were placed at the murder scene, withheld information, and selectively told his story, much like he accused prosecutors of doing to win a conviction.

But Cook wasn't about to drop his quest for complete exoneration.

PART V

A New Approach

TIMELINE:

February 2012
Cook's attorneys file request to retest evidence for DNA and fingerprints.

2012

Appellate review of Cook case begins 7th year

2013

Cook's attorney names Mayfield as actual killer

2014

Mayfield admits lying about seeing victim

2015

2015
Cook's attorneys file request for finding of actual innocence.

April 5, 2016
Attorneys interview Mayfield under immunity agreement.

June 6, 2016
Court hearing scheduled to consider petition for exoneration.

2016

July 1, 2016
Opposing attorneys present final summations before Judge Jack Carter.

July 25, 2016
Carter releases opinion, denying actual innocence claim. His ruling sent to Texas Court of Criminal Appeals for review.

Cook Conviction Tossed; Judge rules against actual innocence

CHAPTER 64

Fight for Actual Innocence

The plea agreement gave Cook a chance to build a new life after nearly twenty years surrounded by brick walls and steel bars, but he found it difficult to integrate into mainstream society, where the stigma of being a convicted murderer kept him on the move.

He now pursued two goals—to be officially declared innocent and to seek compensation for his time spent on death row. Proving corruption within Smith County, as Cook believed there to be, and making prosecutors pay would be the icing on the cake. A finding of actual innocence is the first step—a key requirement in an application for state compensation and health benefits. But proving actual innocence is extremely difficult because it would require "clear and convincing evidence" of Cook's innocence and/or newly discovered evidence that likely would have had an impact on a jury verdict. New evidence generally means evidence that was not available prior to or during the trial.

Under Texas law, a convicted person found to be actually innocent of a crime may receive a lump cash sum, monthly annuity compensation, health benefits, and education costs. The lump sum is calculated using the base rate of $80,000 for each year of time served. For Cook, that meant about $3.2 million in total compensation.[71]

---

71 Texas Civil Practice and Remedies Code Title 5 § 103.052 Lump-Sum Compensation.

But first he had to find an attorney or attorneys willing to help him maneuver the complicated legal system without pay. Cook eventually connected with attorneys—Barry Scheck, for one, at the New York–based National Innocence Project and Gary Udashen with the Innocence Project of Texas—to create a virtual double dream team.

With the help from both organizations, Cook filed a request in February 2012 asking to test certain evidence in his case. The request came more than a decade after a new law gave Texas inmates access to DNA evidence in state files that might help prove their innocence.

The evidence in Cook's case underwent additional testing until 2015. Although the results confirmed Mayfield's DNA on the victim's undergarment, no new forensic evidence was found. But the latter fact didn't deter Cook or his attorneys, who believed Mayfield's DNA was enough to support the innocence claim. All they needed now was a judge to agree. Filing the claim in Smith County proved to be problematic since Cook remained leery of getting a fair shot from any court in that county. The petition for the release of evidence for DNA testing had been approved by an administrative judge. The petition for exoneration was filed in the 114th District Court in 2015, but Cook objected to presiding Judge Christi Kennedy hearing the case because of her connections—albeit distant—with the district attorney's office. Kennedy's deceased husband, Richard, had once served as a prosecutor under Skeen and Dobbs. Kennedy eventually recused herself and was replaced by visiting District Judge Jack Carter from Texarkana. I was surprised Cook didn't object to that judge as well. Since filing his actual innocence claim, Cook publicly claimed his arrest was a culmination of a homophobic witch hunt, claimed Rudolph was a lesbian who killed Linda in a jealous rage, and contended Skeen continued to prosecute him to protect his cousin, A. D. Clark.

Coincidentally, Skeen's two sons are named Jack and Carter.

The state would be represented by District Attorney Matt Bingham, his assistant Michael West, and special prosecutor Keith Dollahite in opposing the innocence claim. Bingham joined the

Smith County District Attorney's office in 1995 as an entry-level prosecutor. He worked his way up the ranks of prosecuting misdemeanor and felony cases before Skeen named him First Assistant Prosecutor in 2002. Bingham served as acting district attorney when Skeen left to accept the position on the 241st District Court bench. In 2004, Gov. Rick Perry appointed Bingham to Skeen's unexpired term.[72]

Cook also had suspicions about Bingham because of his history with Skeen. He eventually voiced his concerns publicly about Bingham during a tirade of Facebook posts. Out of the public eye, Bingham and his team reinvestigated the state's evidence against Cook.

Their filings with the court began to match the growing stack of documents filed by Cook. The pile grew even larger with responses to filings, responses to responses, and so on. Carter eventually set aside a week in June to hear testimony from a string of witnesses— possibly even Cook himself.

---

72 Bingham retired in 2018 and went into private practice.

CHAPTER 65

New Deal

Cook's attorneys outlined evidence supporting their claim that Linda's lover Mayfield, not Cook, killed Linda. Mayfield was a violent-tempered, possessive man who became angry upon learning Linda intended to see other men, they said. He had ordered a book about sexual mutilation murders, asked a colleague how to beat a polygraph, failed some lie detector tests, and was seen rummaging through the victim's desk drawer. Mayfield's suspicious behavior also included making it a point to remind people to recall how calm he was after the murder and telling a coworker that Linda had "ruined his life," according to Cook's written argument.

Mayfield's DNA, not Cook's, was found at the murder scene, and Mayfield had lied about his contact with the victim, Cook's attorneys claimed. They also noted how Mayfield's daughter had threatened to kill Linda, and most of all, Rudolph's description of the man she saw that night fit Mayfield. They rehashed their prosecutorial misconduct claims, too, adding a few other accusations to the pile.

The defense's new evidence consisted of the DNA test and a previously undiscovered written report from a police officer who said Rudolph had identified Mayfield as the man she saw that night. The report had been found among fifty boxes of work product kept in the prosecutor's office that Bingham had allowed Cook's attorneys to inspect.

Cook's new attorney Udashen also had gone so far as to accuse prosecutors Skeen and Dobbs of knowing the results of the DNA tests and withholding that information until after Cook accepted a plea agreement in 1999.

In his written argument, prosecutor West contended Cook willingly accepted the plea even though he knew tests would not implicate him. Cook, he argued, could have rejected the plea agreement and waited for the test results. The state's argument summarized most of the same evidence used in prior trials but focused their argument on the fact that Cook had waited sixteen years after the DNA test result to file a writ, leaving the state at a huge disadvantage because witnesses had since died and evidence had been lost or destroyed.

West contended Cook's plea in 1999, and a judge's final finding of guilt ended the case.

"Mayfield's DNA, not Cook's, was found at the murder scene, and Mayfield had lied about his contact with the victim..."

—Author

CHAPTER 66

More Lies Revealed

The much-anticipated live testimony never materialized after another bombshell pushed both sides into negotiations. Judge Carter himself announced the revelation to a stunned courtroom crowd in June 2016.

Thankfully my longtime friend Marilyn Covey called me just weeks before the hearing or I likely would have missed witnessing another historic moment in this story. My life had been a whirlwind of events since I left The University of Texas at Tyler in 2011. I spent part of that year recuperating from brain surgery, but I also began a freelance career to help support myself while I conducted research for this book. When my cash reserves began running low, I accepted a temporary position as a daily newspaper reporter in Tennessee with a former colleague and boss as my editor. My planned three-month stay turned into three years as I moved from being a reporter/photographer and editor to a lifestyle editor for the same newspaper. The job paid the bills while I continued working on this book. Marilyn had been my mentor at the *Tyler Morning Telegraph,* and we have remained friends ever since. She knew how important it would be for me to attend the hearing. I took a few vacation days to make sure I would be in the courtroom when Cook attempted to gain exoneration. I drove more than sixteen hundred miles in twenty-four hours during the round trip, but I was anxious to witness what I hoped to be the end of this story.

Cook had once vowed never to set foot in Smith County again. He once told me he would rather go out of his way to reach his destination than risk being harassed in a bogus traffic stop he expected to experience in Smith County. His words came to mind as I saw Cook enter the 114th District Courtroom with his entourage of attorneys and supporters the morning of June 6, 2016.

I had arrived earlier, making my way through a line of solemn-looking people being screened by the double metal detectors as they reported for jury duty. Aside from the detectors, the courthouse interior appeared much like it did nearly twenty-five years ago when I was a beat reporter for the *Tyler Morning Telegraph*.

The elevator doors opened on the main floor and out stepped former prosecutor David Dobbs, who recognized me immediately. Dobbs had long since left the district attorney's office and now practiced law with his wife, former Assistant District Attorney Debra Tittle. Dobbs, like everyone else I recognized that day, certainly had aged. His hairline headed north long ago, and he no longer wore eyeglasses.

"It looks like all the old gang is back," he said.

Indeed. The cast of characters—just older versions—roamed the hallways. There was Judge Kent, now retired, a scrunchie holding her graying hair wrapped into a bun on the back of her head. Mayfield's attorney Buck Files was navigating around small groups scattered along the route to the courtroom, and a familiar-looking man with a rolling walker was attempting to seat himself on a hallway bench.

I took a second look and realized the man was a broken version of James Mayfield.

Once a man reflecting confidence, fitness, and style, he now looked frumpy, disoriented, and feeble.

He was dressed in a simple green T-shirt, sweatpants, and slip-on shoes. His short, thin white hair had been combed forward from the back, barely enough to meet a receding hairline that reached halfway

James "Jim" Mayfield waits for a ride outside the Smith County Courthouse.

Photo by Vanessa E. Curry.

over the top of his head. His thin crop of hair and gaunt face made his ears stand out even more.[73]

Of Cook, Nugent, and McCloskey, the former death row inmate appeared the most changed, with snow white hair and a fleshy full face that covered his once sharp jaw-line and square chin.

The hearing had been scheduled for 9:00 a.m. but the courtroom benches had filled much earlier. Crews with video cameras mounted on tripods occupied two corners, poised to record the proceedings. The silence in the room was broken only by occasional hushed voices.

---

73 Mayfield died July 12, 2019.

More than thirty minutes passed the scheduled start before Carter entered the courtroom and immediately cut to the chase. The defense attorneys and Bingham had reached an agreement, he said, thus rendering moot the need for hearing live testimony the rest of the week.

Cook's conviction would be set aside based on false evidence given by Mayfield, and the court would rule upon only the actual innocence claim. In exchange, Cook's attorneys agreed to drop claims that former prosecutors Skeen and Dobbs had withheld the DNA test result. Court records show there was no evidence to support that claim anyway. Cook's attorney Udashen also had noted in the petition a previously undiscovered police report[74] that stated Rudolph identified Mayfield as the man she saw that night. That issue, too, was now moot.

Although the judge didn't elaborate on Mayfield's lie, he did reveal that prosecutors granted Mayfield immunity in exchange for the truth. Carter pointedly noted that Mayfield's false testimony was "without the knowledge" of prosecutors.

Setting aside a conviction equates to legal exoneration, a term often misunderstood outside the legal community. A legal exoneration removes the conviction and returns the case back to the status before a trial. In other words, Cook still could be charged with murder—and tried again—but the presumption of innocence applied.

The written agreement on file in the district clerk's office provided the details. Bingham had arranged an interview with Mayfield in Houston for April 5, 2016, with himself, Cook's attorneys, and Files. Mayfield previously had testified under oath before a grand jury, in several depositions, and in multiple jury trials that his affair with Linda ended three weeks prior to her death and that they did not have sexual relations after that point.

In the April 5 interview, Mayfield admitted Linda had visited him on June 8, 1977, for his birthday and the two had engaged in

---

74 That report was later called into question. Other evidence suggests the statement likely was a recording error.

sexual intercourse. The revelation explained why Mayfield had failed a polygraph in 1977 and why he sought advice on how to beat a lie detector test.

Details of that interview revealed Mayfield was questioned repeatedly about whether he feared Linda would follow him to Houston and continue to cause problems with his marriage.

"Did Linda tell you that she might move to Houston?" an attorney asked him.

"She did not say that to me, no," Mayfield replied.

The attorney posed another question, asking Mayfield if having sex with Linda on June 8 made him think, "Oh, god, I've reignited this whole thing? She's going to be in my life, she's going to follow me to Houston, therefore, I need to kill her?"

"Oh, my goodness, no," Mayfield replied.[75]

With the April 5, 2016, Mayfield revelation out of the way, Carter turned his attention to the final issue he needed to resolve—whether Mayfield's confession and other evidence submitted by Cook's attorneys were sufficient to warrant a finding of actual innocence. The judge already had stacks of affidavits, transcripts, and other documents to review, but he gave opposing attorneys until June 17 to submit any additional supporting documents and set June 29 to hear oral arguments for the ruling on actual innocence.

Before turning over the floor, Carter commended both sides for working together to resolve most of the writ issues—a process that Udashen told the court is "really a model for how these types of situations should be handled."

And within a matter of fifteen minutes, the June 6, 2016, hearing ended. Camera crews rushed outside to position themselves ahead of a mass of people slowly making their way through the hallway, down the steps, and eventually outside the courthouse's front entrance to celebrate and pose for pictures. It was Cook's turn for crushing hugs, backslaps, and high fives.

---

75 From a transcript of the interview previously available at nebula.wsimg.com. The website is now inactive.

"Well, the last time I did this, it didn't feel near this good," the sixty-year-old Cook said as he exited the courthouse.

The mob of television cameras and young reporters jostled for the best angle, oblivious to the fact that Mayfield—now in his eighties—was sitting behind them, waiting at the curb to be helped into a vehicle. Once I mentioned that fact to one female reporter, the attention temporarily switched to Mayfield. She rushed to stick a microphone in front of Mayfield, who did not respond to her questions.

Photo by Vanessa E. Curry.

Celebrating outside the Smith County Courthouse, from left, attorney Paul Nugent, attorney Nina Morrison of the Innocence Project, Jim McCloskey of Centurion Ministries, and Kerry Max Cook.

"Well, the last time I did this,
it didn't feel near this good."

—Kerry Max Cook

CHAPTER 67

Secrets

The agreement to set aside Cook's conviction started his attorneys down a new path that could lead to two possible scenarios—a finding of actual innocence or possibly resolving the case through another plea agreement or trial. After reviewing submitted documentation, Carter could determine that the evidence supported a theory of innocence that would have rendered a not-guilty verdict at trial. In that case, Cook would be exonerated—a ruling of actual innocence—which was required for him to be eligible for compensation.

In an affidavit filed with the court, Cook contended he had suffered significantly from a wrongful conviction and therefore deserved to be compensated. His legal status as a murder suspect had prevented him from obtaining housing for his family in his name and child-care services for his son; cost him friendships, jobs, and career opportunities; caused family difficulties; and prevented him from obtaining a gun permit.

"It is difficult, if not impossible, to describe what it is like to re-enter society and build a normal life after twenty years of being brutalized and nearly executed on death row much less with a murder conviction still on my record," Cook wrote.

He said he suffered from severe depression and post-traumatic stress disorder and had undergone triple heart bypass surgery while living with the stigma of being a convicted murderer.

"The most painful aspects . . . has been the impact on my teenage son K.J.," he added.

Cook contended, if he had known the results of the DNA testing prior to his fourth trial in Bastrop, Texas, he never would have accepted the plea agreement. This didn't make sense to me. If he knew the sample came from someone else, scientific confirmation could create enough reasonable doubt to support just what he wanted—an acquittal from a jury. However, there still was a risk that it wouldn't.

Finding Mayfield's DNA at the murder scene was a major piece of evidence, but combined with Mayfield's confession, Cook now had a nugget of gold that appeared to tip the scales of justice in his favor and elevate Mayfield's status from a suspicious character to a viable murder suspect.

But if that was the golden key to Cook's eventual exoneration, the prosecution had the Kryptonite—a piece of evidence I found buried in the massive court files the writ of habeas corpus petition had created. I wanted to see what additional evidence opposing attorneys had filed for Carter to consider, so I revisited the case files at the courthouse after the 2016 hearing. The eye-opening report was marked as a felony discovery supplement form dated January 19, 2016, and contained two sworn statements sent to defense attorney Udashen.

The first affidavit came from Tyler attorney Duane Stephens,[76] who reportedly had been retained by witness Robert Hoehn within a month after Edwards's death. Although conversations between an attorney and client are legally considered privileged information—meaning it is protected from disclosure—Hoehn's closest living relative, his second cousin Charles Ferris, had waived that privilege, thus allowing Stephens to speak.

Hoehn, Stephens wrote, confessed that he and Cook had entered the victim's apartment that night through the sliding glass

---

76 Stephens died October 26, 2016.

door, and he had watched Cook beat Linda with a blunt object before mutilating her body with a pair of scissors.

Stephens also noted that Hoehn heard Rudolph enter the apartment and made eye contact with her. "Mr. Hoehn believed that Paula Rudolph had mistaken him for James Mayfield, Linda Jo Edwards lover," the attorney said in concluding his statement dated May 15, 2012.

Hoehn's story was eerily like the story Cook reportedly told Smith County prosecutors in plea negotiations before the punishment phase of his 1978 trial. In that story, however, the roles were reversed: Cook claimed he watched as Hoehn killed Linda and removed body parts from the scene, prosecutors claimed.

The second document was a handwritten statement by Kathleen Choate from West Monroe, Louisiana. She wrote that in June 1977 she was visited by her second cousin, Robert Hoehn, who told her he knew a man accused of killing a woman. "We both started crying. When I got my thoughts back, I asked him what the guy's name was and he said, 'Kerry Max Cook,'" she wrote.

According to the statement, Hoehn hesitated when asked if he "had done it." "[He] told me that 'he couldn't tell me,'" she said. Her statement was dated August 8, 2013.

The scales of justice just tipped back again, at least in the court of public opinion. Defense attorneys likely would argue that the affidavits were not admissible unless the actual witnesses were available for cross-examination. Stephens, the author of the first affidavit, however, died in 2016.

With the new evidence presented from both sides, Judge Carter certainly faced a difficult decision weighing the value of Mayfield's and Hoehn's confessions. Understandably, the state's new evidence could tank the actual innocence claim, leaving Carter with no choice but to give prosecutors yet another bite of the apple in hopes of convicting Cook again and sending him back to death row.

CHAPTER 68

Another Team Change

But Cook, as it was revealed three days later, wasn't at all happy about the agreement to set aside his conviction and the scheduled June 29 hearing regarding actual innocence. In fact, he said, he believed he had been betrayed by his own attorneys.

Reviewing the photographs I had taken inside and outside the courthouse during the hearing, I realized Cook wasn't smiling much at all throughout the entire event. He linked arms with attorneys and supporters while posing, but the best he could muster was a subdued smile apparently hiding the seething anger welling up inside. That anger exploded in a statement released to the media days later in which Cook announced he had fired his attorneys from the Innocence Project in New York and Texas. He was livid, he explained, that Udashen had thanked the prosecutor for his cooperation in reaching the agreement.

"I did not authorize you to make that platform speech praising Matt Bingham and the Smith County District Attorney's office in Tyler," Cook wrote. "I told you [Gary Udashen] the night before as the client no."

To Cook, Udashen had publicly humiliated him and had done more to exonerate prosecutors from misconduct than to rectify the injustice committed against him.

"I could go on for pages and pages of everything done over my objections, but the point is, I no longer trust . . . you are . . . in a too friendly relationship with [District Attorney] Matt Bingham," he wrote.

Cook then launched daily tirades against his former attorneys, current and former prosecutors—especially Dobbs—and the Tyler media on his Facebook page[77] while pleading for legal help for the upcoming oral arguments, now just weeks away. He contended the agreement was the product of a "panic and desperate focus" by unprepared attorneys who also failed to take him seriously when he insisted on exposing perceived misconduct within the Smith County criminal justice system. And the deal only set him up for another no contest plea, he claimed.

"I told you . . . I was willing to die to stand up to this horrible Smith County corruption. You would not listen. Well, listen now," he wrote to his former attorneys.

Cook's outbursts were nothing unusual. Once he got started, it was very difficult for him to listen to reason. In my years of interacting with Cook and watching his interactions with others, I believed his paranoia undoubtedly was founded in part from his decades behind bars, where trust is nothing more than a four-letter word. His Facebook posts, however, revealed a deep-seated hatred for prosecutors Skeen, Dobbs, and Bingham and a growing list of assistant district attorneys, special prosecutors, and even the Texas Court of Criminal Appeals. He believed they all only wanted to win to save face, even if it required lying and hiding or fabricating evidence. Cook claimed Dobbs was asked to broker the deal between Bingham, Udashen, and Nina Morrison (his former attorney with the Innocence Project in New York)—a situation that made Cook more determined than ever not to accept anything less than full exoneration.

He characterized the Innocence Project's involvement as a "corporate takeover"—a point prosecutors addressed in documents

---

77 Cook later deleted all his Facebook posts.

filed with the court. Indeed, one of the Innocence Project of Texas's founders, Jeff Blackburn, resigned in 2015 because he believed the New York organization had not remained true to its mission. The Innocence Project in New York, Blackburn said, had become too dependent upon large donations from Wall Street types and celebrities.

"What was once a movement has now become a business," Blackburn wrote in a letter to the organization's board of directors.[78]

Cook now stood alone, as he described, "on the goal line" of one of the biggest legal decisions of his quest to be fully exonerated. Even if he had the money to hire another attorney or could find one to represent him pro bono, there was no time for that attorney to familiarize themselves with such a lengthy, complicated case, let alone prepare for oral arguments. Realizing his dilemma, Cook vowed to represent himself or pro se if necessary, ignoring the old proverb, "A man who is his own lawyer has a fool for his client."

News of the agreement bounced around the social media networks—especially those sponsored by individuals or organizations that supported Cook. However, the sites spread more misinformation about the status of the case than facts. A technically accurate but misleading headline over an Austin-based *Texas Monthly* magazine article (an anti–death penalty advocate) suggested Cook had been cleared of all wrongdoing. Reporter Michael Hill wrote in a June 6 online article that "Kerry Max Cook, a subject of *The Exonerated*, is finally exonerated" and added later in the article that Cook "has finally been legally exonerated." It was not until much deeper in the article that Hill wrote, "Mayfield's material lie means that Cook will now be legally exonerated (subject to the approval of the CCA) though not

---

78 Hernan Rozemberg, "Texas Innocence Project Founder Quits, Accused Colleagues of Selling Out," *San Antonio Current*, May 27, 2015, https://www.sacurrent.com/news/texas-innocence-project-founder-quits-accuses-colleagues-of-selling-out-2440927.

'actually innocent.'"[79] *Texas Monthly* writers also had adopted *The Dallas Morning News* misleading conclusion that witness Rudolph had changed her story over time after initially identifying Mayfield as the man she saw in her apartment that night.

Celebrities also jumped into the fray. Kim Kardashian West and Madonna took to Twitter to show their support. Cook continued pleading for help on his Facebook posts and eventually attracted the attention of Houston attorney Mark Bennett, who later appeared in documents as the attorney of record. Bennett had just a few weeks to familiarize himself with a forty-year-old case and with Cook.

---

79 Michael Hall, "Reversal of Fortune: Kerry Max Cook, a Subject of *The Exonerated*, Is Finally Exonerated," *Texas Monthly*, June 6, 2016, https://www.texasmonthly.com/the-daily-post/kerry-max-cook-exonerated/.

"I told you...I was willing to die to stand up to this horrible Smith County corruption."

–Kerry Max Cook

CHAPTER 69

Final Summations

There's always that awkward moment when arriving early to a courtroom. Those already seated stare as you enter as they try to determine what connection you have to this case. I admit I do the same thing while I'm sitting in the benches waiting. Such was the case on July 1, 2016, the rescheduled date for oral arguments in Cook's innocence claim to be heard before Judge Carter.

Camera crews returned as well as other journalists. I recognized a dozen or so locals who obviously just came out of curiosity, but there were some individuals I pegged as Cook supporters.

Defense attorney Bennett was inside the bar alone, pacing a bit nervously until Cook, Cook's wife, former defense attorney Nugent, and McCloskey arrived. Cook, dressed in a new blue suit, shirt, and tie, embraced Bennett and then sat down.

Cook and I both noticed former defense attorney Udashen walk into the courtroom. Cook got up and walked to the back of the courtroom to greet him. There was an awkward moment when Udashen extended his hand and Cook pushed it away to embrace him instead. McCloskey then encouraged Udashen to join him and Nugent seated in the front row. It seemed all was forgiven.

Carter briefly addressed the courtroom, summarizing the events of the previous month, and concluded by saying the main issue remaining was to resolve the actual innocence claim. And since Cook filed the motion, he and his attorneys now had the burden of proving evidence supported innocence.

Bennett addressed the judge as if he were reading a novel. "This is a story of love and betrayal," he began, and for the next forty minutes he outlined the theory that Mayfield killed Edwards because he was unable to resist her sexually and feared his weakness would ruin his marriage. According to Bennett's scenario, Mayfield planned to move his family to Houston and start a new life away from temptation, but when he learned that Linda planned to follow him, she became a problem that needed eliminating.

In the weeks before Linda's death, Mayfield vacillated between his lover and his wife—abandoning his wife and family in mid-May to move in with Linda and then leaving her four days later to return to his wife. He rescued Linda from a suicide attempt but testified repeatedly that their affair was over after that, replaced by a father–daughter relationship instead.

"We know now Mayfield and Linda Jo were still meeting in the apartment and having sex," Bennett said, reminding the judge of the newly acquired statement in which Mayfield admitted they had intercourse on June 8, 1977.

Cook's fingerprints were found at the scene, Bennett explained, because he had been inside the apartment on June 7, 1977, making out with Linda on the living room couch.

"What evidence supports that?" Carter asked, interrupting Bennett.

Bennett referred to transcripts of testimony given by Randy Dykes, then eighteen, and his then twelve-year-old brother, Rodney, who recalled Cook returning to their uncle James Taylor's apartment with "passion marks" on his neck. Cook told them he got them from a girl named Linda whom he met at the pool, Bennett said.

"It is difficult to dispute that the woman . . . and Linda Jo were the same person," Bennett said, although admitting that evidence was deemed inadmissible at retrial.

Photo by Vanessa E. Curry.

Judge Jack Carter highlights points concerning
the actual innocence claim during a July 2016
hearing in a Smith County courtroom.

The day of the murder, Mayfield helped Linda search for an apartment of her own, but he became increasingly concerned she would follow him to Houston. Linda now became "a problem" for him, so he killed her and arranged the murder scene to lead the investigation away from himself, Bennett said.

Bennett surmised Mayfield must have returned to the apartment on June 9 to have sex with Linda and then hit her in the head with the plaster statue. He contended her body "looks like a composite of photos" from *The Sexual Criminal*—a book Mayfield previously denied ever seeing, Bennett said. Mayfield now admitted he was familiar with the book, he noted.

"Why lie about the book for forty years?" Bennett asked. "Because he used this book to make it look like she was killed by a sexual criminal."

Mayfield's lies then begged the question:

"Why didn't he go ahead and say he did it? He was granted immunity," Carter asked.

"It was difficult enough to admit he lied. That was something too difficult to admit," Bennett replied. "He's not telling the whole truth."

Bennett said Mayfield's actions gave insight to his character. "What does it say about a man who would lie for forty years to preserve his marriage?" he asked. "This was not a white lie. It was a lie that sent a man to death row . . . that makes Mayfield a monster."

Bennett made it through the first part of his arguments well considering he only had less than a month to prepare. Although he occasionally slipped using the wrong names, overall, his argument was clear, concise, and to the point.

For the state, special prosecutor Dollahite stepped up to the podium and began by telling Carter that the defense had clearly failed to meet the legal standards of actual innocence. There wasn't any new evidence, he argued, and Bennett certainly hadn't presented clear and convincing evidence—a Herculean task—to prove Cook was innocent, he said. Mayfield's lie wasn't even enough to create reasonable doubt, Dollahite said, but merely "muddied" the water.

And although Cook told reporters and others he did not know Linda nor had he ever been inside her apartment, his fingerprints were found on the glass door in such a way that disputed that claim. Linda's roommate also "repeatedly and consistently" identified Cook as the man she saw inside the apartment that night, Dollahite said.

"That's a little worrisome," interjected Carter, who noted Linda's roommate Rudolph did not initially identify Cook even though she saw him at least twice during separate hearings shortly after his arrest. The judge questioned whether her final identification was based upon seeing him in court or seeing him in her apartment the night of the murder. Rudolph, Dollahite explained, recognized Cook after seeing him standing for the first time. She previously had seen him sitting in the courtroom.

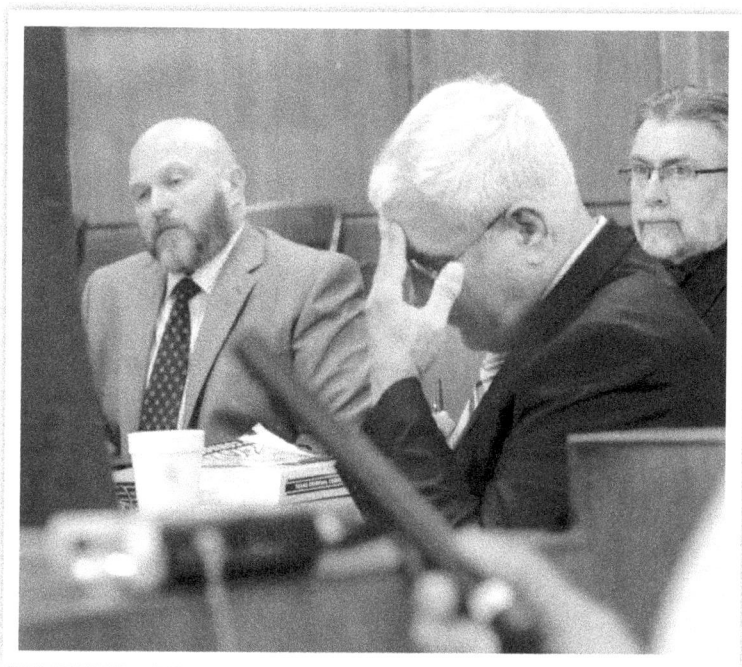

Kerry Max Cook attempts to maintain his composure
during hearing in a Smith County courtroom.

The prosecutor also reminded the judge of Reserve Deputy Bob
Wickham, who testified, Cook admitted killing Linda while being
escorted from court during his 1978 trial—testimony supported by
another law enforcement officer who recalled the deputy's account,
he said.

The mention of Wickham's name sparked a controlled reaction
from Cook this time. He buried his bowed head into his hands,
eyes closed until the moment passed.

As for the book, Dollahite contended it was part of a large
collection of books purchased by the library and was only brought
to Mayfield's attention through a psychology professor who
expressed concern about its contents. And the fact that Mayfield's
DNA was recovered from the victim's underwear wasn't evidence
he killed her since it could not be determined when it was left.

Dollahite said that to accept Bennett's account one would have to believe Linda took off her panties to have sex with Mayfield and then put them back on, only for him to cut them off during the murder shortly after. "No reasonable juror could accept that," he said. The semen stain did not constitute new evidence since Cook knew about it in 1999 before his fourth trial; he knew the results likely would be revealed sometime therein, and yet, he decided to accept the plea agreement, Dollahite said.

"The truth is the DNA does not prove unequivocally Cook did not kill Edwards," he said.

Cook, Dollahite said, was a twenty-year-old with a criminal record who had been diagnosed with an antisocial personality disorder after being committed to a mental hospital. He was living in the same apartment complex as the victim and had admitted to watching her undress through a window. The prosecutor also cited parts of Rodney Dykes's and Randy Dykes's testimony in which they recalled an encounter with some girls at the swimming pool. Cook sent Rodney Dykes over to the girls—one of whom matched Linda's description—with the message that he was interested in them. "Rodney recalled the girls laughed and looked at him like he was crazy," Dollahite said. "There was no interest."

On the night of the murder, Dollahite said, Cook and Hoehn watched a movie and later went to get cigarettes. Cook returned to Linda's apartment, entered through the sliding glass door, and grabbed the plaster statue sitting on a table near the door and used it to hit Linda in the head, he said.

To round out his argument, the prosecutor contended Cook's actual innocence claim violated the doctrine of laches—a legal term referring to a situation when an unreasonable delay leaves the adverse party at an unreasonable disadvantage. In this case, Dollahite said, Cook waited sixteen years after agreeing to plead no contest to a murder charge in exchange for time served. If forced to retry the case, the prosecution, he said, was at a great disadvantage because photos of the crime scene and physical evidence—including the latent fingerprints found at the scene—had been lost or misplaced. As for witnesses, Rudolph, Collard, and others were now deceased, and others could not be located or were too old to remember details of the case. Besides, Cook knew about the DNA results just seven weeks after he accepted a plea deal, the prosecutor said.

And with that said, Dollahite returned to his seat.

Bennett would have the last word, an opportunity to counter any of the prosecution's points. Bennett saw an opening and he took it, criticizing Dollahite for citing the doctrine of laches. "You would think they wouldn't be arguing laches. They should be thankful for an opportunity to see justice is done," he said.

Having no money, it took Cook a long time to find legal assistance—someone willing to represent him for free, he said. "That point shouldn't be glossed over," Bennett argued. As for Rudolph's testimony, the attorney recalled testimony in which the witness told prosecutors she "couldn't swear" who it was she saw in the apartment that night. "Memories of faces don't get better over time," he said.

Bennett claimed investigators and prosecutors "fell in love with Mayfield and betrayed Mr. Cook." That statement didn't seem strong enough for Cook, who interrupted by motioning Bennett to his side. After a quick whispered conference, Bennett told Carter his client requested he emphasize a point more strenuously: "Mr. Mayfield doesn't just look good for this crime—Mr. Mayfield killed Linda Jo Edwards," he concluded.

It took about two hours to complete the arguments, but it left those in the courtroom wondering how long it would take for Carter to reach a decision. Based upon the questions he asked, Carter appeared to have researched the case history. However, he indicated both sides had filed many more affidavits and other materials for him to review. "Obviously, I've got some work to do. It's a difficult case," he said. "I'll make a decision as soon as I can."

The mood was a little subdued as the players and audience slowly spilled out of the courtroom, down the hallway, and out the front courthouse doors with media cameras in front and behind the pack. The group mingled on the front walkway till about noon, when a group of Smith County attorneys—including Mayfield's attorney Files—lined up for their annual public reading of the US Constitution in honor of the upcoming Fourth of July holiday. Bennett and former defense attorney Nugent joined the group, but when Cook took a turn at reading, Files objected. He insisted the event was for defense attorneys, not defendants. Cook immediately shot back, calling Files a "crook," before Bennett and Nugent calmly ushered Cook away from the group. The verbal exchange made the local television news that night.

Kerry Max Cook outside the Smith County Courthouse in July 2016.

Photo by Vanessa E. Curry.

"Obviously, I've got some work
to do. It's a difficult case."

—Judge Jack Carter

CHAPTER 70

Another Ruling to Appeal

The next day, Cook was back on Facebook, expressing his frustrations about being saddled with the burden of proof.

"I have to bring the actual killer to the courtroom and prove he or she is guilty beyond any doubt to be free of a public perception of guilt" he complained. "Imagine being me having to live with this life tragedy. Just imagine."

His contempt for the judicial system in Smith County exploded on July 25 when Judge Carter released an eighteen-page opinion denying Cook's claim of actual innocence.

"This court finds that the exceptionally high burden to prove actual innocence has not been satisfied," the judge concluded.

Cook came unglued, ranting on his Facebook page against the judge and even his own attorney.

"I just want to scream and scream and not quit until my heart gives out," Cook wrote.

In his ruling, Carter specifically dismissed the idea of laches, saying Mayfield's revelation was certainly timely. The judge also noted his ruling was not based on Cook's contention of collateral consequences (difficulties obtaining a job, housing, etc.), although Carter agreed that claim had merit.

The judge's overview of the issues raised in the actual innocence claim noted that Smith County prosecutors had requested a continuance of Cook's fourth trial to await test results of the semen stain found on the victim's underwear and a hair found on her buttocks. The defense, the judge noted, did not object to the DNA testing but wanted to go ahead with the trial. The state's motion was denied, but the trial never materialized because of the plea agreement.

The hair, although found to not microscopically match Cook, never did undergo further DNA testing and was later destroyed— an action Cook's attorneys said violated a 2001 state law. Carter's opinion, however, included a footnote indicating the hair and other evidence were legally destroyed thirty-four months after Cook pleaded no contest, was found guilty, and released.

Finding Mayfield's DNA at the scene, however, was somewhat inconsequential, the judge said.

"The ultimate issue in this case is a determination of who murdered Linda Edwards, not who had sexual relations with Linda Edwards," he said. "DNA evidence convincingly shows Mayfield had sexual relations. It excludes Cook as the depositor of semen. That's all it does."

The judge said the DNA evidence gave the defense "additional armor," but it did not unquestionably prove that Cook was actually innocent. Mayfield's lies about his relationship with the victim and about the book also failed to support the claim, he said.

Assuming a lie made Mayfield completely uncreditable or believing he probably left his DNA inside the apartment the night of the murder required the jury to make "deductive" steps, the judge said.

Carter then focused on what he considered the strongest evidence against Cook—his fingerprints, eyewitness testimony, and Mayfield's admission. Rudolph's identification was "problematic," he said. Describing the fingerprints as "fresh" and the reported admission to Wickham both were subject to criticism, he said. But, Carter concluded, those matters were for a jury to believe or disbelieve.

The explanations did nothing to console Cook, who contended Carter lacked enough knowledge of the case to render a sound opinion.

"The judge was not on my side after all," Cook concluded.

He also accused Bennett of making "some serious missteps" in his final arguments and claimed his former attorneys with the Innocence Project "tricked" him into signing an agreement he couldn't take back, he wrote on social media. In another Facebook post written much later, Cook claimed the agreement to set aside his conviction actually exonerated him.

When Bingham signed the agreement, the prosecutor "agreed to legally exonerate me," Cook said.

The Texas Court of Criminal Appeals would have the final say on that matter.

PART VI

The Waiting Game

2017

June 2017

Cook files a federal lawsuit in US District Court Eastern District of Texas in Tyler against twenty-two Tyler and Smith County entities and individuals citing misconduct in his case

2018

Cook, Attorneys Beyond Frustrated Over Wait

February 2019

Cook's federal civil suit dismissed until criminal conviction is fully vacated.

2019

May 2019

Court of Criminal Appeals requests exhibits missing from files sent for actual innocence claim.

2020

Six Years and Still Waiting Cook Decision

2021

2022

May 2022

Appeals court orders Smith County to comply with previous order.

Kerry Max Cook's name is finally cleared

2023

Sept. 2022

Court receives all the requested records from Smith County.

June 16, 2024

Cook is hospitalized after suffering a stroke.

2024

June 19, 2024

Cook officially exonerated.

"This Was All or Nothing": Kerry Max Cook, Who Spent 19 Years on Death Row, Has Been Declared Innocent
- *Texas Monthly*

CHAPTER 71

In the Meantime

I lost touch with Cook after the 2016 hearing. Although I initially followed him on social media, he blocked me when he read my accounts of his rants. A friend who kept me informed also was blocked when Cook made the connection.

In 2017, I learned through a source that Cook had filed a civil lawsuit in the US District Court Eastern District of Texas in Tyler, naming twenty-two defendants (government entities as well as individuals) who, he claimed, violated his civil rights and led to his initial conviction. He was being represented by the Chicago-based law firm of Loevy & Loevy, which made a name winning civil cases involving wrongfully convicted people and whistleblowers. A judge, however, dismissed Cook's civil lawsuit in 2019, putting it on hold until/if his criminal conviction was fully vacated. In other words, the federal court deferred considering his claims until the Texas Court of Criminal Appeals ruled on the actual innocence issue.

Occasionally, I would learn about Cook's travels to other parts of the world to speak about his experience on death row. He also granted interviews for various true crime podcasts. One in particular caught my attention years after its original airing. In February 2017, Cook was interviewed for a segment on the *Generation Why* podcast in which he claimed Linda's roommate

Rudolph was a lesbian who fit the profile of the killer. He based this information on interviews with apartment residents who described Rudolph as being "very macho," with attributes of a man, and a "very cold person." Cook said information from these interviews was not discovered by his attorneys until just before the 1996 hearing. During the podcast interview, Cook also claimed Rudolph had "positively" identified Mayfield as the man she saw inside the apartment that night and that she "completely changes her story" after police suggested she would become a suspect herself if she didn't. I was stunned and angry. Cook saw Rudolph several times over the years and should have known she did not look or act anything like those descriptions. It was a cheap shot against a woman who lost her husband in the Vietnam Conflict and died in 2013 without the opportunity to defend herself. Making accusations, floating new theories, or sharing "information" after the deaths of those who could neither verify nor challenge it became a habit for Cook.

The waiting game for the appellate court's decision was set to begin its seventh year when Cook and I crossed paths again, although not in person. I was working for a nonprofit online news organization in Tyler and decided to write a story updating readers about the Cook case. I thought it would be interesting to hear Cook describe what his life had been like waiting for a critical decision in his effort to gain full exoneration. His life must have been like the world's longest and slowest roller-coaster ride that never ends. Cook declined my interview request, suggesting instead I contact one of his new attorneys associated with the Exoneration Initiative in New York. The nonprofit organization focuses on the most difficult criminal cases: those lacking DNA evidence. I called at least one Exoneration Initiative attorney, Glenn Graber, a dozen times and left numerous messages that went unreturned. After my article appeared on July 17, 2022, Graber emailed my boss, alleging my story contained "numerous errors" and that it failed to provide a balanced account of Cook's case. He also said neither he nor Cook's other attorneys (Rebecca Freedman or Keith Hampton) were aware of any efforts to previously contact them. He invited someone in our organization to contact him. I called Graber's office and left a message that was never returned. I never learned what "errors" he allegedly found in the story, although, based on my experience, the real issue is usually a difference of opinion rather than factual error. I certainly am willing to correct mistakes; I'm just not interested in arguing the evidence. I strongly suspect Graber did exactly what Cook told him to do—nothing more, nothing less. It's as if we were playing some sort of game.

Cook isn't the only one anxious to learn the court's decision. As a journalist, waiting also is a nerve-wracking experience. I can't even calculate the number of hours and days during my career I waited outside a courtroom for a jury to reach a verdict. Waiting for a decision on an appeal often takes years, but Cook's case set a record (and continues to do so). In Cook's case, I can only imagine how complicated it must be to sort out the tangle of legal issues this case has raised. Leaks are extremely rare in the appellate court, so I'll have to wait just like everyone else.

In Cook's case, the only hint that the appellate court is actively working on it is a request for exhibits in May 2019 that should have accompanied the appeal paperwork. Determining whether that request was fulfilled has been difficult since the current district clerk has failed to return at least six messages I left with her office.[80]

---

80 Messages were left for District Clerk Penny Clarkston.

CHAPTER 72

Waiting

Details of the decision-making process in the state's highest criminal appeals court are not subject to public disclosure to protect the integrity of that part of the judicial system. From the public's perspective it is a guessing game about why it is taking so long in Cook's case or when justices will reach a decision and make it public. The case's unusually long, complicated history involving complex legal issues is unprecedented and likely will intrigue legal professionals for decades to come. The appellate court itself, however, may unknowingly be a part of the problem.

Although justices serve six-year terms, nearly every time Cook's case came before the appellate court, different sets of eyes with different viewpoints of the laws reviewed it. Comparing the opinions overturning Cook's conviction reflect possible shifts created by election turnover.

Consider this: Of the slate of nine justices attempting to reach a decision in this case, only one—Justice Sharon Keller—was on the appellate court bench when Cook's second conviction was overturned in 1996. The remaining justices have forty years of catching up to do.

Previous court decisions also raise other disconcerting issues. Is the court's task now limited to determining if Judge Carter's finding is legally sound? Can the court revisit the fairness question concerning Cook's first trial, or could its ruling include elements of both?

The court's opinions, however, clearly show Cook did not get a fair trial in 1978. Prosecutors lied about making a plea deal with Shyster Jackson, who later said the state fed him details of the crime. The prosecution also pressured then investigator Collard into testifying about the age of the fingerprints, although he knew that was scientifically impossible. The initial prosecutors and police investigators withheld exculpatory evidence that could have strengthened Cook's defense.

Cook's conviction, however, initially was overturned in 1991 because he was not warned of his right to remain silent before speaking with a psychiatrist. Prosecutorial misconduct wasn't a factor until his second conviction was overturned in 1996 although a majority ruled Cook still could be retried. Excluding Hoehn's testimony, however, left a huge hole in the state's case. Coupled with the fact that most of the main witnesses—Mayfield, Collard, and Rudolph—are now deceased, it's unlikely the prosecution will pursue another retrial if Carter's finding is upheld. That leaves a ruling on the actual innocence claim—highly unlikely—as the only way to close the criminal case as a legal issue. When that ruling will be released, however, is anyone's guess.

The court of public opinion, however, is still in session and likely will never adjourn.

"...it's unlikely the prosecution
will pursue another retrial..."

–Author

CHAPTER 73

Breaking News

Just when I thought I couldn't wait any longer to publish this story, another huge monkey wrench came flying into the picture as I was Tyler-bound on personal business.

It was June 19, 2024, and I was on Interstate 30 just outside Texarkana when my cellphone chimed multiple alerts. I pulled into a rest stop to see what the commotion was about.

A text message from a former colleague showed a clip from *The Texas Tribune* that read, in part, "Texas court finds Kerry Max Cook innocent of 1977 murder ..."

I skimmed through the accompanying article. The court had ruled that prosecutorial misconduct prevented Cook from receiving a fair trial and that new evidence supported his actual innocence.

It was a Wednesday, of course—the day the court releases its rulings.

I was stunned for a few seconds before that familiar rush of adrenaline jumpstarted my brain, generating a flurry of questions while I created a list of people I needed to call and contemplated writing a new final chapter.

It was the first time in my journalism career that I had come close to yelling, "Stop the presses!" After thirteen years of researching, interviewing, and writing this story, I was just days away from giving permission to print.

The next twenty-four hours were a whirlwind of activity for me, one of the few nonparticipants still around who knew the case history and had covered most of its major developments. I hadn't brought my laptop on this trip, so I stayed up late reading the court's one-hundred-and-six-page opinion on a screen no bigger than the palm of my hand.

The next day, I appeared as an "expert" on a Tyler television station's evening newscast and granted an interview with the Tyler newspaper. I empathized with both reporters (neither of whom had been born yet when Cook won his first appeal) as they struggled to keep dates straight and to understand the complicated issues the case created.

When I returned to my Tennessee home days later, I carefully dissected the opinion to better understand the court's reasoning behind what it called "perhaps one of the most notable murder cases in the last half-century."

The decision legitimized Cook's claim of innocence in an appeal also notable for the length of time it consumed and as a rare and phenomenal aspect of the criminal justice system.

In general, exoneration means the convicted person is officially cleared of the charges against them. According to the Texas Coalition to Abolish the Death Penalty, only sixteen people sentenced to death in Texas have been exonerated since 1973.[81]

The news must have created a flood of emotions for the 68-year-old Cook, who now can pursue compensation from the state for wrongful conviction. Unfortunately, I wouldn't be able to get Cook's reaction. Two months before the ruling, I contacted him through social media, hoping for an interview. He declined and directed me to never contact him again.

---

81 https://tcadp.org/get-informed/texas-death-penalty-facts/ - :~:text=Since 1973, 197 individuals who,sentenced to death in Texas

I didn't know it at the time, but on the day he was exonerated, Cook was in a Houston hospital, having suffered a stroke days earlier.

Exoneration—especially in a capital murder case—is rare because an appellate court's duty is to decide procedural issues, not to determine guilt or innocence. In Cook's case, the court was forced to take that extraordinary step. In doing so, it overturned numerous rulings by multiple trial judges and previous appellate judges.

Most significant among those prior decisions was Judge Jack Carter's rejection of Cook's actual innocence claim in 2016.

The court's 2024 decision to exonerate wasn't unanimous. Although eight judges agreed that Cook deserved a new trial, two of the eight did not agree on exoneration, and there was one dissenting vote.[82]

Writing for the majority, Judge Bert Richardson addressed a history of misconduct, missteps, and questionable testimony spanning a lifetime.

"This case is riddled with allegations of State misconduct that warrant setting aside Applicant's conviction," Richardson stated. "And when it comes to solid support for actual innocence, this case contains it all—uncontroverted Brady violations, proof of false testimony, admissions of perjury, and new scientific evidence. "It is alarming that for more than four decades some of those charged with pursuing justice for Linda have actually obstructed the search for the truth of what really happened that night."[83]

In a concurring opinion, presiding Judge Sharon Keller agreed that Cook should receive a new trial but did not support exoneration. Judge Mary Lou Keel concurred with Keller.

---

82 The majority consisted of judges Bert Richardson, Barbara Hervey, David Newell, Scott Walker, Michelle Slaughter, Jesse F. McClure III, Sharon Keller, and Mary Lou Keel.

83 https://search.txcourts.gov/SearchMedia.aspx?MediaVersionID=293d06bb-cdce-4301-b1b1-2da73b206309&coa=coscca&DT=OPINION&MedialD=2d8e253f-255b-4fc4-b5de-5dfcfb16cb40

Keller contended that Cook had failed to satisfy the required standard to prove actual innocence. Under Texas law, Cook must show "by clear and convincing evidence that no reasonable juror would have convicted him in light of new evidence."

Keller cited four pieces of evidence that she said would allow a reasonable juror to find Cook guilty, including:

- The testimony of reserve sheriff's deputy Robert Wickham, who asserted that Cook confessed to the crime
- The testimony of Paula Rudolph, who identified Cook as the man she saw in the apartment the night of the murder
- Cook's fingerprints showing that he had to have been inside the victim's apartment
- Cook initially lying about knowing the victim

"I think all of this evidence together is at least minimally sufficient for a reasonable juror to find Applicant [Cook] guilty," Keller wrote.

Judge Kevin Yeary cast the lone dissenting vote—agreeing with Keller's opinion that Cook failed to demonstrate actual innocence but concluding that Cook was not entitled to a new trial.

Richardson also addressed the question of why it took the appellate court eight years to reach a decision.

"The road to this point has been long, much of it unnecessarily slow ... the victim of repeated delays," he wrote.

According to the court's opinion, the delays were due to a combination of dealing with an extremely voluminous number of records, the COVID-19 pandemic, a ransomware attack, two changes in the defense team, and delays on the part of the trial court and Smith County to provide portions of the records.

Cook filed for relief in September 2015. It was granted in 2016, but Smith County failed to transmit the full record to the Austin appellate court.

After "numerous informal requests and phone calls" to the court's staff and Smith County, in May 2019, the court ordered that the missing parts of the record be sent.

Smith County and trial court officials "failed to respond in a timely manner."

In May 2022, the court ordered the county to comply with the previous order.

During this time the effects of the COVID-19 pandemic and a ransomware attack caused further delays.

The court finally received all the requested records on September 21, 2022, but it took the defense another two months to reply to the state's case summary.[84]

---

84 Although the court did not specifically name the Smith County employees responsible for the delay, the district ckerk's office and the individual court employees are responsible for maintaining records. District Clerk Penny Clarkson, who took office in 2019, came under fire in early 2024 when former County Commissioner JoAnne Fleming filed a lawsuit seeking Clarkson's removal from office for "ignoring her official duties" and violating Texas codes.

CHAPTER 74

The Final Word

In exonerating Cook, the court concluded that the prosecutors had "resorted to improper means to achieve conviction" by considering only evidence that supported their theory of the crime and ignoring evidence to the contrary.

Judge Richardson described the state's case—from the flawed expert testimony and undisclosed favorable deal given to a jailhouse snitch to Mayfield's admission that he had indeed had sexual relations with the victim days before her murder four decades later—as "bookends of deception." The court's opinion then systematically dismantled key segments of the state's case.

"Several actions of the State go beyond gross negligence and reach the realm of intentional deception against the tribunal," Richardson wrote.

Among the court's findings were the following points:

- Cook could not have committed the crime according to the state's timeline, which showed he had less than fifteen minutes between the time Hoehn dropped him off at the apartment complex and the time Rudolph returned home. The timeline also contradicted expert testimony that the number of wounds Edwards received would have taken a "considerable amount of time" to inflict.

- Rudolph's testimony was "completely unreliable" due to her inconsistent testimony and because the description she gave (height, hairstyle, clothing, etc.) better fit Mayfield.
- Under pressure from the district attorney in 1978, Collard gave misleading testimony about the age of Cook's fingerprints. The prints found on the sliding glass door could be consistent with grand jury testimony that Cook knew the victim and had been inside her apartment days before the murder.
- Grand jury testimony indicating that Cook had met Edwards at the pool and had been invited to her apartment was not disclosed to the defense for years after the first trial. Evidence that Cook had "passion marks" (hickeys) on his neck within the days before the murder supports that testimony.
- Wickham's testimony about an alleged confession was "inexplicable," and his statements were inconsistent. Affidavits obtained by Centurion Ministries showed Wickham was "untruthful" and a "wannabe" police officer.
- Mayfield lied about his familiarity with the book *The Sexual Criminal*, which contains scenes "strikingly similar" to the Edwards murder scene. Mayfield also lied about the last time he'd had sexual relations with Edwards, and his DNA was found in the victim's underwear, tying him directly to the crime scene.
- The crime classification and criminal profile presented by the state do not fit Cook. Expert testimony profiling Edwards's death as a lust murder was "flawed from its inception" and provided the "final bookend." Evidence suggests that the crime was consistent with a domestic homicide rather than a lust murder. Cook did not have any long-term sexual fantasies, was not a loner or social outcast, and was able to socialize romantically—all contrary to known characteristics of a lust murderer.
- A dark-colored hair with a bloody root found on the victim's buttock was "selectively" destroyed before it could be tested. A preliminary test excluded Cook, Edwards, and Mayfield as the contributor. Prosecutors contended the hair was destroyed

according to law, but the court ruled that the state did not give Cook the required notice of intent to destroy.

- The court's conclusion reflected a scathing rebuke of the prosecutors and the means by which they pursued a conviction.
- "It is clear that Cook never enjoyed the full panoply of protections guaranteed under the Constitution," the opinion stated. "Cook spent close to a decade and a half on death row and from the very beginning based on a web of fabricated testimony and misrepresentation. "Even if Cook had been made aware of the deception, Cook was left with little-to-no legal recourse because it was outside the record on appeal."

Considering the totality of the evidence, the court ruled that the prosecutors failed to prove anything more than "Cook just being in the wrong place at the wrong time to his extreme misfortune."

The court's ruling now stands as the final word since the state cannot appeal.

Upon receiving a death sentence in 1978, Cook vowed to prove his innocence "if it takes me ten years, twenty years."

By my calculations, it took forty-five years, eleven months, and twenty days.

EPILOGUE

During the height of my career, I covered at least sixteen capital murder trials, of which eleven (sixty-eight percent) have since ended with an actual execution.

Of the capital murder defendants I've interviewed, Thomas Wayne Mason truly scared me. We exchanged letters and spoke briefly on his way to and from the courtroom, but the exchanges always were intense. Mason possessed two traits especially dangerous when combined— ignorance and uncontrollable anger.

James Wilkens Jr. was the capital murder defendant who fooled me. When we first met, he was awaiting an execution date. During our first few interviews, Wilkens calmly and convincingly told me he had put his faith in God and was willing to accept the will of the Lord, whatever it may be.

He changed his tune once he was granted a new trial. In his retrial, Wilkens blamed childhood abuse for his shooting rampage, claiming he thought he was seeing his father when he killed another man and a four-year-old boy. He sulked when the jury didn't believe him.

A Smith County jury returned him to death row in 1993, and he was executed in 2001. In his final statement, Wilkens begged for forgiveness.

* * *

Cook's case heightened my complete disdain for hypocrisy, lies, and injustice, especially because human lives and reputations are at stake. The "what ifs" and "buts" this case generated are mind-boggling.

Imagine how different Cook's first trial would have been if the initial prosecutors had followed all the rules or if defense attorneys knew then what subsequent attorneys know now. What if Cook hadn't flip-flopped in explaining his fingerprints at the crime scene? What if Mayfield had told the truth from the beginning? Cook was wrongly convicted in 1978, but does that mean he is actually innocent?

The Texas Court of Criminal Appeals certainly believed so, although I question the role the court assumed in order to achieve it. The judges not only ruled on procedural matters, but they also decided the veracity of witnesses and other evidence—undermining the duties of the jurors and trial judges.

The "facts" surrounding the discovery of Cook's fingerprints and Mayfield's semen at the murder scene still perplex me. Did Linda invite Cook into her apartment or not? When did Mayfield and Linda last have sex?

There is no question that the prints on the sliding glass door belong to Cook, who initially denied knowing Linda or ever being inside her apartment.

Two previous trial judges ruled that grand jury testimony about how Cook explained the passion marks on his neck (and thus gave a reasonable explanation for his fingerprints) was inadmissible hearsay. It didn't necessarily have to be.

If Cook is now telling the truth in saying that Linda actually had invited him back to her apartment, then he is partially responsible for hindering his own defense—a probability the appellate court didn't address in its opinion.

Undoubtedly DNA evidence also connects Mayfield to the crime scene. Although he initially lied about the timing of his last sexual encounter with Linda, this took decades to confirm. In retrospect, the crime scene investigator should have submitted Linda's panties for analysis in 1977 anyway. DNA tests were certainly available in the mid to late – '80s and could have dramatically changed the course of this case.[85]

Unfortunately—although crucial evidence—no forensic tests can determine exactly when the fingerprints or semen were left at the crime scene.

My observations, however, should not be misconstrued to suggest I believe Cook innocent or guilty. This case is a colossal legal tragedy that will no doubt be studied and debated for decades to come.

I am fortunate to have been able to follow this case to its end. As such, I thought it only appropriate to try to get some final insight into the case from some of the key players.

---

85 According to the National Institute of Justice, DNA was first used as evidence in a criminal case in 1986. https://nij.ojp.gov/nij-hosted-online-training-courses/what-every-first-responding-officer-should-know-about-dna/dna-evidence-overview - :~:text=DNA was first introduced as,left at a crime scene

Reaction interviews are the bread and butter of a journalist who covers the legal system. Readers want to know the opinions on the outcomes (jury verdict or appeal) of the people involved, and getting interviews with the defendant, defense attorneys, prosecutors, victim, survivors, possibly a juror or two, and even an expert is an ideal plan to obtain a well-rounded story.

However, reaching that goal, especially on a deadline, can be difficult for a multitude of reasons. Access is key, but the bottom line is this: If someone doesn't want to talk, then there is nothing I can do. In that case, I find myself facing the double-edged sword of a dilemma. Giving readers a reason for excluding someone (did not respond to interview request) is important to avoid appearing biased, but including the explanation often is erroneously interpreted as intentionally embarrassing someone.

My status as persona non grata with Cook apparently extended to Nugent, who did not respond to two separate interview requests. Skeen also did not reply. An effort to reach Jimmy Edwards also was unsuccessful.

I'm not surprised. Sports journalists at smaller newspapers probably can relate. Coaches of a losing team tend not to call in their game scores, and sometimes, winning coaches seek the biggest spotlight.

This saga wouldn't be complete without former district attorney A.D. Clark's answers to some serious questions. To the best of my knowledge, Clark has never granted an interview about the Cook case, so I was surprised when he responded to my request sent via social media.

There was just one catch: Clark would only respond to written questions. That's a problem for a journalist like me who embraces the concept that spontaneous responses reflect genuine feelings rather than carefully worded answers.

Conducting an interview through email or text messaging isn't ideal either because it can be a very slow process and prevents a journalist from being able to observe important nonverbal cues and voice tone.

Live interviews allow a journalist to respond quickly with follow-up questions or requests for clarification. But if submitting written questions was the only way I could get an interview, I had to do it. I waited a week, but in the end, Clark said his lack of access to the original files prevented him from accurately responding to my questions.

I did, however, hear from David Hanners, albeit indirectly. It seems he read my comments about the case in that June 22, 2024, *Tyler Morning Telegraph* article.

He submitted an opinion piece, chastising the newspaper's decades-long coverage that he said, "rarely went beyond reporting what Smith County officials said publicly."[86] He even contended the Tyler newspaper often "defended Smith County authorities."

I adamantly disagree. My coverage of the case included inside and outside the courtroom. I wrote articles about the victim's family. I interviewed Cook on numerous occasions and wrote his side of the story. I wrote articles about Centurion Ministries and its investigation. I even wrote stories about the financial impact the trials had on Smith County. Most of all, I provided accurate and fair coverage of developments in the case, including trial testimony.

Hanners is entitled to his opinion, as am I.

In my overall analysis of their coverage, I credit *Dallas Morning News* reporters, including Hanners, for revealing egregious misconduct, questionable testimony, and blatant lies behind Cook's wrongful 1978 conviction. Exposing that corruption is admirable. But they didn't stop there. Their transition from investigative reporting to becoming a Cook advocate was subtle—not just what they wrote about but also what they didn't write about.

Early coverage focused on finding fault with Smith County authorities, then reflected a disdain for Smith County prosecutors for retrying the case. In the meantime, they ignored the elephant in the room.

What about the lie Cook told and how it contributed to his wrongful conviction? A murder defendant admitting he lied should have been a front-page story. I don't recall ever seeing or reading an article in *The Dallas Morning News* that highlighted that aspect of the case before it was revealed during the 2002 trial.

I posed that question to Hanners in 2024. His answer unlocked yet another secret. Hanners testified in December 1992 (albeit outside a jury presence) that he learned Cook had lied during an interview conducted sometime in the fall of 1991 or the spring of 1992. However, attorneys inexplicably (at the time) did not question him about specifics.

---

86 David Hanners, "Hanners: Be dedicated to courage in future reporting," July 6, 2024. *Tyler Morning Telegraph.*

He was allowed to testify before a jury about the accuracy of the quotes attributed to Cook in his previous articles but not about a subsequent interview in which Cook allegedly admitted he had lied about knowing Linda. Since Hanners didn't write about that interview, he couldn't testify about what Cook said because it constituted hearsay.

But, there was another reason why Hanners wouldn't or couldn't discuss that particular interview. In 2024, Hanners explained that it was "highly probable" the interview had been off the record.

For non-journalists, those three words seem to be a magical force that automatically prevents a reporter from quoting a source either in writing or verbally, directly or indirectly. In reality, though, a journalist must first agree to that condition. It's a tough choice to make: don't agree and lose potential important information or agree and lose the opportunity to share that information.

It's a gamble, especially since a journalist doesn't know in advance the value of the information. Obtaining information off the record, however, can still be useful since it may help a journalist find a different source for the same information.

Breaking an off-the-record agreement raises ethical and legal questions. Most states did not (and still don't) recognize a reporter–source relationship as being privileged. If Hanners had been forced to testify about that interview, he would have faced breaking his promise to Cook or a possible contempt of court charge if he refused.

Determining the total impact of Hanners's agreement with Cook is difficult since I'm not privy to the decision-making process Hanners and/or his editors went through to make such an agreement.

Hanners contends Cook's about-face is inconsequential since his published articles mentioned grand jury testimony from witnesses who reported Cook had told them about meeting Linda at the swimming pool (hearsay testimony ruled inadmissible during trial).

"Given that Cook was under no obligation to testify, his lie had no material impact on the outcome of the case," Hanners wrote in an email to me.

Maybe so, but if Mayfield's lies, Rudolf's alleged change in testimony, and Jackson's lies were newsworthy, certainly Cook's lie deserved the same treatment.

Cook's lie is incredibly important for several reasons:
- It hindered his defense in his 1978 trial.
- It questioned Cook's credibility.
- It's hypocritical since Cook and his defense criticize state's witnesses for doing the same thing.

Not treating Cook's lie (albeit problematic) with an equally critical eye leaves the impression of bias, at best, and represents clear bias, at worst.

In his 2024 letter to the editor, Hanners chastised the *Tyler Morning Telegraph* for not having the "courage" to investigate Cook's case from the beginning. I, however, contend Hanners strayed into the advocacy role.

Hanners also admitted he had formed an opinion about Cook, but he insisted it did not affect how he wrote his articles.

"I became convinced of Mr. Cook's innocence in early 1988, a couple of months after I began looking into the case," Hanners wrote in that same letter to the editor.

I refuse to sacrifice my journalistic integrity just for a good story. I struggled to maintain my objectivity under the pressure to "get on board," and I never will regret not sacrificing my journalistic integrity just for a good story.

* * *

Now, Cook has cleared a major hurdle to seek compensation from the state and pursue his federal suit against Smith County, the city of Tyler, and the dozens of law enforcement officials connected to the case.

Could wrongful convictions such as Cook's be prevented in the future? Possibly. There are some promising new programs and laws in place, as well as advancements in forensic testing, to address the growing concerns.

For example: five Texas counties (Bexar, Dallas, Harris, Tarrant, and Travis) now have Conviction Integrity Units with the primary responsibility of reviewing actual innocence claims.

Although public opinion polls indicate support for capital punishment in America is slipping (with acceptance rate barely over fifty percent), a total ban on the practice is still illusive. Instead, death penalty opponents are tackling — and winning — smaller battles. Since 2000, U.S. Supreme Court decisions have slowly eroded the death penalty's reach.

My final semester in graduate school consisted of one criminal justice class in which I chose capital punishment as my research topic. I reviewed the history of executions in America, the expert opinions for and against the practice, the methods of execution, the wax and wane of public opinion — all the usual stuff — in a fifty-page paper. Although I received an A for the assignment, in retrospect I failed miserably to recognize an important development in the effort to abolish capital punishment in the United States. The evidence was all there in my research, I just failed to connect the dots. In hindsight, I clearly saw a path toward incremental, rather than outright abolishment. That path or strategy came to fruition during the first decade of the new century. In 2002, the U.S. Supreme Court banned executions of inmates who are mentally retarded — a term generally defined as someone with an I.Q. of approximately seventy or less. In another landmark decision three years later, the same court ruled as unconstitutional the execution of inmates who had committed capital murder when they were younger than eighteen.[87] Since 2007, nine states have abolished capital punishment and governors in four others have instituted a moratorium on the practice. The rate of executions, meanwhile, has declined dramatically since 2000. The most recent battle addresses the method of execution — lethal injection — as cruel and unusual punishment. Since 2000, the Death Penalty Information Center has recorded twenty "botched" executions throughout the country, most of which involved the effect of specific drugs used in the process. A nationwide shortage of sodium thiopental — one of the drugs used in lethal injection — also contributed to a surge of legal challenges.

The battles to eliminate, or at least limit the use of capital punishment, rage on.

* * *

Despite its faults, I believe in America's judicial system. I believe in fairness and the premise that the accused is innocent until proven guilty. I admire the

---

87 Napoleon Beazley, who was convicted of killing John Luttig in Tyler, was executed in 2002 and was one of the last death row inmates in the country to die before the U.S. Supreme Court ruling could have saved their life. Beazley committed the crime 3½ months before his 18th birthday.

dedicated prosecutors, judges, and defense attorneys who seek justice for all; the journalists who keep a watchful eye; the private citizens and organizations who help the innocent or wrongly convicted; and those who support the victims and their survivors. I especially appreciate the service of jurors, who often have the difficult task of sorting through the evidence and trying to reach a decision.

Capital punishment is no longer an abstract idea for me. As a journalist, I've studied the death penalty, observed the judicial process from all sides, and witnessed an execution—more involvement than the average person likely will ever experience.

Cook's case has proved to be the one that made me look deeper into the debate over whether the death penalty should be abolished. His case motivated me to read more, listen to debates, and analyze the basis for opposing views. In some instances, missteps in Cook's case—legal and otherwise—were preventable, while others were unforeseen. The judicial system isn't perfect, although every effort should be made to ensure it is fair.

But I've seen photographs of too many gruesome murder scenes, seen the lives of too many victims' families torn apart by anger and sorrow, to dismiss the death penalty just yet. The thought of an innocent person being executed still disgusts me, but unfortunately it can happen. Consider instances when American soldiers are killed by friendly fire. Despite extensive training, US soldiers have killed other US soldiers during combat because of miscalculations and miscommunications. It's tragic. It's unfair. It's preventable, and yet, our military engagements continue with the possibility of it happening again. As long as the public supports laws allowing capital punishment there is a possibility an innocent person could be convicted and possibly executed. It's also possible a guilty person could be wrongfully convicted due to prosecutorial misconduct.

I understand the desire to remove certain convicted killers from society forever—to make them pay, by law, the ultimate price for their actions. And I can support a death sentence as long as the defendant is afforded a fair trial, proven guilty beyond a reasonable doubt, and allowed reasonable appeals.

I also recognize the injustice of convicting the innocent—stories about people who spend decades in prison, their lives forever scarred by the experience.

There are numerous elements involved in the debate, but the most difficult question to resolve is whether executing someone for killing another is moral. Sister Helen Prejean addresses that question in her book *River of Fire: My Spiritual Journey*. I read the book—a prequel to *Dead Man Walking*—after meeting her for the first time in March 2019 during her visit to Tennessee Technological University.

Prejean said the death penalty is an immoral act that defies the sanctity of human dignity and the belief that all life has some degree of worth. She compared her journey of becoming an activist to a piece of charcoal. Waking up to the inviolability of human life, she said, lit a fire in her that took time to get deep inside. Her burning passion now is to use "spiritual power" to change public consciousness.

"I trust the book's power to change hearts and minds," she wrote.

* * *

The future danger issue especially interests me since I have followed two capital murder cases in which former death row inmates were later freed. To the best of my knowledge, both Andrew Lee Mitchell and Kerry Max Cook did not commit any further acts of violence once they were released despite testimony that they likely would continue to be a danger even while incarcerated.

In 2005, Texas became the last of the "death penalty" states[88] to sign into law the option of life without parole (LWOP) in capital murder cases. Previously, a capital murder defendant who received a life sentence could become eligible for parole—a factor some experts claim contributed to the number of death sentences.

Since the law's passage, the number of LWOP sentences has increased (death by incarceration),[89] and the number of death sentences has decreased in Texas.[90]

Smith County District Attorney Jacob Putman said he believes the LWOP option addresses a major concern for jurors, who faced the possibility

88 The Law Office of Greg Tsioris, "What Is Life Without Parole In Texas?," *Parole Law Blog*, January 31, 2018.
89 "Texas Enacts Life Without Parole Law," *Prison Legal News*, January 15, 2006, 27.
90 "The Associated Press, "Nearly 400 Prisoners in Texas Serving Life Without Parole," *The Daily Texan*, November 30, 2011.

of a violent offender eventually being released back into society.

"Life without parole really takes that fear away from citizens," Putman told me.[91]

Since taking office in 2019, Putman said his office has pursued death sentences in three cases—obtaining that penalty in two of those and accepting a plea for LWOP in the third. He estimated his office has elected not to seek the death penalty in as many as eight other cases during the same time period.

LWOP proponents contend the option tackles the potential problem of executing the innocent by keeping the defendant alive in case proof of actual innocence comes to light. Serving a term of natural life is also cheaper than a death sentence, they argue.

Putman said money is not a factor in deciding whether to seek the death sentence in Smith County cases. "Smith County is a very law and order county. We can afford seeking the death penalty," he said. "We take it [the decision] very seriously. We don't do it flippantly."

Before deciding to seek a death sentence, he said, prosecutors consider all the evidence to determine if a jury would likely see the defendant as a continuing threat to society and if there are any mitigating circumstances to warrant LWOP instead.

For Putman, the society being considered is not just regular communities. Proving the defendant is likely to commit violence within the prison community itself also plays a major role in the final decision, he said.

The case of capital murder defendant Steven A. Smith, accused of fatally shooting two Tyler dentists in 2022, offers a unique opportunity to compare how the decision to seek a death sentence has changed in Smith County.

Smith is accused of killing Dr. Blake G. Sinclair and Dr. Jack E. Burroughs during a dispute over a set of dentures. During the incident, Smith reportedly pointed his gun at a clinic nurse but did not fire after the women begged for her life, according to a published report.[92]

If these murders had occurred during Skeen's tenure, I have no doubt prosecutors would have sought a death sentence for Smith. However,

91 Telephone interview with Smith County District Attorney Jacob Putman, December 7, 2023.
92 "Texas Man Allegedly Became Angry with Clinical Staff, Fatally Shot 2 Dentists," *True Crime Daily*, March 17, 2022.

in November 2023, Smith County prosecutors announced they would not seek the death penalty in his case, which was scheduled for trial in January 2024.

Based on my experience, the fact Smith refrained from shooting the nurse favors a defense argument against a death sentence. Putman later told me his office did not seek a death sentence for Smith because he believes there is a "reasonable chance" a jury would not answer the questions concerning future dangerousness and mitigating circumstances in favor of a death sentence.

LWOP may thwart some of the major drawbacks of the death penalty, but it also creates new problems and adds to the divisiveness of the issue.

Prejean's approach, however, hits at the heart. She delivers a powerful message she believes embraces the religious principles of love and forgiveness—ones she hopes and prays will be the catalyst for awakening the masses, who will demand politicians ban the death penalty forever.

She fights for a noble cause but one, I fear, extremely difficult to achieve considering the prevailing belief that justice means capital murder offenders deserve the ultimate punishment.

My spiritual journey isn't even close to accepting Prejean's message—yet. But I do support legal reforms designed to reduce the possibility of error, including holding law enforcement officers and legal professionals accountable for misconduct that results in wrongful convictions. Our system of justice accounts for mistakes— "wrongful" convictions that can be corrected— in applying the law through the appeals process and providing rectification via retrials. Convicting someone who is innocent, however, is a "wrongful" conviction with much greater and often irreversible consequences. Society should not tolerate the use of illegal or unethical means to win a conviction or acquittal of a criminal charge. The devastating consequence of Cook's wrongful conviction—regardless of which definition of "wrongful" is applied—is the loss of truth.

Those who believe Cook is innocent may be somewhat satisfied that at least he was finally exonerated. Those who believe he is guilty may be pacified that he at least served twenty years behind bars. Despite it all, however, the truth about what happened the night of June 9–10, 1977, in Apartment 169 at the Embarcadero Apartments in Tyler, Texas, will forever remain a mystery.

NAME GLOSSARY

Acker, Marvin—Police captain in Jacksonville, Texas, when Cook was released on bond in November 1997.

Aldrich, Donald—Convicted of the 1993 murder of Nicholas West in Smith County. Executed in 2004.

Allen, Tom—Tyler psychologist who reviewed Cook's mental health records. He testified in the punishment phase of Cook's second retrial.

Ament, John—Jacksonville, Texas, attorney who represented Cook in 1978 trial.

Arnett, Mahlon—Juror in Cook's first retrial.

Barron, David—*Tyler Morning Telegraph* reporter who covered Cook's 1978 trial. He retired in 2021 after working thirty-one years as a sports reporter for the *Houston Chronicle*.

Baggett, Donnis—A reporter/editor who investigated the Cook case for *The Dallas Morning News*. He interviewed Edward Scott Jackson when the former witness recanted his testimony in which he claimed Cook confessed to the crime.

Beard, Charlie—Texas Court of Criminal Appeals justice who wrote a concurrent but dissenting opinion in the 1996 ruling overturning Cook's conviction.

Beazley, Napoleon—Convicted of the 1994 murder of John Luttig. Executed in 2002.

Becknell, James B., Jr.—Convicted of murder in the death of Dr. W. Carl Roddy, a professor at Texas Eastern University. He died in prison in 2013.

Bennett, Mark—Houston attorney who represented Cook in oral arguments in 2017 concerning an actual innocence claim.

Bingham, Matt—Smith County District Attorney from 2003 to 2018. Now in private practice.

Blackburn, Jeff—Attorney who resigned from Innocence Project.

Blalock, Amy—Assistant Smith County prosecutor who wrote initial appeals concerning Cook's reversals. Currently in private practice.

Bonebrake, George—Former fingerprint expert with the FBI. After retirement he worked as a consultant. Testified on behalf of the defense in Cook's case. He died in 2011.

Bond, Bob—Police chief in Tyler, Texas, at the time of Linda Jo Edwards's murder.

Brandley, Clarence Lee—Janitor who served nine years on Texas death row before being freed in 1990. He died September 2, 2018.

Brill, Steven—Lawyer and journalist who founded Court TV.

Brooks, Charles, Jr.—First offender in Texas to be executed since 1964 and first by lethal injection.

Brookshire, Jim—Georgetown attorney appointed to assist Cook's defense during his second retrial.

Brumbelow, J. R. "Dick"—Republican candidate for Smith County District Attorney who opposed Jack Skeen Jr.

Brush, Hunter—Former Smith County District Attorney who served from 1967–1979 and 1978–1982.

Carter, Jack—Visiting district judge assigned to preside over Cook's actual innocence claim in 2016.

Chambers, Tony—Convicted of rape, kidnapping, and murder in the 1990 death of eleven-year-old Carenthia Marie Bailey. He was executed by lethal injection on November 15, 2000.

Choate, Kathleen—Second cousin to Robert Hoehn.

Clark, A. D., III—Smith County District Attorney in office when Cook was tried in 1978. No relation to Tyler police investigator Eddie Clark.

Clark, Eddie—Tyler Police Department investigator on the Cook case in 1977. He retired.

Clayton, Joe D.—Smith County court at law judge who ruled in the libel suit psychologist Jerry Landrum filed against reporter David Hanners and *The Dallas Morning News*.

Clinton, Sam Houston—Justice in the Texas Court of Criminal Appeals who was the lone dissenter in the 1987 opinion upholding Cook's conviction and death sentence.

Coats, Bill—Former County Court at Law #2 judge and 7th District Court judge in Smith County. He died April 10, 2002.

Cockrum, John William—Convicted of capital murder in the death of Eva May. He was executed by lethal injection in 1997.

Collard, Doug—Tyler Police Department crime scene investigator who testified about Cook's fingerprints found at the murder scene. He died in 2015.

Cook, Doyle Wayne—Brother of Kerry Max Cook. He died in 1987.

Cook, Ernest—Father of Kerry Max Cook. He died in 1991.

Cook, Evelyn—Mother of Kerry Max Cook. She died in 2005.

Cook, Kerry Max—Accused of murdering Linda Jo Edwards in 1977. He has been convicted twice and won two appeals. He entered a plea in 1999 to a reduced charge in exchange for time served. That conviction was set aside in 2016. As of September 2023, Cook was still awaiting a final ruling from the Texas Court of Criminal Appeals on an actual innocence claim. He is the author of *Chasing Justice: My Story of Freeing Myself after Two Decades on Death Row for a Crime I Didn't Commit* and lives in the Houston area.

Cook, Kerry Justice "K.J."—Son of Kerry Max Cook.

Coons, Richard—Austin forensic psychiatrist who testified for the defense in Cook's second retrial.

Corley, Edward Eldon—Former Texas death row inmate who won a new trial. He agreed to plead guilty and is currently serving a life term for the 1974 murder of Vicki Lynn Morris.

Covey, Marilyn—Former reporter for the *Tyler Morning Telegraph* who wrote the forward to this book.

Dixon, LeRue—Cherokee County attorney who represented Cook during his 1978 trial. He died in 2019.

Dobbs, David—Former Smith County chief felony prosecutor at Cook's retrials in 1992 and 1994. Currently in private practice in Tyler.

Dollahite, Keith—Special prosecutor who worked with Smith County prosecutors in opposing Cook's actual innocence claim.

Dowell, Stuart—A former Texas Ranger who met with news reporter Donnis Baggett and Edward Scott Jackson when Jackson recanted his testimony in which he claimed Cook confessed to the crime. He died May 17, 2006.

Duncan, M. P. "Rusty," III—Justice of the Texas Court of Criminal Appeals who wrote the majority opinion in the 1990 decision affirming Cook's conviction and death sentence. He died in 1990.

Dunn, Henry—Convicted of capital murder in the death of Nicholas West. He was executed by lethal injection on February 6, 2003.

Dunn, Thomas—Smith County prosecutor who testified Cook and his attorneys approached prosecutors in 1978 requesting a plea deal in which Cook would confess to killing Linda Jo Edwards with another person.

Dunn, Thomas L.—One of the first to be tried on a capital murder charge by Jack Skeen. His death sentence was reversed on appeal. He later confessed to two murders and received a life sentence.

Dykes, Randy—Nephew of James Taylor and brother to Rodney Dykes. His testimony involved whether Kerry Max Cook had known the murder victim.

Dykes, Rodney—Nephew of James Taylor and brother to Randy Dykes.

Edwards, Jimmy—Only brother of murder victim Linda Jo Edwards.

Edwards, Linda Jo—Murder victim found dead June 10, 1977, in an apartment she shared with a coworker at Texas Eastern University.

Edwards, Melba Sue—Mother of murder victim Linda Jo Edwards. Died in 1972.

Edwards, Ray—Father of Linda Jo Edwards, Jimmy Edwards, and Carolyn Edwards. He died in 2004.

Ellsworth, David—Author of *Smith County Justice*. Real name is Joe Werner, and he was a fugitive from California.

Engle, Richard—A man interviewed by a Dallas reporter who claimed that, on his deathbed, Robert Hoehn said the wrong man was on death row for killing Linda Jo Edwards.

Erwin, Bonnie—Capital murder defendant convicted and sentenced to death. His conviction was overturned. He was not retried since he already was serving life without parole on a federal charge.

Ferris, Charles—Second cousin to Robert Hoehn.

Fields, Karlos—Capital murder defendant serving a life sentence for the murder of Dennis Price. Codefendant Stacey Lawton was given a death sentence.

Files, F. R. "Buck," Jr.—Tyler attorney who represented Jim Mayfield. In private practice in Tyler.

Flood, Chris—Houston attorney, brother-in-law of Paul Nugent. Helped represent Cook during his first retrial.

Gillman, Todd J.—*Dallas Morning News* reporter who covered two of Cook's retrials. Now the Washington bureau chief for the Dallas newspaper.

Gomez, David—An FBI special agent who worked for the National Center of Analysis for Violent Crimes in Virginia. Testified for the prosecution in Cook's second retrial.

Gonzalez, V. V.—Pathologist who performed the autopsy on Linda Jo Edwards's body.

Graber, Glenn—New York attorney who represents Cook along with Rebecca Freedman and Keith Hampton on Cook's actual innocence claim.

Grigson, James—Dallas psychiatrist who interviewed Cook before his 1978 trial. He died June 3, 2004.

Hanners, David—*Dallas Morning News* reporter who investigated Cook's case. He is now a folk singer/songwriter who lives in Manchester, England.

Harned, Olene—Worked at Texas Eastern University library with murder victim Linda Jo Edwards. She retired in 1990 from what is now called The University of Texas at Tyler and died on June 13, 2015.

Harrington, Eden E.—Former executive director of the Texas Resource Center who worked with Robert McGlasson and Scott Howe on the Cook case. She is now director of the William Wayne Justice Center for Public Interest Law.

Hayden, Gerald—Former Tyler police officer who testified for the defense in Cook's second retrial.

Hill, Michael—*Texas Monthly* reporter who wrote the online article "Kerry Max Cook, a Subject of *The Exonerated*, Is Finally Exonerated."

Heard, Harry—Longview attorney who represented Cook on his first appeal.

Hendrickson, Arlo—College math instructor who ministered Cook while in prison. He testified for the defense in the punishment phase of Cook's second retrial.

Hesskew, Dusty—Austin Police sergeant who is a specialist in reconstructing violent crime. Testified for the prosecution in the Cook trial.

Hoehn, Robert—Tyler hairdresser who testified he was with Kerry Max Cook the night of the murder. He died in 1987.

Howe, Scott—Attorney associated with the Texas Resource Center who worked on Cook's case with Robert McGlasson.

Jackson, Edward Scott—Known as "Shyster" Jackson, a jailhouse informant who testified Cook confessed to the slaying. He later recanted his testimony. He is currently serving a life sentence in Missouri on a murder conviction.

Johnson, Jo Anne—Former prison psychologist who testified for the defense in the punishment phase of Cook's second retrial.

Jones, Robert D.—Visiting district judge who presided over Cook's second retrial in Georgetown and his third trial in Bastrop. He died in 2023.

Justice, William Wayne—US District Judge of the United States District Court Eastern District of Tyler. Served from 1968 until his death in 2009.

Kennedy, Christi—Judge of the 114th District Court in Smith County from 2009–2020. Widow of Richard Kennedy.

Kennedy, Richard—Former assistant district attorney in Smith County. He died in 2015.

Kent, Cynthia S.—Tyler attorney and former judge of the 114th District Court. Currently in private practice in Tyler.

Keller, Sharon—Texas Court of Criminal Appeals justice who wrote the dissent in the 1996 opinion overturning Cook's conviction. She serves as the chief justice.

Knight, Steve—Reporter for the *Tyler Morning Telegraph* who wrote the first newspaper article about the death of Linda Jo Edwards. He still writes for the Outdoor section of that newspaper.

Landrum, Jerry—Tyler psychologist who evaluated Kerry Max Cook when he was in Rusk State Hospital. He also created a profile of Linda Jo Edwards's killer for police. He later testified for the prosecution in the Cook case. He sued *Dallas Morning News* reporter David Hanners for libel, but the case was dismissed. He died November 13, 1999.

Lawton, Stacey—Convicted of capital murder in the death of Dennis Price. He was executed by lethal injection on November 14, 2000.

Lewis, Rickey Lynn—Convicted of murder and sentenced to die for the shooting death of George Newman. Lewis was executed by lethal injection on April 9, 2013.

Loftin, Carolyn Edwards—Sister of Linda Jo Edwards.

Lucas, Baker Steven—Convicted of murdering his mother. Sentenced to thirty-five years in prison. After his release he lived in El Paso, where he died in 2019.

Mansfield, Steve—Texas Court of Criminal Appeals justice who wrote for the majority in the 1996 opinion overturning Cook's conviction.

Marty, Ed—Smith County Assistant District Attorney who defended the state in Cook's appeals.

Mayfield, Elfriede—Wife of James Mayfield.

Mayfield, James "Jim"—Texas Eastern University library director who was having an affair with Linda Jo Edwards. In 2016 he admitted he lied when he testified that the last time he and Edwards had sex was three days before she was killed. He later admitted they had sex the day of her death. He also admitted knowledge of a book titled *The Sexual Criminal*. Mayfield died July 12, 2019.

Mayfield, Luella—The adopted daughter of James Mayfield. Also went by the last name of Raitano.

McCloskey, Jim—Founder of Centurion Ministries, a New Jersey-based organization that works to free those they believe have been wrongly convicted. Author of *When Truth Is All You Have*. Now retired.

McElyea, Joyce—Kerry Max Cook's aunt.

McGill, Peggy—Worked at Texas Eastern University library with murder victim. She died July 3, 2021.

McGlasson, Robert—Attorney with the Texas Resource Center who took interest in Cook's case.

McMillan, Larry Wayne, Jr.—Four-year-old murder victim killed by James Joseph Wilkens Jr.

Mears, Frederick—Former professor at Texas Eastern University who testified he expressed concern about the book *The Sexual Criminal*.

Melontree, Andrew—Former Smith County commissioner. He died in 2020.

Miller, Glenn—Texas Department of Public Safety trooper who testified Bob Wickham told him Cook confessed.

Mitchell, Andrew Lee—Previously served time on death row for the murder of Keith Wills. His conviction was overturned on appeal in 1993. He later plead guilty to a lesser charge and was released for time served. He died on April 18, 2018.

Moore, Evan—*Houston Chronicle* reporter who wrote "Justice Under Fire: 'Win at all Costs' Is Smith County's Rule, Critics Claim." He was sued for libel by Jack Skeen, David Dobbs, and Alicia Cashell. The case was dismissed.

Morris, Vicki Lynn—Murder victim of Edward Eldon Corley.

Morrison, Nina—Former attorney with the Innocence Project. Currently is a US judge in the United States District Court Eastern District of New York.

Newman, George—Murder victim of Rickey Lynn Lewis.

Norris, Amber—Cook's former girlfriend who testified in the punishment phase of his second retrial.

Norton, Linda—A Dallas forensic pathologist who testified for the defense in the Cook trial.

Nugent, Paul—Houston attorney who represented Cook in two retrials. In private practice with Nugent & Peterson law firm in Houston.

Nunnelee, David—Served as a public information officer for the Texas Department of Criminal Justice and often coordinated media interviews with death row inmates. He retired in 2011 and died in 2020.

Onion, John Edward "Jack," Jr.—Presiding justice of the Texas Court of Criminal Appeals who wrote the opinion for the majority in the 1987 decision upholding Cook's conviction and death sentence.

Phillips, Glenn S.—Former judge for the 241st District Court in Smith County, Texas. He died in 1999.

Petty, Charles—Pathologist who testified for the prosecution in Cook's second retrial. He died in 2007.

Prejean, Sister Helen—Author of *Dead Man Walking* and other books about her experiences as a spiritual advisor to death row inmates.

Reasoner, Charles—Tyler resident who served as the jury foreman in Cook's 1978 trial.

Ressler, Robert—A former FBI crime scene analyst whose defense testimony was barred from Cook's second retrial.

Raitano, Luella—Adopted daughter of James Mayfield. Also went by the name Luella Mayfield.

Roddy, W. Carl—An assistant biology professor at Texas Eastern University who was shot and killed in 1977. James B. Becknell Jr. was convicted of murder in the case and received a life sentence.

Rosen, Steve "Rocket"—Houston attorney who represented Cook in his no contest plea in 1999. He died in 2020.

Rowland, Marilyne—Juror in Cook's first retrial in Georgetown. She found the missing nylon stocking when she examined Linda Jo Edwards's jeans.

Rudolph, Paula—Employed in the library at Texas Eastern University and shared her Embarcadero apartment with murder victim Linda Jo Edwards in 1977. She testified she saw Kerry Max Cook inside the apartment the night of the murder. She died in 2013.

Salter, Phyllis—A Cook supporter from Henderson, Texas.

Scheck, Barry—Attorney who defended O. J. Simpson on murder charges. Cofounder of the Innocence Project.

Sessions, James—Convicted of capital murder in the death of Clifford McDougal in 1980. He died in prison of natural causes in 1999.

Skeen, Jack M., Jr.—Smith County District Attorney from 1982–2002. District judge of the 241st District Court from 2003–2022. Retired.

Smith, J. B.—Smith County sheriff who was continuously elected from 1978 to 2012.

Stallings, Danny—Cherokee County, Texas, sheriff who helped identify Kerry Max Cook.

Stephens, Duane—Tyler attorney who represented Robert Hoehn. He died October 26, 2016.

Swindle, Howard—Investigative reporter/editor for *The Dallas Morning News*. He died in 2004.

Szarka, Andrew—Texas Eastern University professor who Linda Jo Edwards confided in before she died.

Taylor, James—Resident at Embarcadero Apartments and briefly lived with Kerry Max Cook in 1977.

Teague, Marvin O.—Texas Court of Criminal Appeals justice who dissented with Justice Clinton in the 1990 opinion upholding Cook's conviction and death sentence.

Thompson, Mike—Smith County Assistant District Attorney who presented the state's case against Kerry Max Cook in 1978 trial. He died by suicide about three months after Cook's conviction.

Ticer, Amy Joanne—Married Kerry Max Cook via proxy while he was on death row. They later divorced.

Tittle, Debra—Former assistant district attorney in Smith County. Now married to David Dobbs.

Trull, Don—A Tyler businessman who met with Donnis Baggett, Trooper Stuart Dowell, and Edward Scott Jackson when Jackson recanted his testimony in which he claimed Cook confessed to the crime.

Tunnell, Joe—Judge of the 241st District Court in Smith County who presided over Cook's first retrial. He died in 1998.

Udashen, Gary—Dallas attorney who works with the Innocence Project.

Wattley, Cheryl—Dallas attorney who worked with Steve "Rocket" Rosen in representing Cook during his 1999 plea.

Weckerling, Alan—Proprietor of Weckerling Laboratory in Dallas. He testified about the "halo effect" during Cook's second retrial.

Wells, Christopher—Convicted of capital murder in the death of Chad Choice. He was spared a death sentence by one vote.

West, Michael—Assistant district attorney in Smith County who assisted Matt Bingham in the 2016 Cook hearings.

Wickham, Bob—Former Smith County reserve deputy who testified Cook confessed to killing Linda.

Wilkens, James Joseph, Jr.—Convicted and sentenced to die for the shooting deaths of Richard Wood and Larry Wayne McMillan Jr. He was retried on appeal and convicted. He was executed by lethal injection on July 11, 2001.

Wills, Keith—Murder victim. Andrew Lee Mitchell initially convicted of the crime and sent to death row.

Wilson, Nita—Former KETK–Region 56 reporter who interviewed Cook. The videotape of that interview in which Cook denied knowing Linda Jo Edwards or being in her apartment was used as evidence by the prosecution.

Winn, Thomas, Jr.—Jury foreman in Cook's second retrial.

White, Ann—She worked at Texas Eastern University library with murder victim Linda Jo Edwards. She died on April 7, 2015.

White, W. J.—Psychologist at Rusk State Hospital when Cook was committed.

Wood, Richard—Murdered by James Joseph Wilkens Jr. in 1986.

Wright, Bill—Former Tyler attorney who defended numerous capital murder defendants in Smith County. He died in 2014.

ACKNOWLEDGMENTS

Becoming an author took more than using my God-given talents of writing and telling a story. I'm forever grateful that He also put people in my life to help me and support my effort.

Thank you to former Smith County District Clerk Lois Rogers and her accommodating staff who allowed me to review dozens of boxes of court records. Finding records also would not have been possible without the assistance of various clerks at the Tyler Public Library and at the Robert R. Muntz Library at The University of Texas at Tyler.

My former colleague and friend, Dr. Marsha Matthews provided patience, sound advice, and encouragement and was always there when I just needed to talk through my thoughts. Lori and Gary Kroll provided a home base for me in the Dallas area whenever I needed it, and special thanks to their daughter-in-law, Brittany Kroll, for a much-needed makeover. I'm also forever grateful to my longtime friend Donna Mills for her endless support.

Dr. Yvonne Thrash opened her home to me as my Tyler base. Her advice, encouragement, and support helped me through some difficult times.

Thanks also to my mentors Marilyn Covey, Betty Gomes, Noelle DeAtley, Chris Fletcher, Hattie Kemp, Jason Waller, Paul Woolley, Nancy Braswell, and Jan White Russell.

And to my mother, Janet Rich, who provided the genes, encouragement, and financial support to nurture my love of reading, learning, and pursuit of a higher education.

Vanessa E. Curry is an award-winning journalist and educator who has covered the Kerry Max Cook case for four different news organizations over the past thirty years.

Her educational background includes a master's degree in interdisciplinary studies with emphases in journalism, criminal justice, and political science. Curry's coverage of legal issues has earned numerous accolades, including the Liberty Bell Award from the Smith County Bar Association, two Gavel Awards from the State Bar of Texas, the James Madison Award from the Freedom of Information Foundation of Texas, honors for investigative reporting from the Texas Association Press Managing Editors, and an award for Media Excellence in Public Awareness from the Texas Corrections Association.

She has appeared on true-crime television shows *City Confidential* and *Forensic Files* for her coverage of a high-profile murder case in Smith County, Texas.

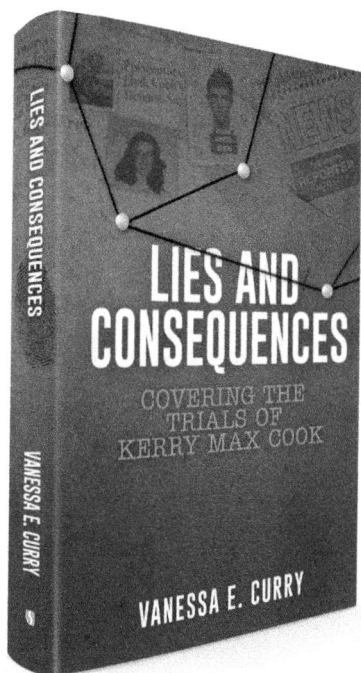

FOR MORE AUTHOR INFORMATION AND TO ORDER
BOOKS IN BULK, PLEASE VISIT:
VANESSACURRY.COM

OR SEND AN EMAIL TO
VANESSA_CURRY@ATT.NET

www.ingramcontent.com/pod-product-compliance
Lightning Source LLC
Chambersburg PA
CBHW052027030426
42335CB00026B/3307